Kid Pro Quo

Essential Parent-Coaching Skills
For Growing Confident, Cheerful Children

James Mackenzie Wright

Fisher King Publishing

Kid Pro Quo

ISBN 978-1-906377-79-3

Cover design by Chris Carroll

Fisher King Publishing Ltd
The Studio
Arthington Lane
Pool-in-Wharfedale
LS21 1JZ
England
www.fisherkingpublishing.co.uk

Quid Pro Quo:
(A favour or advantage granted or expected in return for something)

Kid Pro Quo™:

SO you want a bit of acknowledgement from time to time **for the job you do** for us?

Then send a little our way sometime for the s p a c e we **create** and hold w i d e open for you to explore yourselves too.

This will allow us ***all*** **to** evolve and **grOW**

- N.E. Jung-Pursson

James Mackenzie Wright, MSc

An apprentice Parent (aren't we always, really?) and Head of Training at Performance Coach Training Ltd, James creates coaching cultures in organisations worldwide, speaking and workshopping on respectful communication, leadership and emotional intelligence. His audiences are diverse - corporate, sporting, charities, schools, teachers, parents and young people - although his teaching is constant; creating and sustaining mature communication structures at every level of society.

His philosophies for team and family leadership are identical: To enthuse and empower new leaders (rather than to create followers). His methods target the fundamental people-issues, that support children, parents and families to stay healthy *'from the inside, out.'*

He is committed to the work of Amnesty International and speaks regularly in schools and colleges around the UK on its behalf, as well as to a London-based charity, The Ministry of Entrepreneurship, providing coach-training workshops to disadvantaged young people.

He has published an educational novel, Seven for a Secret (Fisher King) - a new coaching perspective for bereaved children aged 11 to 111.

James lives in West London with Romanie, Loic and Luke, and Slinky the cat.

For Loic and Luke

Two wise, playful and brilliant young men,
waiting in the wings to become
wise, playful and brilliant parents.
When the time comes
your children are going to be so happy
to have you as fathers and uncles...
...and coaches.

Contents

Foreword

There is nothing as precious as that of the mind of a child and nothing as vital, on every level, as to how that mind is nurtured. Everything we become, the world we create, the society in which we live, the way we interact with others and the ability to do great things, all stem from those formative years and the influence of all that we see and hear. How immense the responsibility it is to be an adult with the task of empowering the mind of children so that they are poised, ready for a wonderful, amazing life ahead.

How many times do we hear parents telling expectant mothers and fathers, 'You can read all the books you like but nothing really can prepare you for parenthood'... Maybe this is so, although this book offers far more accessible preparation than most I've read.

This is a book about reciprocity pure and simple. Even the book's title is an insightful choice; Kid Pro Quo - a delightful adaptation of Quid Pro Quo. Bringing up children is definitely a two-way street.

So the definition of 'Kid Pro Quo' (delivered through the eponymous eyes of N.E. Jung-Pursson) becomes a challenge all parents would do well to heed; namely, how aware are we, really, when we attempt to overlay our own childhood/parent scenarios onto our own children a few decades later?

Parents often appear to report that their efforts to raise and shape their children have been met with ingratitude, intransigence and only occasional compliance. I have two stepsons whom I describe as having adopted me when they were about to be teenagers, with the divine help of their very patient mother. We managed to navigate our way through, more by luck than judgement, to a point where I am now, daily, in awe of two young men making their way in the world as successful adults.

This book is a timely reminder to me that, were I to re-frame my view and approach it from my boys' standpoint, at all ages of their development, I would be confronted with the stark truth that ***they had actually been working as hard as they knew how, consciously and unconsciously, to raise and shape me into a more complete parent.*** Where was I, in their eyes back then, on the scale of ingratitude, intransigence and compliance I wonder? And where am I now?

My re-frame indicates they have had only my interests at heart; for if I, the parent, am incomplete, how much of the person they need me to be, can I actually be? There is a delicious paradox about this - are they being selfless in demanding that I too 'grow up'? Or selfish? Or is it me demanding this of them?

Now look. I've started doing what James does all the way through this book - asking questions. There are well over a thousand coaching questions in these pages that we can learn and adapt to use when conversing with our families. And as is the way with coaching questions, each one carries a 'government self-reflection warning.' It's not enough to just ask questions of our children; it should be unavoidable that they cause us to hold the proverbial mirror in front of our own faces too.

The opening chapter is a beautiful and plaintive cry for recognition, written as if from the child's mind, (lest we forget that all our children are TOPCATs - Totally Outstanding People Capable of Astonishing Things). Of course they are, and the exuberant 'Hijack' in Chapter 30 reinforces this right when we need it; in the section on Listening. Are we really listening to our children, so that they - THEY - can hear their emerging voices, and know that we are hearing them too?

It is right to remember also, that coaching cannot happen where the family environment is non-conducive. James devotes more than half the book to understanding ***how to build and sustain the space where coaching our children will be able to flourish***, before introducing the coaching skills.

This is as vital as it is brave - it's all too easy to find books that merely offer encouragement to applying the skills of coaching to one's children, without insisting on the base framework (the 'backdrop of anticipation') which will ***allow coaching to be absorbed*** by children and parents alike.

Spending time nurturing the areas so often overlooked, ***prior*** to expecting respectful, cheerful conversations with our children is, for me, the 'Coaching Gold' in this book. I adore the Chapter headings in Part Two, which are so simple and yet so provocative - (don't they just sum up 'Coaching' in a nutshell)? In fact, that's what really hits me about this book - it so effortlessly models core coaching skills and principles on every page. There is no dissociation - the coaching is the teaching is the coaching.

If you are reading this in hard-copy, keep a highlighter pen handy as you absorb the words - you'll be glad you did. There is so much in this book that you will want to re-discover as you revisit sections time and time again.

Kid Pro Quo should be at the top of every parent's reading list; it will not only help in the way children are nurtured but what is contained within these pages will help us to engage more meaningfully, on every level, throughout life.

Enjoy the profound as it unravels and use the wisdom that this book provides. You'll remember the moment that Kid Pro Quo came into your world. So will your children. When you are speaking to a nervous, expectant parent you'll find yourself saying, 'Don't worry, there is a book that will help you...' And they'll be so grateful.

Rick Armstrong
Managing Director - Mentor Group
Co-author of *The Little Book of Positive Thoughts*
And of *The Little Book Of Visualisation*

Introduction

So there was I congratulating myself on being an evolved, sorted kind of adult. I teach emotional intelligence. I train people to become coaches. I've coached and mentored hundreds of people and I've spoken about creating strong communication structures in organisations to thousands more...

Then I became a parent. Strictly speaking a step-parent; regardless - a father to two boys and a partner to their mother.

This is a role I had long effused about from the safety and relative irresponsibility of bachelorhood. Previously I had played the 'benevolent uncle' to my friends' families as they grew up - hugely enjoyable and wonderfully indulgent; the youngsters all belonged with other people. Ultimately, not my problem then. I had managed, with some diligence and cunning to avoid 'proper parenting' until a few years ago.

Despite my late start, I do feel I have paid my dues in other ways, from which I have some valuable insights into growing the delightful minds of young people as they shape their youthful aspirations into realities. For a twelve year period as a national youth team volleyball coach, I parented, vicariously one might say, with talented young volleyball players, running junior national teams, clubs, camps, and tournaments across Great Britain, Europe, North America and the Caribbean.

In saying this, given the elite nature of some of these programmes, I and my coaching team possibly spent more actual contact hours with some of these players in any given year than their real parents did. And we were, to be fair, pretty good at providing strong *in loco parentis* boundaries and role modelling, albeit within a sporting context. We received some very warm, generous and grateful comments from their parents on their social and emotional development over those years, so our blueprint was fairly rigorously tested and approved as far as it went.

This sort of parenting though, was comparatively easy next to what you all have been doing for so long. I had simply to organise a sporting itinerary, invite players, structure their time and activity, give them instruction and feedback, then send them back to their real parents at the end. If they rocked the boat, their position in the "family" was jeopardised and they risked early ejection. Since these were pretty motivated and talented youngsters, discipline was fairly simple to manage.

I have long held the notion that good fatherhood is the most honourable and worthwhile work a man can do. Note I don't say just fatherhood. Being a ***good*** father is, for me, the test of true honour – the toughest, longest, most relentless and intense leadership training a man can experience. If I may speak for women too, I would surmise that it must be a similar experience, although, given the marvel of pregnancy there must exist the added, magical, biological bond that I doubt men can ever completely fathom.

So from talking the parenting talk for a couple of decades, although managing to avoid walking the walk for even longer, I met and moved in with Romanie, Loic and Luke.

There I am, at the succulent age of forty-seven, finally taking the longest exam known to mankind. Full of untested confidence that my investment in my own personal development would hold me in good stead as a father figure; that my finely honed self-awareness would surely allow me to acknowledge and sidestep any hint of hypocrisy; that I would cheerily dole out perceptive, logical and mature suggestions and solutions to tricky situations; that they naturally would all look up to me for my innate wisdom; that they would love to bask in my humour and whimsy, adopt my common-sensical approach to living and values-oriented outlook; that family life would essentially be a piece of cake.

I absolutely anticipated how important it is for us parents to create that space where youngsters can play pranks on us, tease us, and make us the objects of their fun, particularly in front of their friends. This is very satisfying for them, indubitably, and provides them with a necessary illusion of power, while serving the dual purpose of creating benevolent, accessible bonds which will come in very handy as they work through their intriguing teenage years.

So imagine how baffled I was to be told by my new, supposedly starry-eyed family that they perceive me to be, on occasion, dictatorial, inflexible, power mad, egotistical, mean, a control freak, righteous...you get the picture. Not necessarily all the time or all at once you understand, but still. And until now I had always thought being righteous was an aspiration. **[Dictionary definition: - righteous, rīCHəs, adj: of a person or conduct - morally right or justifiable; virtuous.]**

Increasingly I heard it wielded as a taunt. How mightily unfair. Not to mention ungrateful. Who knew kids would shoot from the hip like this? (Or that 'Significant Others' might occasionally do the same, come to that).

Far from being hailed as an exemplary champion of paternal perfection from dawn to dusk, I encountered some days peppered with vignettes of uncensored scorn, melodrama, tantrums and pure venom. I expected bends in my new road, but was totally unprepared for so many chicanes. They still manage to catch me unawares, although I'm getting better at spotting the tremors before the quake. Mixing metaphors is a trait I find amusing by the way - please just humour me.

So early insights for me then: don't expect a child to recognise (or care) whether you have a coaching 'hat' on or a parent 'hat.' One of the best gifts parents can give is tacit permission for their kids to openly throw hateful, hurtful and hostile comments at them whenever the words just need to come out. It's possibly one of the most counter-intuitive gifts to rationalise too. It can feel like we are being backed towards a cliff-edge and the youngsters are throwing everything they can at us to try to push us over the edge.

Children without parental boundaries are the most insecure in the world

As an aside, we fledgling step-parents seem to be particularly vulnerable to these outbursts, whose aim can, on the surface, appear to be to goad us into deserting our new family, since "everything was fine until [we] turned up." That whole Step-Parent as Coach scenario, and while we are at it, the Foster-Parent and Adoptive-Parent as Coach scenarios too, could be covered in a future book, perhaps.

This behaviour can be massively painful and one's instinct might understandably be to enforce tighter controls, punishments or even retaliation. However, by responding from a high ground, parents learn to show that they are strong and confident in their relationship with themselves and each other and are not afraid of the children's hatred, jealousy and hostility.

parents work towards creating a model of acceptance, confidence and respect in which the child's self-awareness can and will, eventually flourish

All that will pass. Give it time.

It's my view that children without parental boundaries are the most insecure in the world. So for parents and step-parents alike, by standing firm we are also demonstrating that we believe in them as young adults who are capable of experiencing strong emotions and taking responsibility for them in due course.

Most parents do their best to set out their stalls on the path of minimum judgement, I'm convinced. We have simply to tell the child, ***"Well, the things you can't change are that I still believe you're amazing, I still love you and I'm still here."*** We are minded to work towards creating a model of acceptance, confidence and respect in which the child's self-awareness can and will, eventually flourish.

Aha, I thought. This resembles the mindset of a professional coach. That, I know how to do. Let's put the two together. It was at this point I knew I might actually make it as a parent.

we learn to lay aside our egos sufficiently often to allow wisdom to approach our children (and indeed anyone) from any and every available source

So. Whether I'm viewed as Dashing Cavalry Officer or Beleaguered Charity Intern, I'll accept both. Because on the many occasions when we are all in tune, coach-hood and family life truly is a magical space to occupy. Growing myself up alongside two dazzling young men is a joy; all of us interpreting our worlds the best we can; making the fullest use of our own and each other's resources; laughing, playing, learning, living and loving together.

Some time ago I came across the African proverb - you probably know it: '**It takes a village to raise a child.**' I think I'm better placed to understand this now. For me it means we set our boundaries and then we learn to lay aside our egos sufficiently often to allow wisdom to approach our children (and indeed anyone) from any and every available source. And it requires that how they process and action that accrued wisdom ***must be left to them.*** Even if - no, ***especially*** if - it means watching them make what we discern as mistakes. That's still a tough one to manage.

But then again, I don't recall anyone ever saying growing youngsters was easy. My parents certainly didn't.

James Mackenzie Wright,

Kid Pro Quo™

On reading this, if you feel moved to communicate your own experiences, reviews, successes and indeed, outright horror-shows to us, we would be really excited to read them, and perhaps make reference to them (discretely where appropriate and always with your permission of course). Every contribution will be valued and gratefully welcomed at

www.kidproquo.co.uk '

Appreciations

All things considered, I'm fairly comfortable in the knowledge that when I finally decided to join the Honourable Order of Parenting having dodged it for decades, I arrived ready to embrace the role. Meeting Romanie at a dear friend's funeral and moving in with her and her two spirited, insightful and brilliant sons has brought my life full-circle. The daily reflections that accompany the role are predictably unpredictable, and all hugely appreciated.

I am enormously grateful to you, Romanie, Loic and Luke, who, after losing Will, (Romanie's husband and the boys' father) to cancer tragically early in all your lives, have opened innumerable spaces for me to reflect on myself, my values and my responsibilities. Most important of all, you have allowed me to discover and treasure the first-hand realities of growing as a man by growing as a parent.

Many dozens of people deserve far more than a mere mention for their contributions to this book. I am deeply grateful to the hundreds of parents who have attended workshops and talks, and offered their insights and wisdom, and real-life scenarios, many of which appear throughout these pages.

A huge thank you to all the teachers in the schools I have worked with, (and the many millions I'll never get to meet), many of whom see our children far more than we ourselves do in any given week, and who help shape their attitudes and aspirations. Through extended conversations with these teachers I have been able to understand in far greater depth the mind-sets of our children as they become older, particularly the many *alter egos* they freely inhabit, with their teachers, their friends or with us, their parents. How can we possibly know the extent of the teaching influences they are encountering at school, in sports clubs, art classes, music lessons and other out of school activities? All we, as parents, can do, and must do, is trust these wonderful people whose calling is to educate and grow the minds of our children and of all children.

I have been fortunate too, to work with and learn from a number of leading lights in the coaching world; Carol Wilson, Nancy Kline, Sir John Whitmore, Gene Early, Anthony Robbins, Liz Macann and the late David Grove are a few. Especial thanks to Carol Wilson, the woman who has inspired me almost daily over the last ten years, providing work, learning, insight and most precious of all, friendship. Carol, I am so happy we met in Olympia, at the Vitality Show back in 2001 - one instinctively knows when one meets a friend for life, and I love and respect the way you embody coaching to me and all those you touch.

Thank you for taking me under your wing while my own feathers were forming.

Thanks especially to Martin and Vivian Wright for your thorough and insightful editing.

Once again, much admiration for the patience, good-humour and attention to detail shown by the irrepressible Rick Armstrong at Mentor Group and to Chris Carroll at Fisher King Publishing for his instinctive, spot-on designs right through this book from the front cover to the back.

And if it's not too presumptuous, then I'd like to thank you, my readers for buying this book - if indeed anybody has. Not just because you will have deemed it worth the financial outlay, and for finding precious time to read it, but more because it identifies us all as kindred souls whose demonstrated intention is to work to create cheerful, cordial communication at home, and by extension, everywhere else too. And there's further, renewed and heartfelt acknowledgement at the end of the book too for actually reading it through to the end.

I hope you find you can.

Prologue
When Ajay Met Annie

How do we look at our children when we talk to them? What filter do we create, through which to view them? What intention do we subconsciously deliver as we converse? How many times might we catch ourselves daily relating to our children through a filter of, **"You have a problem,"** or maybe, **"You are a problem"?**

The following is a true story, although I may have added a dusting of literary licence with a few of the details, names and dialogue.

* * *

Annie had been offered a generous allowance from her employer to take taxis every morning and evening to and from work. However, she chose instead to walk the few blocks to the main road and take the bus downtown, so that she could experience the sights and sounds and smells of Mumbai. She would leave her hotel after breakfast and turn left into a backstreet, a short cut along which there were some small, straggly trees for added shade - any protection from the intense early morning heat was welcome.

Arriving at the main road, she passed a boy of about fifteen years old, whose legs were crippled and useless to him, and he sat on a skateboard, begging. Annie smiled and nodded at him the first two mornings although she chose not to give him money. The third morning, he recognised her coming from a distance and aimed his skateboard towards her, using his hands wrapped in ragged cloth as oars on the dusty concrete to propel him. He was exceptionally agile on his board and span it round as she walked towards him, and he wheeled himself alongside her, again asking for money.

She laughed spontaneously as he performed a couple of tricks, tipping his board so he was driving on the back two wheels only, and spinning 360 degrees before continuing alongside her. He smiled too, in response to her laughter, an uncertain, tentative smile, but he seemed to be enjoying himself.

"That's amazing," Annie said. "You're a real master navigator on that board! What else can you do?"

"I am dancing, if you like," said the boy, and proceeded to rock the skateboard backward and forwards on its front and back tips, and spinning it one way, then the other, full circle.

Annie laughed again. "What's your name?" she asked.

"I am Ajay," the boy told her.

"Thank you, Ajay. You've really brightened up my day. I have to get that bus now, so I'll see you tomorrow, I'm sure."

And she waved to him, crossed the road and boarded the bus.

That evening, she returned as usual, stepped off the bus, and there, looking slightly apprehensive, was Ajay.

"Hello, Ajay. I don't normally see you this late."

"I wait for you, Madam," he said. "Look, I am dancing for you."

And once again, he performed some surprising moves on his board. She laughed, delighted.

"My goodness, have you been practising or is that just natural rhythm?" she teased him. They turned together into the short cut street, a bumpy mud lane which was difficult for him to wheel himself down.

"Madam, I stay here. Big road. More people. More money..." he seemed almost shy this time, as if his statement, undoubtedly his truth, was somehow embarrassing.

"Of course, and this little road is difficult to negotiate. I'll see you tomorrow morning, will I?"

"I be here. I always be here."

"Bye then."

"Goodbye, Madam. Ah, Madam?" Ajay called after her.

She turned.

"Madam, please what is your name?"

"It's Annie, Ajay. My name is Annie."

"Annie," he repeated, as she smiled and waved to him once more, turned and walked on.

The next morning, he was waiting at his corner.

"Hello, Madam Annie."

"Good morning, Ajay. How are you?"

"I am well, Madam Annie. How are you?"

"I'm very well, and already in better spirits for seeing you, Ajay. And today I am only working half day, so that's better still."

"So you come back before tonight evening?"

"Yes, probably around two o'clock. In fact, I had an idea last night. Will you be here at two?"

"I always here, Madam Annie."

"May I ask you a favour? It will take about two hours."

"What is a favour?"

"A favour is help. I'd like you to help me."

"How I can help you, Madam Annie?"

"You'll see. See you at two."

And she smiled mysteriously, and waved as she crossed the road to her bus stop.

Soon after two, she appeared off the bus and there was Ajay, waiting.

"I wait for you to come, Madam Annie. How I help you?" He seemed excited, though nervous.

"Come. Let's go this way, the road is a bit longer but easier."

They journeyed together and she told him about her work. Two or three times a year, Annie flew to faraway countries to paint racehorses and pets for wealthy owners. She told Ajay she would be in Mumbai this time for a week, mostly painting horses and dogs. He told her he had never seen a horse before. She promised to show him some of her sketches.

They arrived at the hotel, and watched, intrigued as he bounced himself up the low steps to the reception area. They attracted curious and slightly displeased attentions from the reception staff, but Annie smiled politely at them and beckoned Ajay towards a door leading off the lobby. She found the key in her purse and unlocked it and invited Ajay inside.

"This is a room they let me use for my painting," she explained. "It has a nice light from the garden and I can spread out my things."

"I can see horse?" asked Ajay.

"Of course you can. Look at these." Annie emptied some sketches from a large cardboard folder and spread them out across the floor where he could examine them easily. He spent several minutes poring over each sketch, carefully shifting himself in between the papers with his hands, careful not to touch them. His skateboard was abandoned by the door.

"I love to see real horse," said Ajay.

"Maybe one day you will," replied Annie. "Ajay?"

"Madam Annie?"

"Ajay, I asked you here because you said you might be able to do me a favour. Can I tell you how you could help me?"

"Of course, Madam Annie."

"Well, some clients have asked me if I could paint their children too, as well as portraits of their animals. And I need a little practice as I haven't painted people for some time now. Would you allow me to paint you? I would need to see you for a couple of hours every day for the next four days until I leave. What do you think?"

A look of consternation appeared on Ajay's face. He was obviously uncomfortable.

"Madam Annie, you don't paint me. I am not good for paint. I only must ask money in street. Two hours... Must ask money in street..."

"Ajay, I'm sorry, I didn't mean to make you uncomfortable. And I want to pay you for being my model. You have such a fabulous energy, and your face is so beautiful and natural. It would make me so happy to practice with you and it would teach me so much. Please say yes. I will pay you one thousand rupees each day you come. Please say yes."

Ajay was silent and turned away from her.

Annie remained seated on the stool, leaning forward, still, silent.

After some seconds, Ajay turned himself around to face her, his eyes were moist and tear-streaks had washed a thin path through the dust on his cheeks.

"*Nahi, nahi,* Madam Annie, you laughing to me. I not beautiful. I am nothing. Not beautiful, not for paint. I only for ask money in street. I go back."

And he shuffled his way between the papers to his skateboard, pulled it flat and reached for the door handle. Annie said nothing. As he turned the handle, he looked towards her. He noticed she hadn't moved. Neither to stop him, nor to contradict him. He paused.

"You...are serious, Madam Annie? You no laugh to me?"

"Ajay, I'm not laughing at you at all. I would be so happy to spend more time with you, and to study you and to paint you. If you will let me. And of course I will pay you a modelling fee. It will just be until the end of this week."

Ajay looked intensely at Annie. After a long minute he released his grip on the door handle.

"Then I stay with you. And you give me one thousand rupees?"

"One thousand rupees. Each day for two hours. I promise. Now then, while I set up my materials, perhaps you would like to freshen up in this bathroom? I will bring a chair for you to sit at the sink, or you may shower if you prefer. Be ready in fifteen minutes if you can. I'll call you when I'm ready. Tomorrow, we will find fresh clothes and we can wash and dry your own while we work if you like."

Annie met Ajay at the bus stop each evening and he accompanied her back to the hotel where they talked, modelled, painted and laughed until dusk.

He told her how he had been left to fend for himself after his parents died young, and his uncle had brought him up and taught him some English, until he too was killed in a car accident when Ajay was ten years old. Since then he had been living in a small room in the slum house of his uncle's friends, bringing back whatever money he could to pay them for his survival. She told him about her children and her life in Scotland, where there were hills and huge open, green spaces and animals in the fields.

Both were deeply fascinated to hear the life stories of the other and their time together passed quickly.

On the second day he changed into a clean T-shirt and shorts she had bought for him, and the hotel washed and dried his own clothes while they worked. The hotel staff were relaxed now at this intriguing couple entering the lobby and disappearing into the Drawing Room, as they now called it. They had grown fond of Ajay and his bright, positive outlook, and had invited him to come each weekend to the hotel to shower, while they would wash and dry his clothes.

On the fourth day, they arrived at the hotel as usual, around four-thirty. But today, Annie asked Ajay to wait outside, while she prepared the room. He waited, still a little nervous of the scrutiny of the receptionists until Annie reappeared in the doorway a few minutes later.

"Please come in. All of you. Please come in and take a seat." She waved an arm at the two receptionists and the concierge too. Inside the Drawing Room were three chairs in a row, with a fourth set sideways in front facing an easel. The easel was covered with a beige sheet. "Ajay you sit here, in the seat of honour. And you may sit here," she gestured to the hotel staff to sit in the three remaining seats.

"As you know, I have been painting Ajay, who has kindly allowed me to practice on him. And now I would like to show you the painting. I have stayed up each night and into the early hours of each morning, and I think it is probably the most beautiful painting of the most beautiful person I have ever done. Here, Ajay, what do you think?"

She pulled a corner of the sheet towards Ajay and gave it to him to hold.

"Ready?"

He shrugged, uneasy.

"Pull."

He pulled slowly, and then tugged and the sheet billowed to the floor.

The three hotel staff gasped and clapped. They turned to Annie, and threw compliments at her.

"It is so wonderful! It is identical! It is perfect! It is like it is him in a mirror!" they gushed.

Annie though, never took her eyes off Ajay who had frozen in his seat. She saw his forehead crease, his eyes widen and fill with tears. She saw his lips begin to tremble, all the while transfixed on the painting in front of him. She knelt next to him and took his hand. His hand too was trembling and as she did so, the tears ran freely down his face, and a low humming sound came uninhibitedly from his throat.

She squeezed his hand and he looked into her face. She too, had tears in her eyes, which overflowed silently and ran down each cheek to her chin. She hadn't anticipated the intensity of his reaction.

"Ajay, do you like it?" she asked, softly.

Noticing her tears, he reached across to her face with his other hand and dabbed her tears from each cheek and looked at the wetness on his finger.

"Madam Annie. No-one ever look at me so long before. And no-one ever hide feeling that they see only ugly person, nothing person. They throw money towards me but they never speak. Money and pity. Money and pity. I can only use the money - the pity I cannot use. They pass all day, but me, ME they never notice. They only notice pity person. You never throw money to me, Madam Annie, you throw to me only respect. Like a person, not a pity. Not a nothing. And now you show me ***me***. And you make me feel beautiful just for this day only. Thank you Madam Annie. *Tum bhi khoobsurat ho*."

Annie leaned forward, looked into Ajay's eyes and kissed his forehead lightly before wrapping her arms around his muscular shoulders in a tight hug. Slowly his arms raised to her shoulders and he allowed himself to hug her too. They stayed locked together, both crying, both laughing, unable to break the embrace for nearly two minutes.

"So you like it!" she whispered against his ear, smiling.

They gently broke the embrace and sat back from each other, their hands and fingers tightly entwined. Annie noticed the room was once again empty, except for the two of them. The hotel staff had tactfully, silently exited and closed the door.

Ajay started to speak and then checked himself. He swallowed and cleared his throat and started again.

"If I like or if I do not, not so important. If I like or if I do not, not change that this is most happy moment of ever in my whole life. This moment I feel beautiful. This moment I feel like person of something, not person of nothing. This moment I can never forget." He paused, and watched as Annie's tears started to spill from her eyes once more. "But, Madam Annie," he continued, "I can tell you, this painting I like so very, very much. Really I look like this? I not see what I am looking like since I was ten years."

"No mirrors in your house, Ajay?"

"No mirrors, Madam Annie. Anyway, why I want to see ugly, pity person? But you make me look like handsome man, Madam Annie."

"No, Ajay, I paint what is real. You are a handsome man."

"*Agar main is tasveer ki tarah hoon, toh main sundar hoon!*" Ajay was laughing.

"What are you saying?"

"I say you, "If am like painting, I am indeed handsome man!"

"One moment Ajay, wait here." Annie stood up and walked to the wall where she unhooked a round, gilded mirror. She held it up next to her painting. "Now look. This is Ajay. And this is Ajay."

He looked intently at the mirror, then at the portrait, then back again.

"Same same Ajay," he said.

"Yes, same same Ajay."

"This painting show me ***me***, this painting show Ajay, handsome man. It is magic painting! You are magic woman!"

"No, I'm not a magic woman, Ajay. I'm an artist, but more, I am a mother, who has her own children. Back home, far away. And every time I look at them I see beauty too. And they are fortunate in that they know their beauty. They understand beauty to mean finding beauty everywhere. And so do I. Ajay, I want you to have this painting. It's for you. And every time you look at it, you tell yourself how beautiful and strong and decent you are. This is the real Ajay. Always remember, 'beautiful you.' "

"*Main sundar hoon.* Beautiful me. *Tum bhi khoobsurat ho,* Madam Annie. Beautiful you also." Ajay was almost chanting the words. "This I always remember," he said simply, smiling happily.

PART ONE
READ THE RULES OF THIS COACHING GAME CAREFULLY!

"How far can this [young] mind go ***before*** it has need of mine?
And how much further? And how much further still?"

Nancy Kline - More Time to Think

1.

I Am The Square Root Of Infinite Potential

Let's allow the children the first words in this book. Their voice is our voice, a decade or two or three later. How do we heed their words, our words, now we believe we have left childhood behind?

meX*me*=i**P**

(I AM THE SQUARE ROOT OF INFINITE POTENTIAL)

Let me spell things out for you...

Actually, you are fortunate to be my parents because I am best placed of all to know how to teach you what you most need to learn. Whether you choose to learn it or not is up to you.

I am a fabulous person capable of extraordinary things. Consequently, I expect you to expect me to excel.

I am very wise already and there is little I can't grasp when I'm well motivated. And all I need to be motivated is to be given enough space to first discover how far my mind can go before it has need of yours.

And yes, I can handle the truth – just present it kindly.

I do process every single thing I encounter every single day - you just might not notice me doing it. And most likely I am going to take many years (maybe as many as it is still taking you) to get everything to where it all makes perfect sense. So let's all be patient.

I reserve the right to experience making some magnificent mistakes and to explore them thoroughly and at length if, and whenever, I feel I need to. Trust me to be the judge of when they've stopped serving my education and enjoyment. Even then I'll probably look for some new ones. Just like you still do, incidentally.

You probably believe you preside over my experimental approach to life. Truth be told, the opposite is more accurate: I preside over your experimental approach to parenting me.

Take a closer look if you're really interested, and you might eventually notice I am continually doing the best I'm currently able given the opportunities and the limitations of the world you have created for me.

I will let you know what my strengths are when I'm ready. And then I'll expect time and your support to develop them. And on that subject, there are plenty of people who excel in the areas where I'm weak. So I'm comfortable with my weaknesses too, and so should you be.

So if you're still looking for that square root of infinite potential, look no further.

You've found me.

2.

Starting Out (Or Starting Again)

Coaching Conversations Are *Not* Normal Conversations

Let's be clear about this right up front.

Well, alright, for some people they may be commonplace, usual, the norm. (Like coaches for example). But they are not normal in the same sense that a chat between friends is normal. Or in the same sense that classroom teaching conversations are normal. Or family squabbles. Or flirting couples. Or dialogue with parking wardens or ambitious athletes.

coaching conversations are NOT normal conversations

Each of these dialogues generally involve two people talking, often at the same time; they are peppered liberally with interruptions, advising, commiserations, opinion, helping, empathy, sharing. They can be great fun and frivolous and they can be moody and violent. They can be unstructured, theatrical, two-way, emotional and inconsequential. They often involve an exchange of ideas, pronouncements, insults and compliments. They can be dishonest, manipulative and self-serving. They can, of course, also be authentic, selfless and empowering.

Does that about cover it? We could probably add more qualities of normal conversations ourselves. So what then, makes these 'normal' and therefore different from ***coaching conversations***?

coaching conversations have only one purpose – ***to be useful***

In a word: ***questions***. Or, if I may allow myself? Two words: ***searching questions.***

Normal conversations have any number of purposes - to be helpful, funny, supportive, mean, informational, educational, frightening, loving, assertive... an endless list.

Coaching conversations have only one purpose - to be useful.

So if we put these two together, the key components of a coaching conversation are simply ***asking searching, useful questions.***

It may well be that coaching conversations touch on some of the components of normal conversations. Some of the above list may fit perfectly well into a coaching conversation. Let's see now... **authentic, empowering, selfless, fun** and... that's all.

OK, not so many then.

Then which components of our 'normal' conversations above definitely ***don't*** fit into a coaching conversation? Well, by a process of elimination... **two people talking, often at the same time, interruptions, commiserations, helping, sharing, unstructured, theatrical, two-way, emotional, inconsequential, frivolous, moody,**

violent, pronouncements, insults, dishonest, manipulative, self-serving.

That just leaves a few from our list above which may surface in coaching conversations at certain times and in certain circumstances: **opinion, advising, empathy, exchange of ideas, compliments.** These can be introduced sparingly and ***only when useful.***

So I hope that makes for a more accessible distinction between normal and coaching conversations. It's certainly the distinction I will be following through with in this book, and every aspect of how to set up and hold a coaching space in our families will be explored in the following pages.

* * *

It is for each of us to ascertain our starting points. If we have picked up this book and our children are already teenagers, we may find ourselves spending longer on the initial chapters. We can take whatever time we feel is required for creating that special space where coaching can take hold. I'll explain thoroughly how to do that if you'll agree to read just as thoroughly. Deal?

At a school in London where I held a workshop, the Head Master asked whether the content was appropriate for parents of under 11's or over 11's. "Both," I replied without hesitation, "Coaching is for everyone." A little later I reflected on this - had I been right to be so dogmatic? Is there a difference in the way we can coach young people according to age?

It may be the vocabulary would vary slightly; it may be the child has a greater or lesser awareness of irony, patronisation, ego, humour, purpose, contribution; it may be that some children define their social hierarchies by age, height, strength or cleverness; it may be any number of things. But coaching 'is what it is,' and as we will see it pretty much fits the bill for children of 1 to 101.

This book is primarily offered to parents whose children are still living with them at home, since therein lie the greatest opportunities for regular, daily, accumulative coaching to take place. At home, on holiday, more or less every day, we've got 'em where we want 'em. They ***will*** submit to our coaching and ***thank us*** for the privilege!

Joking aside, this daily, family coaching is a win-win no-brainer, since on one hand the regular coaching benefits and grows the children immeasurably, and on the other it provides relentless and much-needed emotional intelligence reminders for us parents. And the more the coaching skills and mindset are embedded, the easier it is to relate these to our older, grown-up (dare I say, mature?) children who have flown the nest. So now, a little later still, I feel I can safely stick with my earlier declaration; the coaching skills outlined in this book ***are*** for everyone.

As for where to start with the coaching, that's up to each family and each parent to ascertain. Teenagers with little experience of coaching and being coached will have years of habits and strategies around doing things their way, which, as parents know all too well, can often be at the expense of others around them. Of course, this may be doing some youngsters and teenagers a huge injustice - apologies all round if so. So coaching young adults like these may need more work from us parents on the foundation stages first, to prepare the space before the 'coaching proper' can commence.

At the earlier end of the development spectrum, where our children are either babies or still at primary school age, (4-11 years), then we'll more likely find that they are at a relatively malleable stage and are still open and accepting of our parenting experiments. In which case we may find we need to stay a shorter time establishing the foundation stages and we can jump straight in with the coaching.

Only we, and they, are best placed to make the call as to their readiness to become coached, and indeed, to become coaches themselves. The starting point of each one of us is our own call.

3.

The Stakes And The Ladders - How Best To Use This Book

coaching is for LIFE, not just for visits to grand-parents

LAYING THE FOUNDATIONS

They say that to fully understand what young people are going through, we should walk a mile in their shoes. Now of course, as adults, we can legitimately lay claim to having been there, done that many times over, so it's easy to say we don't need to go through it all again. But it's not a bad metaphor to consider, and of course if it all goes horribly wrong, at least we'd be a mile away, (and we'd have their shoes).

Stay focused - we must keep our eyes on the prize. Coaching is for LIFE, not just for visits to grandparents.

focus in on the parts of young people's development we can *always* predict – their extraordinary capacity for resourcefulness, innovation, energy, brilliance and fun

Children entering primary schools this year (this book is written in 2013) will be retiring around the year 2075. We cannot really have a clue what the world will look like in even five years' time and yet we are supposed to be preparing and educating them for this. It is said that seven out of ten jobs our teenagers will soon hold on leaving education ***haven't even been invented yet***.

There is an enormous degree of unpredictability. However, unpredictability, like spontaneity, is born of structure. If there were no boundaries there would be nowhere to deviate from. As a coach and a parent I find my life becomes much simpler when I focus in on the parts of young people's development I can always predict; namely that they all possess an extraordinary capacity for resourcefulness, innovation, energy, brilliance and fun. There are not many life guarantees but that capacity is a 'given.'

I am proposing a structure in this book born of thirty years' experience of observing, coaching and teaching young people. (And, in fact, forty-five years if we count early recollections of being parented, but then I suppose most people have these). So I should make it absolutely clear that:

This book IS NOT... a guide to good parenting (which is another set of skills altogether).

Absolutely not. You and many gazillions of others would be giving ME the talk on that one and I would be an avid and eager listener.

This book IS... a guide to practical coaching skills, and how to use those skills with our parenting.

For me, given that my nature inclines towards 'coach first' and 'parent second,' I am fully confident that (what I now term) 'pure' coaching lends itself to any audience, and doesn't require any shared expertise to be effective. This is very convenient (and fortuitous) for coaches. As it is also for all parent-coaches. So feel free to assimilate the skills, philosophies and intentions that make up coaching. Let's practice the exercises and work them into our own parenting as much or as little as makes sense.

this book IS NOT... a guide to good parenting, (which is another set of skills altogether)

However, I am not for one moment suggesting that parents may not be directive, nor set firm boundaries. There are many occasions that necessitate good, firm advice - basic hygiene, for example, road safety, violent reactions, drug and sex education - and many more besides. What we can do of course, is introduce our children to which 'hat' we may be wearing at any given time. By letting them know ***"I am going to take off my 'coach hat' for a moment, and put on my 'parent hat' to answer that question..."*** allows them to start recognising that there will be times when we will ask them for their solutions and times when we will offer them ours.

good coaches know exactly where they are in their conversations at all times, the purpose and impact of one question over another, when to leave pauses, what to chase through and what to expand

You will notice as you read through, that the chapters in this book often present more questions than answers. I also make a number of suggestions (but, in line with received coaching protocol ***I must not be overly attached to whether anyone follows them or not***). Make some time to reflect on these questions where they appear to be pertinent, (and even where they don't), and throw them open to the family for their thoughts too.

Likewise, I've presented numerous example conversations. Most are family-oriented; parent to child, parent to parent and some are workplace oriented too. My reasons for this are simply that strong, respectful conversations need to happen in any and every circumstance and I don't believe in differentiating between audiences when it comes to coaching. The more we practice conversing respectfully and usefully, the more we are modelling and practising 'coach-speak' for any given audience. Especially of course, at home.

this book IS... a guide to practical coaching skills, and how to use those skills with our parenting

Coaching conversations, when well executed by an experienced coach, can appear seamless or sometimes even scatter-gun. However, make no mistake, good coaches know ***exactly*** where they are in their conversations, and what the purpose and impact of each question they ask is likely to be. Good coaches know exactly why they choose one question over another, why they are leaving pauses, what to chase through and what to expand. This takes time to practice and to achieve (fortunately there is no shortage of time or practice partners for us parents) and it is essential to be well-grounded in the right mind-set.

Good coaching is a mindset - more an attitude than a set of language skills. There are theories, rationales, real life stories, typical scenarios, exercises and useful coaching questions and tips. There are opportunities to explore our efforts, mistakes and link them to the other chapters. For coaching to be useful, it is required to be very much an integrated process; there are very few coaching skills that work optimally in isolation.

good coaching is a mindset – more an attitude than a set of language skills

So, metaphorically speaking, we are going to design and build a Coach House. Or, (to complement the aspirational nature of coaching), let's make it a Castle; a Chateau perhaps? We are going to stake out our chosen plot of land, taking into consideration the most attractive and useful aspects of the ground we are preparing. Once we are sure of our perimeters, we can begin to map out the areas we want to build and shape, work out where to dig the foundations and how deep it might be necessary to go. Then we can steadily build upwards, wall by wall, floor by floor.

And then move in and live there happily.

In the initial chapters, this book focuses on outlining solid frameworks within which to embed our nascent foundation skills. The coaching **'Stakes'** are represented by Chapters 5-26; each stake needs to be driven firmly into our coaching landscape, one by one, so as to create a safe, calm and considered enclosure. Once this enclosure is secured, it serves to protect the **'Ladders'** (represented by Chapters 27-32) as the Chateau slowly takes shape.

So the invitation is to spend as much time as we can in Part Two, (chapters 5-26). Weeks preferably, *at least*; months if needs be. That means twenty-three more chapters after this one still to ponder on and all of them are designed to set the scene from which our coaching can productively commence. As we become more proficient in the new skills and techniques with which to reach our children, the emphasis on the framework and support structures becomes more illuminated. A chapter we have read today will have a new significance in three months' time, with that much more coaching under our belts.

Read a chapter. Practice a little. Reflect a little more. Drive that stake in further. Re-read.

Repeat with the next chapter...and so on.

Be ***patient*** with each and every one. Patience will serve us well, as our coaching embeds at home.

The first half of this book is concerned with setting up a coachable environment with our children. The second half is concerned with the skill of coaching them. I understand totally that we may be keen to get going with the practicality of coaching our children, and we may, therefore, want to skim through the first half of the book to arrive at Part Three more quickly. Just bear in mind that coaching cannot be effective if the child's mind is unprepared or unreceptive. The first half of this book is aimed at creating prepared and receptive minds. Spend that extra time reading Part Two - all of it. When we have really invested in that preparation, our coaching will be received so much more easily - we will notice the difference.

coaching cannot be effective if the child's mind is unprepared or unreceptive

My first strong suggestion (and it is just that - a suggestion), is that the messages and exercises in each chapter of this book should be learned, implemented and practised ***IN THE ORDER IN WHICH THEY ARE WRITTEN***. Read, understand and practice the 'stakes' and the 'ladders' as they appear. Ascend and descend each ladder mindfully, (the first ladder leads to the basement and foundations), and don't skip too many rungs. Don't skip ***ANY*** if possible - stay patient. If we miss too many rungs we may slip and it becomes more challenging to re-cover the same ground. Trust me, it's not worth it for the want of speedy progress to new aspects of our coaching ambitions.

My second suggestion is to ***take at least one month*** practising on each of the Ladders in Part Three. Let's not be tempted to jump ahead. By all means, we can read ahead, then re-read as many times as we can find time for. But reading alone will not produce practical mastery. So by all means too, let's start ***practising*** the skills and ideas immediately if we're so inclined. However, for a culture of coaching to even begin to take hold in a family there is so much to consolidate, embed and settle.

Then in Part Three there are six, expansive chapters (27 to 32) to complete our grounding in coaching.

The First and Second Ladders serve to further consolidate the initial framework and foundations too. These are the basement and ground floor of our Coach Chateau. Then, we put up the Third, Fourth, Fifth and Sixth Coaching Ladders - these are, if you like, the upstairs living quarters in which we practically explore the skills and techniques that we'll use in our families. If we feel impatient to get stuck in, we can be using and trying out these skills and techniques simultaneously with the framework chapters. Just let's make sure if we do, that we always keep one eye firmly on the groundwork in Part Two.

we ***absolutely*** need to embed structure and framework ***before*** coaching can have a chance of taking hold permanently

I view coaching as an accumulative process; the ladders can be approached one by one. We can practice and evaluate our own levels of emotional intelligence and bring these qualities to the forefront of our children's consciousnesses too. Coaching conversations are heavily structured, although in the care of a seasoned coach the structure is all but invisible, so don't be fooled. We absolutely need to embed this structure and framework before coaching can have a chance of taking hold permanently.

Setting up the frameworks to suit our own families will take more or less time depending on where we feel our relationships with our children are right now. And only we can judge that for ourselves - no-one else is qualified to advise us, nor should they try. I'm certainly not going to preach on that one. Common sense dictates that it's best to err on the side of caution if we're unsure - so let's keep coming back to the chapters in Part Two throughout our coaching journey. We will ***always*** find that a new nugget or reminder will pop out at us - ***every time.*** How do I know this? Because the brain, once we learn to kick start it, loves to make associations, so it has a unique ability to find evidence and relevance for the exact stage of learning each of us is ready to embrace.

our brains have a unique ability to find the exact stage of learning each of us is ready to embrace

There is a misconception that coaching is about skills. However, ***it is the intention behind the skills that matters the most and without doubt the key to this intention is Emotional Intelligence. Without this, no amount of coaching skills will make parenting easier.***

Are we all familiar with this term 'Emotional Intelligence'? I've mentioned it a couple of times already and will mention it many, many times more. In the late 1980s, two American psychologists, Peter Salovey of Yale and John Mayer of the University of New Hampshire were looking for a term which would sum up human qualities such as empathy, self-awareness and emotional control. They coined this phrase ***'Emotional Intelligence.'*** A few years later, in the early 1990s, Daniel Goleman, a writer with The New York Times, brought the term into the public domain through the production of his book: 'Emotional Intelligence: why it can matter more than IQ,' which became a bestseller.

Emotional Intelligence then became abbreviated to EQ. Most of us have come across IQ - the Intelligence Quotient which guides us towards an assessment of our abilities to manipulate data, facts and statistics. EQ - the Emotional Quotient - guides us towards our emotional reflexes to situations and is undoubtedly the underpinning of coaching. Chapter 27 (The First Ladder) in Part Three covers this thoroughly and these qualities will be continually referred to throughout the rest of the book.

EQ is undoubtedly the underpinning of coaching

SKILLS, TECHNIQUES AND TOOLS

It may well take several weeks, maybe even well into the second or third months, before we reach these Ladders in Part Three. If this is the case, we should pat ourselves on our backs for our patience and thoroughness. Seriously, do just that. Regularly.

Self-acknowledgement as a parent is a dying art and certainly hugely neglected - far too often we look for the things that are not working, the things to improve on, and ignore the millions of opportunities to appreciate the sincere and laudable efforts we make to help grow our children.

> ***Like buying this book - there's one.***
> ***Actually reading it - there's a second.***
> ***Making decisions to act on it - dozens more, instantly.***

use Permission as a master key to unlock the doors that open onto the more useful coaching spaces

With several weeks of groundwork under our belts we can start exploring and practising the skills highlighted in our Six Ladders of Coaching. We start our learning by acquiring and consolidating real emotional intelligence (First Ladder). This ladder is the one we descend into our basement, where we will construct strong foundations. The Second Ladder takes us up to the ground floor, the floor on which we would welcome people into our Chateau. On this level we are creating an understanding of the importance of being open and respectful with our children.

In order to go up the stairs to a higher floor in the Chateau, the respectful tradition would be to ask Permission, (Third Ladder), the power of which is massively underestimated in building rapport and trust - two central pillars of the coaching process. I considered portraying Permission as part of Emotional Intelligence, and including it in the basement but I have chosen instead to give it its own floor, the first floor, of our Chateau, where we can fully explore and work through all aspects of it.

the power of asking permission is massively underestimated in building rapport and trust

When used well, Permission creates a profoundly attentive social space, welcoming in deep thinking and self-exploration as enthusiastic, informed visitors. We will come to use Permission as a master key, unlocking the doors that open onto the more useful coaching spaces; the secret rooms, the hidden balconies of the child's mind and interpretations.

They'll be thrilled to re-discover them with us too.

one cannot be truly effective as a coach without an advanced level of EQ

Above this floor we will discover the traditional skills of Listening, alongside Insightful Questioning. The Fourth and Fifth Ladders will lead us up to build these second and third floors. Most people with just a smattering of understanding of coaching, associate Listening and Questioning as central to good coaching. Rightly so. However, even with the highest level understanding of the mechanics of wonderful listening and asking insightful questions, ***one cannot be truly effective as a coach without an advanced level of EQ***. That may sound a contentious statement - but I'm sticking to it. I like to believe I still have an open mind on most things, but I'd struggle to think otherwise on this one. (Which is why I insist on using EQ bricks to build the Chateau foundations).

That word of caution notwithstanding, enjoy these chapters 30 and 31 - there is a lot in them. Spend time mastering the much admired and sought after ability of spontaneous question formulation which involves fluently creating a further insightful question straight off the back of the response to our last. Much easier said than done.

Listening, processing, creating searching questions, asking them, and then listening once more. Each coaching conversation is a brand new performance, or at least a full dress-rehearsal; scripts no longer allowed on stage, safety nets are down - it's us and our audience, and the audience (our children) don't have the faintest idea where their minds might lead them.

> coaching skills will never leave us and will be copied and enhanced by our children when they become parents

Some major wins can, and frequently do, appear very quickly - immediately even. Sometimes on the very first try. Effective listening and questioning are the evergreens of the coaching woodland - resilient, constant, lush and deliciously challenging to climb.

And lastly, Feedback could also, (along with Permission), justifiably have been included in the foundations section but something has to come first and my own experience guides me to the conclusion that it is best delivered once one has some coaching tools readily available on one's workbench.

Our Sixth Ladder however takes us onto the top floor of our Chateau, where we explore The Gift of Coaching Feedback from an appropriately elevated position. The views are spectacular from up there. We'll see soon enough.

Learning to appreciate others effortlessly, and in the process becoming more aware of ***who we are*** as we do what we do, are inescapable by-products of coach training. Becoming more able to diffuse sticky situations, where sensitive Feedback is required, is explained here from a coach's standpoint. Let's spend time exploring and practising all aspects of Feedback with our children. It wouldn't surprise me to find that we immediately notice more respect and attention surfacing as we get to grips with them. Truthfully, it would be more surprising if we didn't.

> the beauty of coaching, once embedded, is that it becomes hard-wired very quickly and passes on to following generations naturally

Then with all this in place, or at least front of mind, we can spend the rest of our lives applying these skills to all sorts of family situations: preventing and resolving conflicts, setting goals and actions or unravelling the limiting beliefs and assumptions that may have implanted themselves. The integration of the coaching skills in these applications, (daily, hourly, for several weeks and months, please - minimum)! - will never leave us and will be copied and enhanced by our children when they become parents. That is the beauty of coaching - once it is learnt well and embedded daily, it becomes hard-wired very quickly, and passed on to following generations naturally.

Nobody I have ever met, has found reason to later reject the skills or renounce the effects of coaching at its best. Yes, I did say nobody. Ever.

Well, not yet anyway...

So if we're really adhering to the long, rocky road approach, we'll enjoy finding time for a little self-evaluation. How have we been doing? What are the main changes in our relationships? And don't just think that it's our family relationships which will be transformed. We will find changes at work, socially and in ourselves too. Make time to stop and really notice them. Remember this is a small step by small step process and the idea is to be a ***FULLY***-rounded and competent parent-coach by the ***END*** of the process over a few months or more. (Not a ***PARTIALLY***-informed and optimistic parent-coach in a couple of weeks).

I don't resort that often to capital letters for emphasis in this book but I feel fully justified in doing so here.

'(And here): Be Patient. Trust My Process. Do The Groundwork.'

Coaching at its purest requires us to be very aware of the words we choose, our intentions and our shared agendas with our children. And we will be after working through this book. Read through the examples and practise them rigorously if they seem appropriate. Also, the spirit of Openness will most likely have become far more ingrained, consciously and subconsciously, in our relationships at the end of Chapter 32 than we may feel is possible or appropriate right now as we read these initial pages on Day One.

Coaching skills can help us deal with some of the more tricky subjects that parents often feel poorly equipped to tackle. Our efforts will be measurably rewarded if we really spend time investing in these foundations, and have heavily prepared and grounded our families in what we are attempting. We may want to practise using these techniques and philosophies to uncover some rarely talked-about subjects. This is vulnerable, exposed, Triple 'A' coaching territory (Access-All-Areas). This is no mean feat we are embarking on - it's a deep dive and it's not for the faint-hearted.

If we can do this well in six months, we truly deserve an honorary Coaching PhD. But be happy if it is still taking shape in twelve. Pats on the back all round for sticking with it.

Spending time together as a family for a number of days can bring its own tensions as well as rewards. As someone said, "Fish and families stink after three days on top of each other". So when we find ourselves mildly dreading the next Birthday/Eid/Hanukkah/Christmas/Diwali where the family is assembling under one roof - let's work through this book now in anticipation of the same date in twelve months when I can GUARANTEE we will look back over our coaching investment and smile indulgently. Coaches don't make many guarantees, but I'm happy in this case to be sticking my neck out.

(Although if there's been no change in your own family dynamics, pass the book on to another family and write to me for a refund. Alternatively, re-read and re-affirm the techniques. It will take hold eventually!)

I know I have repeated many times the wisdom of taking several months to work through all the sections. If you purchased this book, or were given it as a 'present' by a friend (possibly a subliminal hint there)? ***persist through the ups and downs*** over the full term, then in twelve months' time our next special date with the family all together ***WILL*** be markedly and beautifully different.

Because by then, we will have read and absorbed all sections of this book, some sections several times over, and we will have assimilated the messages, stories and learning into our everyday communication. We will have practised the exercises, hopefully made some magnificent mistakes and taken risks - (we're not getting the full learning benefits if we haven't) - jumped ahead, back-tracked, laughed, cried, shouted, mediated, moaned and marvelled.

But in doing so we will have been there. Really been there. Fully present with our own children ***and with ourselves*** at each and every moment, each junction, each backward step, each breakthrough. Our intentions will have been minutely tested, but remained resolute, positive and intact. Our emotional intelligence will be fortified and our sense of self-awareness will never have been stronger.

We are already demonstrating a commendable desire to understand, grow and shape our children just by buying and reading this book in the first place. Parenting is a long-haul lifestyle choice, probably the longest-haul we can undertake. Some say, perhaps ungenerously, a life sentence, with little possibility of parole, even for good behaviour. So let's stay our impatience and allow this book to take us through a 'step-by-step' to these happy habits of coaching.

In an enlightening twelve months we ***will*** find an authentic coaching voice. And the good news is that it is worth it when we do. It will be a full, rich and compelling voice. When we notice it in others, we'll recognise it. When we notice it in ourselves, we'll smile. Embracing this monumental responsibility is courageous and noble and right.

So now let's come back to the present and begin at the beginning. I wish you all the adventure, fun and joy that coaching has brought me and my relationships. Ever consuming, ever challenging, ever fascinating.

4.

James Mackenzie Wright's Handy 'CASE' Principle

Just before we really get cracking with our endeavours to create a cordial coaching culture at home, I feel now is a good time to introduce my CASE principle of learning. Anyone yet come across this as a learning model? In the true spirit of the CASE principle, I invite you to Copy And Steal Everything – if it works for us, let's make it our own, and offer it to other people. (When I say 'my' CASE principle, it doesn't really matter if I made it up or someone told it to me. I can't remember either way and anyway, it's mine now and it's certainly my least 'audacious' acronym among those whose acquaintance we have yet to make in this book).

I'm sure I haven't originated most of the ideas in this book. Coaching has been around far longer than I have. Certainly I may have developed them or reshaped them, but I doubt my brain has actually come up with much real honest-to-goodness 'new learning' in this book. Whose has? Interpretation is everything, everything is interpretation.

By way of illustrating just one CASE example from the millions one could quote, I have chosen this one from the world of art. Roy Lichtenstein is a name you may know. He was a family man of nearly forty years of age when he started to produce his now iconic Pop paintings derived from comic books and newspaper advertisements in the early 1960s. He created an artistic technique, and therefrom a style which is instantly associated with his name. However, it is widely recognised, and accepted, that he 'borrowed' his inspiration for his clean-cut, humorous and youthful images from the available low-culture mass-media sources at the time.

In his own words, he admits without difficulty, ***"I am nominally copying, but I am really restating the copied thing in other terms. In doing that, the original acquires a totally different texture."*** The technique, too, relied upon his 'restating' an existing technique using 'Benday dots' (the name comes from their originator Benjamin Henry Day), and combining them with flat areas of solid print colour and unyielding lines.

Carol Wilson, Nancy Kline, Sir John Whitmore, Liz Macann, Khalil Gibran, Deepak Chopra, Gene Early, Anthony Robbins, David Grove - all are wonderful coaching, spiritual and literary gurus, alongside dozens more authors, workshop participants, teachers, parents and children I have met, worked with and been delighted by. All are represented in these pages and their inspiration and sincere efforts copied and stolen for our coaching delectation. Sorry, maybe that should read, *'nominally copied and restated in other terms'* for our coaching delectation.' Whatever - hey, if it's OK by Lichtenstein, it's OK by me.

I should add though that I always make strident attempts to locate and accurately reflect the sources of information and facts in this book. Where I am aware of the source I have, of course, always given credit - that's fair and proper. All the remaining associations, examples, stories and interpretations are mine and everyone is welcome to them all.

What I am sure of is that all this 'coaching-ness' is an immensely powerful thing, and our missions, should we choose to accept them, are to spread the word and ***try to live it*** by coaching our own children. So now I offer all these thoughts openly and anything that grabs anybody, use it – it now belongs to all of us.

Simply ***reading*** about it and ***knowing*** it is not enough.

Bring it to life, have a go, make a difference - any way we can let's ***GET IT OUT THERE***!

Let our coaching games begin.

PART TWO
COACHING STAKES

PREPARING SPACES FOR CHILD-FRIENDLY COACHING

Timothy: Here's what I know: if you came to me and said,
"There are two people in the world who want you more than anything;
they will do their best and they will make some mistakes,
and you will only get them for a short time;
they will love you more than you can ever imagine;
well, when that's true I'd say so much is possible."

The Odd Life of Timothy Green, 2012

5.

Why Youngsters' Brains Don't Behave As Parents Want Them To

What I have observed about the early years of human development, from birth to around twelve years old, is that these years seem to pass relatively smoothly compared to the next ten or so years. Am I eagle-eyed or what? And now 'teenage-hood' is generally acknowledged as a *bona fide*, stand-alone stage of human evolution since the mid-twentieth century. But, strangely, just knowing this fact, and having practised ***being*** a teenager for seven (in truth, more like fifteen) years doesn't seem to make a blind bit of difference to the occasional bewilderment I still regularly encounter when attempting to ***manage*** the blighters these days.

Compared with other animals that apparently manage the change from youngster to adult fairly predictably and harmoniously, human adolescence is a period fraught with emotional turbulence. Why should this be so? And from a more solutions-focused angle, how could it be most sensitively understood and managed by those who have assumed a role of developmental responsibility? And among that population specifically, by us parents, whose job spec includes the tricky hot spots of the early morning and evening shifts?

Scientists currently tell us that our brains, far from being a finished article at twelve years old as previously thought, continue to undergo major structural changes right through our teenage years and into our early twenties. The frontal cortex thickens before the onset of puberty and slowly shrinks back to normal size over a further dozen or so years.

Social cognition appears not to kick in till age twenty-one or even later. Very convenient if true. No wonder the youngsters' bedrooms resemble bomb sites, the telephone is answered brusquely and the dirty clothes don't make it to the laundry basket. I wonder, since parental efforts are made to hardwire the child's brain at this early pre-social cognitive stage with worthy messages of personal responsibility, big-picture awareness, tolerance, consideration, etc., whether this is actually a mightily ineffective use of our vocal chords? Or conversely, whether social awareness may actually be accelerated by insisting on these messages? And if so, would it have to be at the cost of other hardwiring? In which case what might we miss least? Or most?

For all we lecture young people about the way they should behave, society - of which we adults are the epitome - very often is perceived to condone behaviour that does not warrant respect for another's person, possessions or indeed thoughts. How adversarial are our politicians in parliament, for example? How dictatorial do we expect our business leaders to be?

Interesting that the reality show 'The Apprentice' starring Alan Sugar, multimillionaire founder of Amstrad, (now elevated to Lord Sugar) is given prime-time TV slots and repeat series to showcase the business tycoon disparaging and belittling his would-be employees. Those same 'no-longer-going-to-be' employees generally slope off after receiving the triumphant "You're Fired!" catchphrase, muttering and chuntering petulantly to the cameras and anyone else who will listen about how they were wronged by Sugar and betrayed by their fellow contestants.

A similar programme featuring Richard Branson, billionaire founder of Virgin, (now elevated merely to Sir Richard Branson) received only late-night TV slots and no repeat series. Could it be that the reason for this is that Richard Branson was unfailingly polite and respectful to his would-be employees, who almost all without exception accepted his dismissals maturely, graciously, praising him, his organisation and the other contestants?

Evidently, conflict is still king.

So it transpires that the resulting mood swings, need for excessive sleep, (are you among the parents who often wonder how ***anyone*** can sleep that much?) apathy, indifference to apparent risk, exaggerated emotional response, are all normal responses to the brain's development at this age. So could it ***actually*** be that our youngsters are not ***deliberately*** trying to cause us maximum suffering? Could it actually be that the ***opposite*** is the case? That, in fact, ***they too are baffled by their reactions to seemingly innocuous everyday situations, and are valiantly attempting to wrestle themselves back towards their innate intelligence and goodness?*** All the while flying in the face of the treacherous desertion of responsibility by their brains?

The brain, the one organ that could assist them to make sense of their world has decided mischievously to engage in stretching and shrinking experiments, and coincided the timing with its young patron's critical years. Outrageous behaviour. And not content with that, it unchivalrously chooses to compound the confusion by triggering spontaneous floods of chemicals and hormones to further unbalance any possible moments of stability. Here's just one brain chain reaction: emotional behaviour triggers floods of cortisol in the pre-frontal cortex, restricting dopamine flow, inhibiting rational thought, causing ill-considered responses and leading to... more emotional behaviour. Catch 22.

On the face of it, it seems to be very poor timing by Mother Nature. But then is there ever a best time for a human brain to go AWOL? It is as if Mother Nature has weighed up the odds over several million years and plumped for the teen years as the ***least worst*** socially acceptable ten year period to fine tune a brain. So now it stands a fighting chance of operating for another hundred years without further intrinsic restructuring. Just a thought.

Fortunately ***all*** of us adults grow through these random, childlike episodes and have now left them far, far behind (haven't we?)... We ***all*** long ago chose to discard them as the flotsam and jetsam of an adolescent rite of passage leading to adulthood (didn't we?)... Ah, adulthood - where all ***our*** conversations are now such well-reasoned, balanced templates of respect and consideration (aren't they?)... Because all things considered, if we hadn't chosen this new high ground, and if our dialogues with one another weren't so exemplary, think how stressful and precarious adult (grown-up) life in shops, offices, classrooms, courtrooms, planes, cars, hospitals would otherwise be...

So, irony aside, just maybe, since children and teenagers are in a position to be overseen by us adults while they make their howlers, on balance it's probably a lot safer for everyone. Although even as science tries to rationalise their irrationalities, the practical and emotional challenges of managing our children and teenagers remain as acute as ever.

Did Mother Nature plan around that too - returning our wayward, fully serviced brains to us as young, vibrant adults, just in time for parenthood? Very timely if so.

6.

Ten Core Principles Of Coaching

It would be difficult to exclude any worthy principle that we currently live by, like Honesty, Integrity, Respect, Kindness, Warmth, Playfulness and so on, from a list of Coaching principles. Whenever I ask a workshop group for their ideas about coaching principles they usually come up with a good core list and nearly always a number of outliers too - view points by which individuals live with good intentions and purpose. One's point of view after all depends on one's viewing point. So I have chosen the ten that seem to me to be most indispensable to coaching. Add others by all means if they fit for your coaching.

They are:

Action	**Responsibility**
Awareness	**Self-Belief**
Blame Free	**Self-Directed Learning**
Challenge	**Solution Focus**
Detachment	**Trust**

Action

actions are the coaching glue

Coaching uncovers new perspectives and awareness. By being asked coaching questions, children gain new insights. New insights inevitably lead to thoughts of more things to do, which in turn lead to a desire to take action and change things. Naturally there is a point in coaching purely for awareness and insight, although, while these are useful, they cannot effect much actual tangible and measurable change until converted into actions and new behaviours. With action comes the opportunity to replace old outdated habits with newer ones, and since parent-coaches have day to day access to children, they are best placed to monitor this process.

Actions are the coaching glue. With no actions to complete, from one session to another, there is little to bind the accumulative thoughts together. Actions are under constant review and the completion or non-completion of this week's actions determines the actions to be identified for completion next week. And so on. It is rare to have a coaching session and not feel that some sort of actions should be

undertaken as a result, which puts it right at the core of the coaching continuum.

aware children radiate confidence, decisiveness, empathy, grace and fun

Awareness

Coaching delivers many beneficial outcomes, given time. It is not always perceived as the first choice of intervention by parents, mostly on grounds of just that: time. ***"We just don't have the time to wait while Simon works out things for himself. Sometimes you just have to tell kids what to do, they have to learn that the world doesn't stand still and wait for them, nowadays."*** Few parents wouldn't sympathise with this viewpoint, and there is probably some truth in it. The problem comes with the word 'sometimes.' I notice we parents can be very fluid with the definition of ***'sometimes'***; how often it seems to metamorphose as ***'always.'***

handing out relentless advice to save time is a false economy

This outlook, repeated innumerable times as the child grows up, serves only to deny a child the opportunities and infinite benefits derived from developing its own awareness. Awareness is the most beneficial outcome produced by coaching. Awareness of oneself means becoming one's own observer, one's own inner critic, and noticing how one's inner actions are relating to the outer world.

everything the parent-coach says and does is focused on raising the child's own self-knowledge and awareness of its place in the world

As we have noted earlier in the book, there are still misconceptions that coaching is solely about skills. There are also misconceptions that coaching is about pushing people, or cajoling them, or leading them to awareness or solutions. It's not. Let's be very clear. That is personal training or advising or instructing.

Coaching takes the opposite road of purely ***asking searching questions*** and yet the result is that children still move forward, identify goals and make changes. Aware children radiate confidence, decisiveness, empathy, grace and fun. Meet a child like this and one can bet there is a level of coaching going on at home. This is because everything the parent-coach says and does is focused on raising the child's own self-knowledge and awareness of its place in the world.

awareness is the most beneficial and far-reaching product of coaching

Creating awareness in children, in ourselves, in adult friends, in colleagues, in anyone takes time. Of course it does. However, handing out relentless advice to save time is a false economy, not to mention stressful. We might expect ***adult*** friends and colleagues to be relatively aware over a lifetime of experiences, and therefore we don't feel inclined to invest quite so heavily in their development. But it doesn't work with children. Creating 'advice-addicts' is lazy parenting. Young advice-addicts can never be self-aware until they can kick the habit. And how can they kick the habit while living with their 'dealer?'

What would be our answers to the questions:

"How many adults do I know who show little awareness and perception of how the world works?"

"How much energy do they seem to drain from me and others to support their lives?"

Or to this one:

"Do I want my children to become radiators or drains?"

Creating 'advice-addicts' is lazy parenting. Young advice-addicts can never be self aware until they can kick the habit. And how can they kick the habit while living with their 'dealer?'

Blame Free

Two example situations, one theme:

One: In Hatha yoga there is a very tricky balancing pose known as Standing Bow-Pulling Pose. To arrive deeper and deeper into this pose week by week, it is necessary to twist, stretch and maintain balance and...fall out of the posture. No-one in the history of yoga has ever managed to master this pose without falling out hundreds and thousands of times. Indeed the Yogi will tell the students, ***"Mastery of this posture can only be achieved by falling out and learning how not to."***

No yoga student will ever be chastised for not holding this, or indeed any other pose.

Two: Considered one of the best basketball players ever, Michael Jordan dominated the sport in the USA from the mid-1980s to the late 1990s. He led the Chicago Bulls to six national championships, and earned the National Basketball Association's Most Valuable Player Award five times. He says of himself ***"I've missed more than nine thousand shots in my career. I've lost almost three hundred games. Twenty-six times, I've been trusted to take the game winning shot and missed. I've failed over and over and over again in my life. And that is why I succeed."***

in a coaching culture, mistakes are viewed as learning experiences, not reasons to look for a scapegoat

His coach, Phil Jackson was convinced of his superstar qualities and in the time-outs he would call in the dying seconds, where games are won and lost, he would tell the team, "Get the ball to Michael." And the team understood that Michael would know what to do and would never blame him if he missed the shot.

In a coaching culture, mistakes are viewed as learning experiences, not reasons to look for a scapegoat. Children learn more from 'failure' than from 'achievement' although they are not always as articulately equipped to rationalise those failures in this way, as an adult might be. Indeed, in the wider learning scheme, suppose we were to follow that logic through, the failures would become the desired outcomes and the achievements the consolation prize. Regardless it is therefore crucially

Children learn more from 'failure' than from 'achievement'

important for the parent-coach to provide support and encouragement rather than blame during times of failure.

Challenge

> in the wider learning scheme, the failures would become the desired outcomes and the achievements the consolation prize

Most children like to be challenged and stretched, provided they feel they are within a supportive and encouraging environment. If they don't perceive this support, and yet are still challenged, they can feel isolated and wary. Outcomes can be negotiated with the children and they can come to understand that "Shooting for the stars and only reaching the moon" doesn't have to equate with being a failure.

Only one outstanding athlete in any given competition can ever win the gold medal - the second placed athlete is not now a failure, simply an outstanding athlete with a silver medal. And, most likely, given the nature of competitiveness, a hunger to come back for more. A parent-coach helps the child to step back and look for new perspectives. Coaching is sometimes described as 'holding up a mirror' to the child. Seeing their lives reflected back enables children to see their lives in proportion, often for the first time.

> it is crucially important for the parent-coach to provide support and encouragement rather than blame during times of failure

When we have been allowed to coach our child, we can ask to be further allowed to negotiate challenges. (Gaining these permissions opens so many doors to new dialogue - we'll see more in Part Three). If our son says that he would like to sing in the school choir, we can offer, ***but never insist on,*** the idea that he might want to consider an even bigger challenge. By appreciating his decision; ***"Good for you! You have a lovely singing voice,"*** and asking, ***"What might be an even bigger stretch for you right now?"*** he might reflect on the possibility of eventually singing a solo part.

If our daughter says she might like to become the class representative, we can ask the same question - "what might be an even bigger stretch for you right now?" Whether or not she might be interested to challenge herself further, the gauntlet has been thrown down, along with an implicit belief that, should she choose to stand for election as house captain in due course, we, as her parents, fully believe in her strong leadership qualities.

Challenge is core to coaching. The only caveat occurs when our agendas and theirs 'diverge' and we find ourselves "suggesting" that our children might wish to reach for ***our ambitions for them***. This may add stresses and pressures they have not chosen to undergo and may well be less healthy for their personal growth. Make sure that if they agree to further challenge, they must search for their own challenges.

Whatever they decide is ambitious enough for now, must be allowed to be, yes... ambitious enough for now.

Detachment

Pure coaching (i.e. asking searching questions) often succeeds in capturing the trust and buy-in of young people where instructing, directing and assisting may have failed. Why might this be? I believe that in many cases, detachment is the key. Although it appears counter-intuitive for parents to distance themselves from the outcome of their child's choices, by doing so they are creating a learning space for the child to fill independently, without judgment and without aid. This is immensely empowering for the child and ultimately for the parent too.

How do we feel as parents when we realise our children have sorted out tricky dilemmas by themselves that we were unaware of until after they were resolved? ***"Relieved,"*** is a common response from parents, and the children will often report a sense of pride and probably a tangible boost to their self-confidence. All very positive. So why then, when our child's next dilemma ***is*** brought to our attention, do we automatically offer 'help' when that help might well be to deprive our child of the opportunity to experience more of that same self-confidence and pride? On the other hand, would we prefer to have been kept in the dark, if there was a possibility of knowing the dilemma?

A tricky dilemma for us parents then, too. But let's look around us. We won't see our children clamouring to help us sort our tricky dilemma out. Maybe they just trust us to find a way through whatever comes our way, so they decide not to pry into our affairs too much. They choose to believe in us and maintain a blissful detachment - very empowering for us adults, especially since there's a pretty good chance that given space and time we ***will*** find the right answer...

So detachment seems to be a function of treating people equally and respectfully. If we appreciate the benefits we feel from sorting out our own situations, we can better appreciate the benefits of allowing others to sort theirs. If it works for me, it will work for them. If I can trust myself, I can trust them to trust themselves. Quid Pro Quo. Kid Pro Quo. Wonderful. No longer any need to meddle.

if we appreciate the benefits we feel from sorting out our own situations, we can better appreciate the benefits of allowing others to sort theirs

[Dictionary definition: meddle, *medl*, verb: to interfere with or busy oneself with something that is not one's concern]. (The parental definition of meddle seems to have a slightly different slant to it: help, advise, suggest, be useful). The truth is, if we parents weren't around, the children would likely work 'it' out, whatever 'it' was. Do adults maybe forget too easily that other (younger) people have brains that work well too, given the space to do so?

Some parents I meet often question 'detachment' as a core coaching principle. They can see the value of it, though they feel that some expression of concern, caring, would also be in order. Instead of,

"What might happen when you leave yourself so short of time?" they suggest:

"When you leave yourself so short of time, it makes me feel anxious".

Nothing wrong with this really - straight out of the Non-Violent Communication handbook. But let's pick that up another time.

it's no accident that 'listen' is an anagram of 'silent'

The fact is that children love to be able to demonstrate their abilities, knowledge and common-sense. They ask for chances to prove this in so many ways. Sadly, we parents register their requests in so many ***other*** ways, and override the opportunities by hastily concocting our own quick-fixes. Let's slow down and listen from the outside a bit more often. And when I say listen I mean listen ***without comment***. I'm convinced it's no accident that 'listen' is an anagram of 'silent.'

It's not that we're not compassionate or empathetic or knowledgeable or experienced. It's more a question of whether demonstrating these qualities is going to be useful to our children's thinking at all times. And if not, I must trust that my TOPCAT* children will know what to do, and what the right course of action is ***for them***. Because they will.

(*See Chapter 19)

Let's establish a new alternative from here on in, to that tried and mistrusted management maxim of 'command and control.' Here it is:

Trust and Detach. (See Chapter 19)

Responsibility

'Trust and Detach' - the new command and control

Remember the day our child took its first few steps? And inevitably fell over? Did we pick the child up and explain to it why it fell, or tell it where to put its feet next time? Did we advise it to wait a few months till it gets stronger and then try again? I'm guessing we didn't do any of those things. I'm guessing we, like every other parent on the planet, were ecstatic and praised the child for its cleverness and encouraged it to take more steps while we took photos? We probably cleared a space too on the floor so that it had the least number of obstacles to navigate. In coaching vocabulary we 'created a learning space conducive to optimum success.' And to complete the picture I'm guessing we probably repeated this process when the child spoke its first few words?

We understand an acorn has inside it all the 'oaktreeness' it requires to fully develop; we don't feel the need to inject it with genes to create an even bigger oak tree or stronger branches or greener leaves. We allow it the responsibility to grow itself using the nutrients and environment it finds itself in.

In the same way we understand that, as they decided to begin the journey of walking and talking, our children had inside them all the 'walkingness' and 'talkingness' knowledge they required, and that all they needed from us was support and encouragement. Which we all willingly gave, I'm sure. We allowed them then the responsibility of learning to walk and talk naturally. Granted, we would input with vocabulary, or grammar as they grew older, and perhaps balance exercises and sporting techniques too in the fulness of time. ***But the ownership of the initial responsibilities is theirs and theirs alone.***

So, some pertinent (and responsible) questions we parents might do well to ask ourselves could be:

"At what point do we decide our child's latest learning venture doesn't merit our ecstasy?"

"When do we decide not to create that optimum learning space, and instead choose to criticise, advise, inject, supervise?"

(In other words, *'meddle.'*)

"What might our drivers be, for us to decide not to create that optimum learning space?"

Questions from a more supportive stance might be:

"What if we were to support and encourage every learning step that our children are likely to take while under our guidance?"

"How much space might we create within which they could take responsibility for successes and failures?"

"How can we parent-coaches therefore remember to take this stance (more often) with our children?"

Parent-coaches have only one agenda: to offer opportunities for self-reflection. Other than that, parent-coaches must allow children to drive their own agenda for learning. Parent-coaches instinctively support and encourage, admittedly from a less detached point of view than 'pure' coaches might.

we learn better when we discover things for ourselves than when others tell us what to notice

We cannot therefore ignore responsibility as a core principle of coaching. Taking ownership of our decisions, self-responsibility in other words, is central to the coaching process. Simply; we learn better when we discover things for ourselves than when others tell us what to notice. We like to create our own solutions rather than be told what to do.

At home this is not always feasible, but if we can parent in a coaching style and delegate responsibilities wherever possible, our children will be more engaged and motivated even when receiving direct instructions. This means focusing on making our children feel as comfortable and confident as possible and treating them with respect, even when it is necessary to be directive.

There may be twenty ways of carrying out a task; the most satisfying way is always the one chosen by the person who has to complete the task. Particularly if that person has had the opportunity to try out several of the other ways first. If our children are allowed to work in a way which suits their styles of learning and performance, they are likely not only to get better results more quickly, but to enjoy the task as well.

the more we parents critically check up on our children's efforts and behaviour, the less effort the children will want to put in themselves

It's tricky to accept, but the more we parents critically check up on our children's efforts and behaviour, the less effort the children will want to put in themselves. I'm not advocating total abdication of parental responsibility towards boundaries, just more awareness of how tightly we need to police them.

Self-Belief

There are three components to building children's confidence (anyone's confidence come to that):

1. Allowing them the space to practise until competent or perfect,
2. Encouraging them to stretch themselves through making mistakes,
3. Giving them appropriate recognition for their achievements.

By 'appropriate' I mean authentic, specific and deserved. (There is more on giving feedback in Chapter 32 - The Sixth Ladder. But please don't jump ahead just yet - these foundations are so crucial to understand first!) Appropriate recognition, especially from people we perceive to be in authority over us, builds confidence, and when we ***believe*** we can achieve something we are more likely to embrace the inevitable obstacles, follow through and achieve it.

Psychologists are adamant that having the ***confidence*** that we can do something is a key factor in our achieving it. Giving people (and particularly ***young*** people) praise when they have done something to deserve it builds immeasurable benefits. Praise ***builds*** their confidence that other people have faith in their abilities, ***builds*** their belief that they can achieve more and ***builds*** their energy to continue doing and improving whatever it is we are praising them for.

Returning to the earlier analogy of the child learning to walk; parents, instead of explaining why the walking is wobbly or unbalanced, praise the child excitedly for every new attempt. A large percentage of the incentive for the child getting up and trying again is to receive that heady mixture of attention and praise. We don't need to tell children how to walk because everyone understands that they will eventually work it out perfectly for themselves. Wholehearted encouragement simply energises the process.

On the other hand, if we shout at or scold a child for a mistake we immediately take the fun out of the learning experience which will affect the motivation and slow everything down. And, similarly, if we over-engage with children's tasks and try to micro-manage their creative processes we will achieve the same tensions. Tension is not a natural companion to fun learning. Neither for children nor for adults. There's a chapter coming up (Chapter 10) provocatively entitled 'Stay Calm, Stay Light.' If we can achieve this feat, in the face of all everyday family adversities, our children's self-belief will soar. So will ours of course, too.

tension is not a natural companion to fun learning

Self-Directed Learning

This is undoubtedly the mummy and daddy of all coaching core principles. Parents who parent in a coaching style focus on empowering their children to identify and develop their own resources so that they may achieve their potential in a fulfilling and stimulating way.

There is nothing new about coaching, only the application of the term. As a national team volleyball 'coach' over many years, I understood myself to be 'a performance coach.' Back then, I understood the term 'coaching' to mean I should advise and direct players how to win matches and improve. I now look back on those years, understanding my 'hobby' spec to have been that of 'instructor and manager.' My understanding was that I had to be the 'best expert' and that I was required to take responsibilities for every outcome, every success, every failure.

Result? Stress.

Many years later, when I encountered afresh the term of 'performance coach' in its purer, more detached iteration, I saw how I could make myself less present in the interactions, and could allow the players themselves to assume the 'best expert' mantle. My hobby spec, (it doesn't seem appropriate to call it a 'job' any more), has become to find ways to grow people by challenging their own perceptions of themselves.

Result? Serenity.

Socrates famously said: "I cannot teach anybody anything - I can only make them think." The concept of 'making people think' is at the core of coaching, where it is referred to as 'self-directed learning.' Parent-coaches can encourage this approach by asking the type of questions which direct the child's focus inward. We must never lose touch with the belief that all children have the capability to be fully active participants in solving their own problems and to decide for themselves how best to move forward in that moment.

all children have the capability to be fully active participants in solving their own problems and to decide for themselves how best to move forward

But let's be in no doubt: self-directed learning is not the only approach to any given situation, though it is the only coaching approach.

There are times when it is absolutely necessary to instruct or tell someone what to do; certainly in family situations where young children are learning to experience the world it is often vital to protect and guide them by giving firm instructions. However, ***directive parenting can still be delivered in a coaching style because the fundamental underpinnings of coaching are about respecting people, creating trust and building confidence.***

Over time, and with practice, we will develop a natural coaching style in our communication, creating rapport, improving our children's responses to challenging situations, and by extension, our own too. We will notice it becoming easier to understand others' viewpoints and to see clearer paths ahead.

self-directed learning is not the only approach to any given situation, though it is the *only coaching approach*

In the spirit of self-directed learning then, let me offer, but not insist, that we consider practising and absorbing the coaching skills covered in this book. I encourage us all then to trust our own judgment on the best way of dealing with our own family situations. There is a lot in this book for us to learn and practise thoroughly and different aspects will appear important to different parents. The likelihood is that this importance will change too, with different children and at different ages and stages of their lives.

Coaching children can never be an exact science, nor a prescribed formula. Each of us is uniquely placed to respond to these coaching aspects, whatever they may be, and in a way that feels right for us and our families. We must work through at a pace to suit us, and then, when the skills and techniques feel more fluent and automatic, modify the rules so they fit most naturally with our own intuition.

And one more thing: trying to emulate someone else's style of coaching, or parenting for that matter, if it is not congruent with our own personality, can be a recipe for distrust and confusion.

We are well advised only ever to coach in one personality - our own. So if we find ourselves unsure who we are or what we stand for, now would be an ideal time to find out.

we are well advised only ever to coach in one personality - our own

Solution Focus

Keeping a sense of an outcome ***at all times*** is essential to being able to ask strong, useful questions and keep children on track. As we will see in Chapter 31, coaching conversations always begin with setting an outcome or goal, which serves as a useful measuring stick as the tasks are undertaken. I am not including a full methodology for goal-setting in a coaching style in this book for the simple reason that young brains do not develop a strong meta-view of what they can realistically control until well into their twenties. This is not to say that children cannot set goals and follow through on them, but generally the support and focus is provided strongly by adults, particularly for longer term and more significant goals.

Setting goals and identifying solutions are an integral part of coaching. The goals for children do not have to be huge and life changing, although they can be. They may be simple, modest or fun goals that just require organisation or time management to complete. The challenge with children's goals is that in many cases there are so many distractions to interrupt the flow of their energies on any given task, it often falls to the parent to disentangle them from the various activities they have become embroiled in and help them focus on just one at a time.

Learning to focus on achieving one solution at a time is often a major step for children, and can be very empowering. Asking open questions like,

"How is this helping you move towards that goal?" or

"What would you like to have achieved in twenty minutes from now, that will make a difference?" or

"What will it be like when you have accomplished that?" or

"I notice we are now moving towards a new direction - how useful is this to the main goal?"

and similar, can be very empowering for young minds, once we can get them to focus fully on the task.

Parent-coaches encourage their children to focus on solutions. When children dwell on a problem, it seems to get bigger and drains their energy, and with it their motivation. When we can assist them to focus on a solution, their problem seems smaller and they find more energy and resources to deal with it.

Trust

Children and young people often report that they feel comfortable opening up to other young people after a surprisingly short space of time. They seem to be more willing than some adults to trust their instincts and allow themselves to be vulnerable after a relatively short period of friendship. They also, however, report that these trust bonds can be regularly, and often hurtfully, broken when the friendships break up. This can be a precursor to them being more wary of establishing trust bonds as adults.

How many people can we think of that we could happily tell anything to; our secrets, our misdemeanours, our mistakes and our fears, and KNOW that we would not be judged or ridiculed or gossiped about? Most adults I put this question to can think of less than five, and usually just one or two. When I then ask how long does it take us to build those relationships to that point, where we are completely sure of that person, most report that it takes a long time; the commonest answer is, "many years."

So why would we expect that as coaches, people will open up to us in the same way, ten minutes after introducing ourselves for the first time? Or certainly within the next few weeks of a coaching relationship? It's a big ask, and yet people do just that. And the only reason I can think of as to why they would do that is that as coaches we ***guarantee*** that we are to be trusted with all that personal information from a dispassionate yet involved perspective.

That's a bit of an oxymoron, yet I believe it is the essential component to the success of any coaching relationship. Liz Macann, spent twelve years as Head of the BBC's award-winning in-house Executive, Leadership and Management Coaching Network. Her words on coaching are to be carefully attended to, she coined one of the most enlightened phrases I have yet encountered to define and describe coaching: ***'listening with riveted detachment'.***

listen with 'riveted detachment' -Liz Macann

Ten minutes after meeting Liz for a coaching conversation, I imagine most people would have little difficulty in deciding not only to access but also to externalize their deeper thoughts, fears, insights and expectations of themselves, and would easily continue to do so in the following weeks and months of a coaching relationship. We would realize that she would be fully engaged with the responsibility of our self-exploration, while allowing enough space for challenge and respectful confrontation. In the same way, we should always feel we can fully trust our own coach. If we don't, we have the wrong coach.

coaches don't guarantee a lot but they can, and must, always guarantee they are trustworthy

As we've read earlier, coaches don't guarantee a lot. Coaches don't guarantee success, for starters. Top tennis stars all have coaches, as do top golfers but only one can win a tournament at a time, which means several 'losers'. None of these stars are unbeaten so their coaches are evidently not guaranteeing wins for them. Coaches don't guarantee we will achieve our goals, they don't guarantee we will gain promotion, get picked for the basketball team, be happier, or richer or have more friends, a bigger house, better health or a longer life.

But what coaches can and must always guarantee is that they are trustworthy. We must feel we can trust our coach to hold a leak-proof, fully confidential learning space for us to explore ourselves without passing judgment on us, without giving us unsolicited advice, without blaming us for our indecisions and inactions, all the while demonstrating their total belief in us.

It's already a 'big ask' of a seasoned coach, and as a parent this is a tremendously tricky juggling act. The detachment component is a major test of how far we find ourselves able to trust our children to make strong, 'learningful' decisions. If we should decide to practice coaching our children (in addition to the natural day-to-day mentoring, directing, instructing, leading, advising and making helpful suggestions to them), we will find ourselves practicing that juggling act every day for the rest of our lives.

So, the bottom line then, is that without trust it is not possible for coaching to take place. Trust, in all its components is fundamental to every coaching relationship.

* * *

Here's a challenge to all parent-coaches. Read the following question. Now we've read through all the ten core coaching principles, our challenge is to see how many of the principles we can identify that are implicit in this question. Then, whether we can re-word this question so that it becomes more useful from a coaching standpoint by, in effect, wrapping it up in a mantle of any one or all of these principles. Here's the question for the challenge:

"How come you've managed to go a whole week without managing to complete this project despite everything we've told you about managing your time, and now you're rushing it to get it finished and expecting us to drop everything to help?"

Here's what I identify. On the plus side, the question seems to have elements of **responsibility** and **awareness** in it - therefore potentially some learning. Unfortunately the whole question is wrapped up in blame and criticism and attachment, so its effect as a *coaching question* is now severely compromised.

What re-phrased question can you formulate?

My attempt is:

"What could you focus on, that would leave you feeling you've given it the best chance of being acceptable?"

The blame has disappeared, along with (crucially) the attachment to the drama. It now has elements of **action, awareness, blame free-ness, challenge, detachment, responsibility, self-directed learning, solution focus,** wrapped up in it. That's eight out of ten of the principles in one succinct, to-the-point coaching question. Although the other two, **self-belief** and **trust**, are not included in the actual question, this approach is likely to encourage them too.

In essence though, it is not so important to wrap up all the core principles in every question, so long as we ensure that we don't include any anti-principles, like blame, judgment, advising, attachment, and so on. These instantly dilute the effectiveness of any coaching question, and can inflict lasting damage on the coaching rapport we have been building with the child. As we develop our coaching we can check our questions against this list of core principles and see how many we are wrapping up in them.

7.

Creating A Generative Learning Space

A teacher friend recounted a story of how she was introduced to her first teaching post after leaving Teacher Training College. She was told that her tutor-group, whom she would meet for 20 minutes twice a day for registration, had a reputation for being quite boisterous and difficult to manage. They were aged 13 and 14 years old. The Principal told her that if she found them too unruly then she should send the pupils to her and she would discipline them. My friend made herself a promise that she would try to find her own ways to win their trust and respect. In her own words:

"When I met them I told them I would like each one of them to prepare and present a short five minute project on a subject of their choice, which the class could then discuss until it was time for the next lesson. But the first couple of presentations were hopeless. It was not that my tutees hadn't prepared well and done their best to present to the group, but more that the listening group was too raucous, restless and disruptive.

"I let them know I was going to postpone future presentations until they could maintain an attentive listening space. I devised a game I called "Sitting Still and Keeping Quiet." The rules were simple: that after register had been called, they had to sit still and keep quiet for Sixty Seconds. If there was any disruption - noise or movement - the Sixty Seconds would start afresh.

TICK...TOCK...
TICK...TOCK...

"To begin with it was a nightmare. The kids would cough, clear their throats, flick paper balls, kick the chair in front of them, make farting noises, giggle, ssshhh each other - anything they could think of that might sabotage the game. In fact the sabotage for them became the game. But gradually they tired of the monotony of the continual Sixty Second re-starts, and little by little they started to self-police, and then to police each other.

"I kept it light-hearted i.e. "Oh, was that another giggle I heard? Ground control to Stopwatch - commence countdown at sixty seconds. Again..." and so on. Three weeks later (!) we achieved our first full minute of stillness and calm. So we moved onto Two Minutes. This, interestingly, only took one more lesson to achieve, although I could see some of them were bursting with the effort.

whatever ages our children are at the first thing we need to create is a calm, coaching space

"I asked them if they would like to try for Three Minutes and they negotiated, saying they would, but only if they didn't manage to listen well enough to the next few presentations (which, by the way, they were now really keen to re-start). So we started the presentations again, and with just a few minor hiccups, we managed to hear from every tutee by the end of that first term. A lot of my tutees told me they had started "having a word" with other pupils outside the classroom so that they could concentrate on the learning and presentations, and certainly the Principal was very impressed by the turnaround in my tutor group."

Whatever combinations of ages and stages our children are at the first thing we need to create is a calm, coaching space – this needs time, application and a determined but light touch to set up.

it is more tricky to impart wisdom when the atmosphere is tense

I have coached and spoken at hundreds of schools in the course of my work over the past few decades and worked with thousands of children. As a visitor and a guest, I am generally politely received by the school-children. There is evidently a sense of novelty in having a guest coach, and that novelty fairly easily sustains an engaged discipline for the short time I am typically with them.

The same was true, as I mentioned earlier, when I first met and moved in with my new family. The difference there came, as many other step-parents can probably testify, when the novelty wore off (eerily quickly for my liking) and the responsibilities of being a parent as well as an educator turned permanent.

I speak to many teachers in Britain who report that up to eighty per cent (!) of their lesson time can be spent simply maintaining discipline. This situation may resonate with some parents too. Who has ever stopped to count the minutes spent managing conflict at home, or at school, in a given school-week? And observed that total multiply during a holiday-week? Try it as an exercise while we begin constructing our stage for our own family coaching. It can be a real eye-opener as well as highlighting how, and from where, conflicts arise. It is more tricky to impart one's wisdom when the atmosphere is tense.

when children choose to allow coaching they are anticpating some sort of magic. When coaching is pushed at them, expect resistance

So it seems that once we have created a window of attention and focus we can begin to introduce interesting dialogue and by extension, employ any number of coaching techniques and tactics to allow the child to appreciate its situation and respond to it. (Or, put in a coaching vocabulary, to allow the children to become self-aware, responsible and create their own learning).

A bonus result of this process seems to be that by creating that window, we also create an eager anticipation of what is to enter through it when it's opened. Recall how we felt as we waited for our favourite singer, or comedian, to take the stage, or our favourite football team to emerge from the tunnel. That same anticipation plays a huge part in the creation of the eventual positive experiences that coaching may bring about. We chose to come to that concert, gig or football match. We have spent days waiting for it to arrive. We are ready to rapturously engage. In a similar way, when children choose to allow coaching they are anticipating some sort of magic. When coaching is pushed at them, expect resistance - certainly to begin with.

"how can I get my child to have a proper conversation with me in the first place?"

This chapter is focused on setting up the coaching environment - creating a learning space - where we are encouraged to be fully open and transparent to our families about what we are intending to do. Continue to do this for... well, let's just say for the rest of our life shall we? – (we can negotiate later). There is more - much more - about Openness and Transparency in Part Three of this book and its there for a very good reason, because probably the single most-asked question to me at Coaching for Parent workshops is:

"How can I get my child to have a proper conversation with me in the first place?"

when was the last time we gave our children a 'thoroughly good listening to?'

It's such a common question that I have decided to give it its own sub-chapter and it's coming up next where we'll examine some tactics. Let's make sure we read and heed that section, fully, over and over again if needs be. Creating a conducive environment within our families may need to be practised in its own right, thoroughly and often.

Listening is not confined to just one person at a time, of course. How can we make sure each member of the family is heard - really listened to and acknowledged - when the family gets together to chat about a holiday, or moving house for example? There is an art to being able to run a meeting and have everyone come away feeling they have been given a 'thoroughly good listening to.' Let me defer to Nancy Kline and the following points adapted from her work which are designed to create an enlightened "Thinking Place."

Nancy wrote a seminal book some ten years ago called "Time to Think." It was a radical way of looking at making time for ourselves so that we can process our own thoughts and really take ownership of them and gain insight and responsibility.

She has a company called Time to Think, Inc. (it's a US based company) and her book was so successful that she found time to write another book..."More Time to Think." So her strategies evidently seem to be effective; for her anyway.

* * *

HOW CAN I GET MY CHILD TO HOLD A PROPER CONVERSATION WITH ME?

good ideas can come from anybody - we want the best ideas regardless of who thought of them

Her assertion is that exhibiting any one of her ten behaviour guidelines is capable of improving people's thinking and if people can embody several, or even all ten of these behaviours at once, their thinking can be transformative. They will be creating a "culture of superb thinking and graceful human connection."

That, right there, is surely the ultimate intention of any meeting - whether a family meeting or a business one - to create great ideas from what Nancy terms ***'generative listening.'*** Such an astute and brilliantly simple phrase. Generative listening involves aiming to listen to each person present, to ignite each other's minds, not to simply listen and wait for our turn to reply or challenge. It also means trying not to lead others towards our own thoughts (otherwise it has become a briefing session in disguise).

Good ideas can come from anybody - we want the best ideas regardless of who thought of them.

Here are guidelines to the behaviours which allow generative listening.

If you give Attention of generative quality, born of deep interest in what the person thinks and will say next, they will think better around you than they will if you interrupt them or listen only in order to reply.

If you regard the person thinking as your thinking Equal, regardless of any power differential between you, they will think better around you than if you see yourself as better than (or less than) they are.

If you are at Ease inside yourself, regardless of the degree of (mostly manufactured) urgency and rush outside you, people will think better (and faster) around you than if you are in a hurry yourself.

If you genuinely Appreciate people five times more than you criticise them, they will think more clearly and imaginatively around you than if you focus on their faults.

If you Encourage people – build with them their courage to go to the unexplored edge of their thinking by championing their excellence – they will think better around you than if you compete with them.

If you offer accurate and complete Information to people, and if you show respect for them for facing what they have been denying, they will think better around you than if you collude with their assumption that what is true is not true, or that what is not true, is.

If you welcome the expression of people's Feelings and are relaxed in the face of whatever emotions may surface, they will think better around you than if you race to anaesthetise them.

If you are interested in the Diversity between you and others, the differences both in your ideas and in your group identities and cultures, they will think better around you than if you indicate, however subtly, that being just like you is best.

If you can ask an Incisive Question, one that replaces an untrue limiting assumption with a true, liberating one, they will think better around you than if you abandon them to limiting assumptions.

And if you can prepare the Place where you and they think together so that it says to them, "You matter," they will think better around you than if you allow the place to be intimidating, inaccessible or culturally and aesthetically barren.

Nancy Kline - *More Time to Think*

let all children become used to being heard. They may or may not ultimately get their way, but they will always know they have a voice

Don't skip on this - we may need to concentrate ***ONLY*** on understanding and creating these learning spaces for some weeks. And we must let our children know what we are doing, and why. This is fine, in fact, I'd go even further. Not only is it fine, ***it's essential*** - it is part and parcel of the coaching framework. This part of the foundation work, creating a generative learning space, is probably ***the single most important thing*** that we will introduce during our entire parent-coaching career. For however long we decide to take to implement it, be it weeks, years or lifetimes. It really serves as an essential reminder that if the child is in the "wrong" learning space, then coaching, or any form of productive communication, cannot happen.

This applies equally to toddlers as to teenagers. Let all children become used to being heard. They may or may not ultimately get their way, but they will always know they have a voice.

So, once a coachable space has been established, let me bang my drum once again, to advocate that we move through each chapter ***in the order I have presented them*** (we have discussed the strong reasons for this earlier). Stay with each chapter and its exercises until we and our children are fluent and familiar with using them. This way we are building a robust and permanent foundation ***together***, which we can refer to for ***the rest of our lives.*** Whenever a new chapter and its messages and exercises seem not to be taking hold, ***revisit these points on creating a generative listening space.***

MORE DEFENCE OF YOUNG BRAINS

It's important to give young people and their young brains a break. They really are working as hard as they know how, to make sense of things. We mustn't expect a fully formed adult brain in a ten year old. Although, truth be told, we may well often get more lucidity from a ten year old than from a fifteen year old, since the fifteen year old's brain is likely going through more maintenance and modernisation and as such may not be as consistent as the ten-year-old's. Ever noticed that?

However, there is nothing wrong with expecting our children's brains of all ages to absorb and 'park' information for use (several years) later. ***Know that the information is all going in.*** It just might not be noticeable that it has gone in, right there and then. Keep plugging away, particularly with the niceties, the politeness's, the courtesies, the considerateness and consequential stuff. How many of us can imagine a conversation like this occurring in our homes?

Mum: "Max, now you're fifteen, I'd like you to watch how I dead-head these tulips and re-arrange them in a new vase for the dinner table."

Max: "Sure Mum, give me twenty seconds to shut the X-Box down

and I'll be alert and receptive to your request in a jiffy."

Sure, why not? I know many women who would be mightily impressed with Max's ability and willingness to learn to arrange cut flowers. I concede too that it may be that this utopian conversation is still fairly distant on the Horizon of Good Hope. But there will come a time, along with a reason, why such a conversation will likely re-surface in Older Max's brain and he will relegate his X-Box to a distant second priority in order to fully engage in trimming and arranging some flowers for someone special. His mum might not be present to witness it, the flowers may not be intended for her, but it will probably happen at least once in his life, and her faith in his brain's ability to absorb and park that botanical snippet all those years previously will have been validated.

What is interesting is that we are just now starting to understand how the methodologies of coaching come into play in the brain; as a result, opportunities to recognise and reinforce essential learning will most likely become reality.

More and more these days, we hear the term neuro-science appearing when we talk about coaching and learning. There is an insatiable need to understand the brain, so that we can regulate and normalise behaviour, presumably so that we can control it, or at least explain it more easily. It may yet prove to be a fad and yield little, but then again it may be the harbinger of an era where a fuller understanding of the astonishing mechanisms of our brains becomes known. I'm plumping for the latter. Maybe soon, the mysteries of how and why coaching questions really work will become standard, accepted fact rather than conjecture.

So let's dwell a little here, just temporarily for those of us who are a little nervous around science, and I include myself here.

Even a few years ago it was considered:

that brains became unable to learn new things after a certain age
that children are stuck with the mental abilities they are born with
that damaged brains cannot reorganise themselves
that if brain cells die they cannot be replaced
that basic circuits and reflexes are hardwired and permanent

And from a little research now, even I understand this is absolutely not the case with any of these. So that's progress. Read a very approachable book by Norman Doidge - 'The Brain That Changes Itself' for more detail if you, like me, have a mind that would like eventually to make some sense of how our brains seem to work.

With neuro-science comes another new phrase - neuro-plastic. 'Neuro' being the nerve cells and nerve systems, and 'plastic' meaning 'changeable, malleable, modifiable'. In other words, **nerves and neural pathways that are able to change.** It had long been thought that significant shifts in this plasticity and in the brain's wiring occurred mainly in the childhood years. We now know, empirically and scientifically, that ***the brain can change its own structure through thought and activity at any time*** in the human life cycle.

When we perform an activity, our brain requires specific neurons to fire together. When they fire together, they release nerve-growth factors to consolidate and strengthen the brain map and allow the activity to be repeated. One of these nerve-growth factors is called Brain-Derived Neurotrophic Factor or BDNF and this helps the neurons to wire together and fire reliably every new time the activity is repeated.

The BDNF also switches on the part of our brain which allows us to focus our attention and to remember that experience. This part is known as the ***nucleus basalis.*** It is like having a permanent teacher in our brains saying - "Now *this* is really important - *this,* you *must* remember for life!"

all children need to build neural connections ***by themselves*** in order for their own freshest learnings to be truly effective and sustainable

Imagine the benefits of being able to illuminate our attention and focus, to be signposted effortlessly to learn just what we need to learn, and switch it off again when we need to relax. Imagine if our children were trained to access and respond to their own BDNF every time we asked them to engage in something we felt might be a learning opportunity.

Since the guiding principles of coaching include, among others, creating self-awareness and being solution-focused, every time children embody these principles, they are supporting the formation of new neural pathways. The accountability structures of coaching also play a role; this time in holding the children's focus on their desired outcomes. Likewise all the other coaching principles outlined earlier in this book. These too then, provide them with new structured neural pathways that allow them to experiment, assess and create powerful insights for themselves.

The formation of new neural pathways is known as 're-wiring' which is occurring continuously and automatically in our children's brains, ***but only when*** we encourage them to explore new options and to consciously experience new ways of thinking and behaviours.

Another thing we know about brains is that no two are alike. Studies have shown that when any two people are asked to undertake the exact same activity, each brain activates differently. Each brain is wired to respond via a certain neural pathway when approaching a task. When confronted with a different approach, requiring a different neural route, (i.e. someone's advice) the brain may hesitate to make a connection.

This explains why we often experience a sense of 'disconnect' when people are too quick to direct or give us advice on what, or how, to do something; because our brain is loyal to its existing wiring and explores that route as a default, first.

So if each individual brain operates differently, then all children need to build neural connections ***by themselves*** in order for their own freshest learnings to be truly effective and sustainable. Until we embed these learnings over a prolonged period we are much more likely to revert to the old hard-wiring.

Only constant, focused thought and application hardwires these neural pathways over time. These pathways move from becoming chemical links to stable, physical changes to the brain's structure. We are eventually able to operate effortlessly once this wiring is established. The good news is, much of this is within parents' and children's control. New and compelling research is emerging all the time highlighting the links between healthy eating and strong brain development and the wiring can even develop through visualisation alone. We don't necessarily have to have physically performed an activity even once for the brain to be able to recognise and activate the appropriate neural pathway. Here is an illustration of this:

Bob Bowman was the swimming coach for Michael Phelps, who, after the 2012, London Olympic Games has officially become the greatest Olympian ever, after winning 22 Olympic medals, 18 of them gold. What Bowman gave Phelps were habits that would make him the strongest mental swimmer in the pool. All he needed to do was to target a few specific habits that had everything to do with creating the right mindset.

Each night before falling asleep and each morning after waking up Phelps would imagine himself diving off the blocks, swimming flawlessly. He designed a series of "videotapes" in his head - not real ones, but visualisations of the perfect race, with every tiny detail included. Over the years the visualisations expanded to include everything that could possibly go well and badly - Phelps ran and re-ran them in his head hundreds of times, in meticulous detail.

Charles Duhigg describes an astonishing Olympic race, in his ground-breaking book - The Power of Habit.

Back in Beijing, it was 9:56 A.M. - four minutes before the race's start - and Phelps stood behind his starting block, bouncing slightly on his toes.

When the announcer said his name, Phelps stepped onto the block, as he always did before a race, and then stepped down, as he always did. He swung his arms three times, as he had before every race since he was twelve years old. He stepped on the blocks again and when the gun sounded, leapt.

Phelps knew that something was wrong as soon as he hit the water. There was moisture inside his goggles. He couldn't tell if they were leaking from the top or bottom, but as he broke the water's surface and began swimming, he hoped the leak wouldn't become too bad.

By the second turn, everything was getting blurry. As he approached the final lap, the cups of his goggles were filled. Phelps couldn't see a thing. Not the line along the pools bottom, not the black T marking the approaching wall. For most swimmers, losing your sight in the middle of an Olympic final would be cause for panic.

Phelps was calm.

Everything else that day had gone according to plan. The leaking goggles were a minor deviation, but one for which he was prepared. Bowman had once made Phelps swim in a Michigan pool in the dark, believing that he needed to be ready for any surprise. Some of the videotapes in Phelps's mind had featured problems like this. He had mentally rehearsed how he would respond to a goggle failure. As he started his last lap, Phelps estimated how many strokes the final push would require - nineteen maybe twenty, - and started counting. He felt totally relaxed as he swam at full strength.

Midway through the lap he increaseed his effort, a final eruption that had become one of his techniques in overwhelming opponents. At eighteen strokes, he started anticipating the wall. He could hear the crowd roaring, but since he was blind he had no idea if they were cheering for him or someone else.

Nineteen strokes then twenty. It felt like he needed one more. He made a twenty first, huge stroke, glided with his arm outstretched and touched the wall. He had timed it perfectly. When he looked up at the scoreboard it said,"WR" - world record - next to his name. He'd won another gold. After the race, a reporter asked what it felt like to swim blind.

"It felt like I imagined it would," Phelps said.

Being coached (i.e. being asked searching questions) supports the children's ability to ascertain which habits do or do not serve them. Through reflection and experimentation the brain ascertains which neural pathways are useful and need consolidation.

Naturally, before all of this can begin to occur, let me emphasise as strongly as I know how that the first step is still to ***establish a strong 'backdrop of anticipation' before commencing any coaching.*** The child will work best and hard-wiring will occur most rapidly, when the child is expectant and eager. Where there is resistance to input, the brain is reluctant to activate new nerve-growth factors - remember the BDNF? - and the nucleus basalis remains dormant. No new learning can occur while a child chooses to remain in that resistant state.

If the child's mind has not been prepared for new thinking its brain can be as potentially plastic as we like but the chances are that it will not begin to allow us to even start the re-wire. So this preparation involves paying even further attention to setting the scene strongly for coaching. Learning to do this takes just as much practice as learning the coaching skills themselves. We will look at opening and closing a coaching session in the following two chapters - now neuro-science is making it apparent why doing this well is so crucial.

"Coaching is the most least selfish job ever!"

I know from bitter experience, as I know millions of other parents do too, that trying to conduct a worthy, positive, enriching conversation with a youngster whose eyes and thumbs are transfixed with Modern Warfare, Call of Duty 2 on X-Box, and any number of other brain-numbing activities is always likely to be a non-starter.

Let's be fully open with our children about what we are intending. Inform them of everything we want to accomplish. Get their buy-in as far as we can. Bring them to workshops too, by any means possible. It is a joy to see the plastic brains of youngsters re-wiring uninhibitedly as they embrace the phenomenal wonderment of positive, dynamic communication. One teenager, who attended a workshop was enthralled by how the parents around her were working to communicate more relaxedly with their children, prompting her immortal (and forgivably ungrammatical) observation, "Coaching is the most least selfish job ever!"

8.

Opening A Coaching Session

CONTRACTING

If we have slightly longer to set up the chat or meeting, we might like to try introducing a learning contract. With family meetings we may only feel the need to do it once, or just occasionally, and the contract can serve for numerous meetings.

When both or all are settled, ask:

"Now, can we first make a note of a few things that we would like to see happen in this meeting that will allow us all [both] to be thinking at our best?"

We can write down their answers, and stick them on the fridge door, or just remember them. Remember too, to introduce things that we personally feel are important to keeping people energised and focused. This exercise allows all family members to have a voice to begin the meeting too, so we must try not to make anyone 'wrong' - just accept and include pretty much all answers as far as we can. We may well hear (or introduce) a selection of the following typical replies:

We are working at our best when we are...

Honest *Punctual*
Allowed to be controversial *Respectful*
Open minded *Participating* *Positive*
Fully engaging *Patient with one another* *Clear*
Managing our energies i.e. hydrated, moving, sitting up straight
Seeking to be understanding *Considerate*
Observing confidentiality *Staying relevant*
Open to all ideas and diversities *Flexible*
Mistake-allowing *Trusting* *Using anecdotes*
Humorous *Light and fun* *Connected*
Giving everyone a voice
Listening attentively *Not interrupted or interrupting*

BACKDROP OF ANTICIPATION

The key to setting the scene for a productive coaching conversation involves ensuring that the child is prepared to put its mind to something. Getting youngsters to commit to conversations we want them to have, when we want to have them is always challenging. When they want a conversation about something they are motivated about on the other hand, their sense of immediacy and commitment is startling and insistent. So fair enough - many parents complain to their children about not being present enough - let's try to recognise a motivated conversation opportunity from wherever it may spring.

getting youngsters to commit to conversations ***we*** want them to have, when ***we*** want to have them is always challenging

Just checking on the small stuff is important right at the start, though. Simple questions like...

"So we've got about 15 minutes - is that enough time for you?"

"I'll just check my mobile is switched off while we have this chat - can you check yours too please?"

"You're not expecting any friends to call or pop round in the next 15 minutes are you?"

"Where shall we go that has the most relaxing view and the least distractions?"

"What other distractions are on your mind that you can let go of before we start?"

...all help to create a sense of importance around this conversation.

Set up as many of Nancy Kline's behaviours for generative listening as we can too; they make a huge difference - particularly ***'diversity,'*** (See Chapter 7).

when ***they*** want a conversation about something ***they*** are motivated about, on the other hand, their sense of immediacy and commitment is startling and insistent

SETTING OUTCOMES

It is very effective to start any thinking-session or coaching conversation by looking ahead to an overview of what the child wants to achieve before getting into the nitty gritty. It's okay to include our own desired outcomes and 'wants' at this point too, so long as they do not overwhelm or replace the child's. Looking towards a positive future has a side benefit of raising energy and clarity of purpose. To accomplish this we can ask the child for an outcome using questions like,

"What would you like to know by the end of this conversation that you don't yet know?"

"What takeaways might be useful for you from this chat?"

(Make sure we remember to check in at the end of the meeting to ascertain to what extent their outcome was achieved - we will come to 'Closing a Coaching Session' in the next chapter).

We set these outcomes in order to:

Focus the children's (and parents') minds.

Highlight any differences or misunderstandings with regard to intention and expectation.

- Ensure both child and parent can go in the same direction
- Ensure both child and parent are happy with the planned direction
- Set a bench mark to measure how far the child has come at the end of the session

Try to encourage children to be succinct and specific - it comes with practice. Examples of thinking-session outcomes can be about anything, e.g.

If they are thinking by themselves:

"To be as well prepared as I can be with my packing for a fun summer camp,"

"To think of all the things I have to put on my CV."

If it is a meeting between two people:

"To choose all the things and colours I want in my new bedroom."

If it is a family meeting:

"To decide where we want to go on holiday this summer and who to take."

the purpose of the 'outcome' question in any instances is simply to get the child used to casting its mind forward to the future

Sometimes, it is possible that the child will not know what its desired outcome is – to find that out is an outcome in itself. Take, for example, a conversation about planning university choices or options for a birthday outing. In these cases, there may be no need to spend time identifying a specific goal for the conversation, it may be that the outcome is simply ***"to be a bit clearer about my options."*** The purpose of the 'outcome' question in any instances is simply to get the child used to casting its mind forward to the future, in line with the solution focus of coaching.

At this stage of a young brain's development, (and until the age of twenty-four according to some research) children have not reached the sufficiently advanced cognitive reasoning level needed to ascertain how they can actually influence events personally. Therefore the child may well defer to the parent for larger, more complex or longer term goals, in which cases there is no need to chastise the child for poor thinking skills; it's fine to be ready and willing to assist with some suggested outcomes too.

MANAGING THE TIME

A conversation can take as long as it needs to or as long as agreed. There is no optimum time for coaching to be effective. My feeling is, once a strong outcome is agreed, then a time duration for the conversation can be agreed too. It is good practice to manage time effectively, and good parent-coaches not only know why they are asking each question and what sort of question they are asking, but also at what stage of the conversation to ask it, too.

So if we take a conversation where we have agreed not to exceed 15 minutes to discuss something, it is useful to remind our child at least twice of how much time is left. Ask:

"We're about half way through our time now - how are we doing so far?"

"How would you like to use the last seven minutes or so?"

"We've only got a couple of minutes left - what are your freshest thoughts on this now?"

Remember also that coaching is very demanding on young brains. As adults we are more accustomed to listening intently, processing what is being said (and what isn't), concentrating and focusing, managing emotions, formulating incisive questions and keeping an often difficult framework on track and to time. But an hour long session for a young brain is a major ask. For this reason, I recommend several 'sprints' rather than occasional 'marathons.'

We can make the decision on the durations of sessions if we feel that's best, though it is always preferable to ask the child how long it would like to talk with us. Then we can 'contract' that time, and do our very best not to overshoot.

Even if we have time to let the session run over, the child may not. And *vice versa*. Time is an important discipline in the coaching process and is our responsibility. If our children's minds wander, or get anxious that they are going to miss a favourite TV programme or an event with friends, the coaching concentration we were planning to appreciate them for is in danger of evaporating quickly.

Start with short sessions - we can build up as we become more used to structured conversations with each other.

9.

Closing A Coaching Session

TYING UP LOOSE ENDS

At the end of a coaching session it is important to leave the children, and the family if it is a group coaching session, feeling comfortable and motivated about their next steps. To do this, parent-coaches can make a few brief comments about any or all of the following, keeping them positive and appreciative, and then invite the others to do the same.

Appropriate comments and questions might focus on what has been achieved in relation to what the children set out to achieve and how we and they feel about it. Try using any of the following:

"I'm really impressed by how much we've been able to get through in these [fifteen] minutes. How are you [is everyone] feeling now?"

"What are your 'takeaways'?"

"What question or questions are now most important for you to think about?"

"And what are your thoughts about that/them?"

"What more do you think or feel or want to say about that?"

"And what else?"

"And now what is your freshest thinking about this now?"

(NOTE – this is NOT us making a summary of all points already covered; we are *still asking their brains to engage,* even in closing).

"What would you like to write down so you can remember?"

Remember too, to come back to the outcome originally aimed at, to check in on where the child or family feels it has reached.

"Do you remember at the beginning of this chat you mentioned you wanted to use this meeting to [be as well prepared as possible for your summer camp?] So how do you feel you have progressed with that?"

It is less important whether the child feels it has or hasn't made huge strides towards the stated outcome. What is important is that it allows the meeting to come to an easy and definite close, with no loose ends, no hanging threads. Therefore, *open* questions are essential here in the closing section to prolong the learning. Asking,

"How do you feel you have progressed with that?"

...is better than,

"Do you feel this coaching has helped you to progress with that?"

This is a leading question - we are clearly angling for the answer ***"Yes."*** Coaches avoid leading questions.

APPRECIATION

Appreciative comments are always well received:

"Thank you for being so focused during that meeting. I really admire your concentration to make sure we are covering all the points - I am really starting to look forward to these discussions with you - we get through so much! What would you like to say before we finish?"

Thank the children every time for their concentration, mindfulness, politeness - anything at all really, though it must sound, and be, authentic. And when we are modelling the concept of appreciation, they may feel they want to thank us too.

Closure is a good opportunity for building self-belief and confidence by giving positive feedback on the child's achievements. The parent should generally 'close' first, to model good 'closing,' and then invite the child to close. Closure helps to round off coaching sessions and family meetings positively so all parties can resume a new focus on the next element of their day.

It is really important to try to properly close conversations. All conversations, not just coaching conversations, and not just conversations with our children. By compartmentalising our last conversation, it is completed in our minds and we can turn our full attentions to our next activity. Brains need this ability to 'tidy things away' for optimum efficiency.

At-A-Glance Coaching Template

Things to include in a coaching conversation

CREATING A GENERATIVE LEARNING SPACE

Consider Nancy Kline's ten guidelines to the behaviours which allow generative listening.
(Refer to Chapter 7 for a fuller picture).

Attention, Equal, Ease, Appreciate, Encourage, Information, Feelings, Diversity, Incisive Question, Place.

CONTRACTING

Some useful questions we can use here:

"What needs to happen so you can be thinking at your best?"
"What can we commit to do, to ensure we will be as focused as possible?"

SETTING THE SCENE - (creating a 'backdrop of anticipation')
Some useful questions we can use here:

"So we've got about [15] minutes - is that enough time for you?"
"I'll just check my mobile is switched off while we have this chat - can you check yours too please?"
"You're not expecting any friends to call or pop round in the next [15] minutes are you?"
"Where shall we go that has the most relaxing view and the least distractions?"
"What other distractions are on your mind that you can let go of before we start?"

SETTING OUTCOMES

Some useful questions we can use here:

"What would you like to know by the end of this conversation that you don't yet know?"
"What 'takeaways' might be useful for you to take from this chat?"
"What would you like the next twenty minutes to highlight?"

MANAGING THE TIME

Some useful questions we can use here:

"We're about half way through our time now - how are we doing so far?"
"How would you like to use the last seven minutes or so?"
"We've only got a couple of minutes left - what are your freshest thoughts on this now?"

CLOSING A SESSION

Some useful questions we can use here:

"What question or questions are now most important for you to think about?"
"And what are your thoughts about that?"
"What more do you think or feel or want to say about that?"
"And what else?"
"What would you like to write down so you can remember?"
"Do you remember earlier you mentioned you wanted to use this meeting to [....?] So how do you feel you have progressed with that?"

APPRECIATION

Some useful questions we can use here:

"Thank you for being so focused during that meeting. How are you feeling about things now?"
"I really admire your concentration to make sure we are covering all the points. What would you like to say before we wrap up?"
"I'm really impressed by how much we've been able to get through in these [fifteen] minutes. What are your takeaways?"

10.

D-Day
Don't Say Don't And Don't Say Do

I now, after many, many years of coaching, become instantly on edge when people give me advice where I didn't ask for it. I have developed a strong aversion to it, even though I know people are just trying to be helpful and I would almost go as far as to say I find it tedious, even demeaning in a way. A coach would view seeking to solve a dilemma in another's life as a distinct lack of faith in that person.

People, mostly, are well-intentioned. But to me, now, when I am 'given' spontaneous advice, what I hear is, "Actually, James, you probably won't be able to work this out for yourself - you need me to do that for you." You probably wouldn't guess my discomfort from my outward reaction. I simply smile and give a fairly gracious stock reply along the lines of, ***"Thanks, I'll bear that in mind,"*** although these words tend to leave my mouth through gritted teeth.

"How far can this young mind go before it has need of mine? And how much further? And how much further still?" - Nancy Kline

Am I being ungrateful? Well, look at it from this perspective. I, like many of us I suspect, believe myself to be perfectly capable of making decisions and finding things out. I have made some super choices in life, and I have made some duff ones. I have taken and rejected advice, both options have variously turned out advantageous or otherwise. How was I to know what might transpire? But if I'm to make mistakes, I like to fully own them. And I suspect, I'm little different from most others.

So, on the other side of the dialogue, as a Coach, I now find it vaguely ridiculous to be asked to give advice or suggestions when someone has clearly not invested much time searching for their own answers. My sense is that coachees will probably feel patronised if I don't at least find out what they may have already tried to do about the situation, before putting my brain to work on their problem. I shy away from it wherever possible, saying things like,

"Well some thoughts have sprung to mind while you've been talking, although I'm sure that with a little more exploration of what's happening for you at the moment, you can probably find some much better solutions than ones I might come up with."

Let's recall Nancy Kline's lovely phrase once again:

"How far can this young mind go before it has need of mine? And how much further? And how much further still?"

The key point is that there is learning in all choices and we will grow from that learning.

Whether we say "Don't..." or whether we say, "Do..." to our children - either way we are shutting down their thinking.

whether we say "Don't..." or whether we say, "Do..." to our children - either way we are shutting down their thinking

Here's my D-Day coaching challenge: Pick a day each week - we'll call it D-Day. Can we go a whole meal-time, afternoon, evening, day, without saying either 'D' word ('Don't' and 'Do') to our children? And instead, ask them open questions, like:

"What are your thoughts about that?"

"How could you sort it out, so you're happy with it?"

"Where could you find the information you'd need?"

We'll soon learn their brains work every bit as well as ours.

11.

Stay Calm, Stay Light

You'll have noticed I have designed a few acronyms to accompany the learning (as it seems no serious book worth its salt can afford to be without them). They are admittedly a little tenuous - I think, the adjective I used earlier - 'audacious' - is probably appropriate. You may remember the CASE principle from Chapter Four - and here's another one: **Levity And Understanding Go Happily together - LAUGH together.** Geddit? (To be honest, I wanted to say Levity And ***'Learning'*** Go Happily together but, audacious or not, that would also have been gobbledygook as an acronym so ***'Understanding'*** works well enough too).

levity is the key to coaching young people

So we are now starting to set some rudimentary boundaries to facilitate learning input. In effect, the children may now be starting to perceive that they have some real control within the dialogue. As we have now highlighted, at whatever combinations of ages and stages our children are, the first thing we need to create is a calm, coaching space. This needs time, application and a determined but light touch to set up.

Levity is the key to coaching young people.

REMIND OURSELVES EVERY DAY TO KEEP IT LIGHT! This will be our single, biggest challenge. I'll keep the reminders going throughout this book too.

Fun ways to ask insightful questions...

"Which part of 'intelligent' escaped from your brain just before you decided to do that?"

"How would a brother who remembered that deep down he actually does love his sister resolve that situation?"

"How would a girl who wasn't grumpy ask for another fish-finger?"

"If you did want to choose a less aggressive tone of voice, what would it sound like?"

Fun ways to make insightful observations:

"Of COURSE you're going to screw up from time to time – that's your job – that's what teenagers are meant to do – and it's great that

you're fabulous at it. Now that you know what happens to a light bulb in a microwave, would you please make sure you pick up every one of those pieces of broken glass?"

Fun ways to make insightful mediations:

"I know, I know, brothers are always going to wind up brothers – that's what brothers are for – I'm thrilled that you're normal, I really am. (Now would you stay out of his room for the rest of the evening please...?)"

And as responsible parents we will probably consider that it might not be a bad thing to then focus in on the consequences - but still in questions.

"What do you think would be an appropriate action to take to remind you that the kitchen is not a laboratory and expensive microwaves are not toys for your personal physics experiments...?"

However irksome the situation, it doesn't hurt to keep the playfulness going a little while longer, does it really? The point will have been made, and we've kept our cool and our high ground.

the only way to safeguard against rigidity and authority setting in is a playful attitude

The only way to safeguard against rigidity and authority setting in is a playful attitude. Children don't tend to dwell on things for too long. There's too much else going on to attract them. We don't see too much grass growing under their feet. Nor see them volunteer to mow it if it did, but that's yet another issue. They don't stand on ceremony, they don't notice lack of ceremony. The point is that new things are happening daily in their lives which will revise their approach even to yesterday's successes.

Baffling, often. Inconsistent, inevitably. Irritating, for sure, although only if we choose to let it become so. Breathe and choose our next battle questions with a smile.

12.

Ask Ten Times More Than Tell

ask first, *listen* second, *tell* third.

Coaches probably talk around ten per cent of the duration of most of their coaching interactions. Parents probably talk for around sixty per cent of their interactions with children. No specific scientific proof of that - we can come to our own percentages just by noticing ourselves with our children, and observing friends with theirs, over a couple of weekends. My observations reveal that the majority of our sixty per cent talking is comprised of giving direction and advice. If we do use questions, they tend to be judgmental or leading the child to a course of action desired by the parent, i.e.

"Why have you done that?"
"Wouldn't it be better if you did it like this?"

Most of us have spent a lifetime learning how to impose our opinions on others, make decisions for others and be assertive with others. Society rewards us for this in many professions by promoting us to Team Leaders, Department Heads and Managers. So let's not imagine it's going to be a quick journey to unpick those directive habits. But unpick it we must, if we are going to add Coach to our impressive list of job titles. And of course, no-one has promoted us to the revered rank of Parent. We did that all by ourselves. So let's remember to be patient as we learn to prioritise:

asking first
listening second
telling third

Make it a household rule to ask questions of our children ***at least five times more*** than we tell them what we think. Ten times more is even better, and is for the experienced practitioners of parent-coaching - this requires stamina to consciously stay away from too much telling!

There are thousands of times when we parents don't necessarily know what might be the best course of action to take, for ourselves, let alone for our children. But we make it our responsibility to decide on one anyway, on their behalf, and follow it through regardless of the consequences. And most consequences are regularly unpredictable at the outset. We follow through regardless too of the ideas and thinking of the people around us (often our children) whom we drag into our decisions with little consultation and even less attention to their thoughts.

Children quickly learn that they don't need to think around us if we habitually override their ideas

We give ourselves permission to make decisions on their behalf immediately they tell us they "don't know," which becomes a default since what they do know is that ***they don't need to think around us*** since we have acquired the habit of overriding their ideas anyway.

This habit, like any other, can change, and change for the better. Here's a challenge for starters. Let's challenge ourselves to only ask questions of our children for the whole of next Saturday morning, from breakfast to lunch. Or for the whole of next Friday night from dinner to bedtime. ***Ask only open questions*** and be accepting of the replies, which we then question further. The even bigger challenge is to aim to detach from the outcome - our children will relish the freedom of genuine open planning without inhibitions (a.k.a. 'helpful' suggestions) from us.

Some questions we can use to start with:

"What would you like to do today?"
"How much homework have you got to do before Monday?"
"What's good on TV we could watch later?"
"What would you like for lunch?"
"What could we all do together that we haven't done in a long time?"
"Who would you like to see this weekend?"

and then question the replies:

"What time would be good to do that?"
"How long should we do it for?"
"What would it be like if we were to be able to do that today?"
"How do you feel about doing that?"
"How important is that to you?"

and if the child asks for our opinion or help, these and similar questions will serve as our "right answers":

"How do you think we could find that out?"
"What sounds like a good answer to you?"
"What are your thoughts on that?"
"What would you like the ending of your story to look like?"

If and when our child finds this weird, or sees through the game, we should come clean and admit what we are up to and in the spirit of openness and transparency, explain fully why we are trying to ask more than tell from now on.

There is an unwritten but essential coaching tenet observed by coaches when we don't know where to go next or even what to ask, which is simply to ***ask the coachee***. The coachees, and in our cases, our children, will always know, because they are talking about things that are meaningful to them, things that concern them directly. I've lost count of the number of times I have used this question to coachees, and to my family:

"What would be useful for me to ask you about next?"

if in doubt as to what to ask next, simply ask the child what we can ask

It's a wonderful, open question for when we find ourselves stuck as to where next to take a conversation, (even though it might sound a bit like a cop-out). If we are both sufficiently engaged in working on the challenge, dilemma or situation, just asking this question will free us from the need to demonstrate a lead in the conversation. Persist, and the chances are our children will show us they know exactly where to put their focus and will say something like "well, you could ask me more about..."

Here's a respectful coaching tenet: If in doubt as to what to ask next; ask the child what we can ask.

* * *

This widely publicised, desperate and eloquent rant from a father to his grown-up children appeared in British newspapers in December 2012. It's unfair and impossible to comment on such a letter and the lives of the people it was written for, although I suspect millions of parents may well feel some sympathy for him. There is much in this email concerning judgments, blame, hastily made decisions, complacency, indifference, lack of focus and the courtesies required from giving and receiving advice.

Retired Royal Navy Officer Nick Crews sent this email to his son and two daughters in February 2012 expressing his and his wife's disappointment in them. (One daughter was given permission to publish it to gain publicity for a book she wanted to write, to prove herself more worthy of his approval).

My only comment would be that it highlights the importance of starting early with all the basic values - respect, trust, grace, levity and so on - responsibility and self-awareness can be instilled by ***asking strong, adult questions*** from birth.

Dear All Three

With last evening's crop of whinges and tidings of more rotten news for which you seem to treat your mother like a cesspit, I feel it is time to come off my perch. It is obvious that none of you has the faintest notion of the bitter disappointment each of you has in your own way dished out to us. We are seeing the miserable death throes of the fourth of your collective marriages at the same time we see the advent of a fifth.

We are constantly regaled with chapter and verse of the happy, successful lives of the families of our friends and relatives and being asked of news of our own children and grandchildren. I wonder if you realise how we feel — we have nothing to say which reflects any credit on you or us. We don't ask for your sympathy or understanding — Mum and I have been used to taking our own misfortunes on the chin, and making our own effort to bash our little paths through life without being a burden to others. Having done our best — probably misguidedly — to provide for our children, we naturally hoped to see them in turn take up their own banners and provide happy and stable homes for their own children.

Fulfilling careers based on your educations would have helped — but as yet none of you is what I would confidently term properly self-supporting. Which of you, with or without a spouse, can support your families, finance your home and provide a pension for your old age? Each of you is well able to earn a comfortable living and provide for your children, yet each of you has contrived to avoid even moderate achievement.

Far from your children being able to rely on your provision, they are faced with needing to survive their introduction to life with you as parents.

So we witness the introduction to this life of six beautiful children — soon to be seven — none of whose parents have had the maturity and sound judgment to make a reasonable fist at making essential threshold decisions. None of these decisions were made with any pretence to ask for our advice.

In each case we have been expected to acquiesce with mostly hasty, but always in our view, badly judged decisions. None of you has done yourself, or given to us, the basic courtesy to ask us what we think while there was still time finally to think things through. The predictable result has been a decade of deep unhappiness over the fates of our grandchildren. If it wasn't for them, Mum and I would not be too concerned, as each of you consciously, and with eyes wide open, crashes from one cock-up to the next. It makes us weak that so many of these events are copulation-driven, and then helplessly to see these lovely little people being so woefully let down by you, their parents.

I can now tell you that I for one, and I sense Mum feels the same, have had enough of being forced to live through the never-ending bad dream of our children's underachievement and domestic ineptitudes. I want to hear no more from any of you until, if you feel inclined, you have a success or an achievement or a REALISTIC plan for the support and happiness of your children to tell me about.

I don't want to see your mother burdened any more with your miserable woes — it's not as if any of the advice she strives to give you has ever been listened to with good grace — far less acted upon.

So I ask you to spare her further unhappiness.

If you think I have been unfair in what I have said, by all means try to persuade me to change my mind. But you won't do it by simply whinging and saying you don't like it.

You'll have to come up with meaty reasons to demolish my points and build a case for yourself. If that isn't possible, or you simply can't be bothered, then I rest my case.

I am bitterly, bitterly disappointed.

Dad

We can only guess at what manner of parenting styles these beleaguered parents must have tried to introduce over the years. How might it be if we were to ***ALWAYS*** assume that our children know what they want to do, or say, or think about, or be asked, at any given time? It's such a generous and respectful way to be with them. Our children will enjoy the feeling of having more control in conversations, and the long term effects will surely be a level-headed confidence in ***their own ability*** to choose ***their own paths,*** (and take responsibility for all the ups and downs).

Oh yes - and grow strong, independent children of their own in due course.

13.

Praise Ten Times More Than Criticise

Now we are creating this culture of asking questions in the family, rather than selfishly advising every child that crosses our path, here's another positive challenge we can work at too: **For every one thing we find that we are not happy with, find *ten* things that we like.**

Yes, ***ten***. This can apply to our family, to our work and to our friends. We can apply it to buildings, landscapes, decorations, homework, sporting effort, art, music, aspirations, confidence, listening skills, happiness or coping with a crisis. And everything else.

most of us hear around eight times more criticism than praise

For homework, and for inspiration, watch or re-watch the sublime Australian movie, The Castle. In it, the blue-collar Kerrigan home is filled with love as well as pride in their modest lifestyle, but their happiness is threatened when developers attempt the compulsory acquisition of their house to expand the neighbouring airport. Their house is built in a largely undeveloped housing tract, on a toxic landfill, beneath power lines, and directly adjacent to an airport runway. Blissfully unaware of his family's lack of style or sophistication, the sweet-natured father believes that he has created a luxurious lifestyle for his family and he busies himself by driving a tow truck, racing greyhounds, and constantly adding tacky renovations to the house. The rest of the family shares and supports his enthusiasm in every way.

look for ways to reframe and rephrase tired, repeated, negative gripes in an upbeat, fun style

There is no better illustration of a father praising his family and choosing to find positivity at every juncture.

It's been estimated that most of us hear around eight times more criticism than praise so here's our chance to redress the balance. Find appreciative things to say as often as possible, and remember to play to the spirit of calmness and levity that we are cultivating too. Find the positive components of any person, thing, action or behaviour that we might otherwise criticise. Look for ways to reframe and rephrase tired, repeated, negative gripes in an upbeat, fun style. Make a game of it. Better still, become known for it. Encourage others to play our game.

For example, instead of,

Dad: "What's the point of having rules if you're just going to ignore them?"

Jameel: "Get lost! You're always criticising. I'm going to my room,"

...which leads to a communication *cul de sac* (and acrimony), how about:

Dad: "What I admire about you is your unflagging ability to innovate and challenge!"

Jameel: "Are you being sarcastic?"

Dad: "Well, possibly a tad, yes, although your way of looking at things is always imaginative - that will serve you well later in life."

Jameel: "I just find some rules a bit ridiculous, that's all,"

...which is far less judgmental, keeps it light and allows Jameel to express himself which is ***so*** crucial.

Even when talking about other people's children, whom we may not know so well, there are never any shortage of things to appreciate, even if they are simply about clothing or a feeling we have:

"Josh, I love your casual un-tied shoelaces and ripped jeans 'look' - very in-fashion these days!"

"You strike me as a really determined and focused dancer, Mylene; I bet your friends really look up to you for that!"

"Great first-time listening, Teddy. My kids would have been pleased to have been able to focus immediately like that and getting instant understanding like you just did, and we've been practising for a while!"

infuse consistent, authentic praise into our everyday dialogue with our children and they will come to expect it and see it as normal

Keep it authentic. If we don't mean it, we shouldn't say it, and it has to come from a place of real belief in the child. Start this positive praise game from birth and don't let up when the children start working on asserting themselves and becoming disparaging about our positivity. Children are so over-exposed to sarcasm and malicious irony on TV and in movies nowadays that by the time they reach high school they might want to take our comments as insincere, patronising or veiled criticism.

And of course, start doing it themselves. How fabulous it is to see teenagers with a heightened sense of gratitude and admiration for others.

Another advantage of exhibiting this aspect of a coaching mentality here, is that since we are commenting only on the pleasurable sides of the children's actions and behaviours we are able to detach ourselves more from judgmental and critical aspects. By so doing therefore, we take the ***overview*** wherever we can so as to not allow blame, disappointment or, indeed, excessive complimenting to cloud the acknowledgements.

When we arrive at Chapter 32 on The Gift of Coaching Feedback, we will learn yet another level of being able to create trust and positivity in the children. BUT...as always, be patient - fill in the gaps first; we would do well not to read too far ahead too soon. (Have I said that enough times yet?)

14.

Observe Ten Times More Than Analyse

One of the greatest coaching phrases we can employ is:

"I notice..."

It's easy to be neutral, or at least give the impression of being so. And the only way to authentically use a phrase like "I notice..." is to be very present and observant at all times - which coaches must be anyway. Whatever we notice, no-one else can dispute, and there is little judgment wrapped up in the phrase.

"I notice that seems to be making you agitated,"

...is better than:

"Why are you getting so agitated?"

As will see later, 'why' questions are rarely effective as coaching questions, and just 'noticing' the emotion or behaviour is often a powerful way to show empathy and engagement, without becoming analytical or in any way involved in the drama.

"I notice..." will salvage any number of situations, and not necessarily just the emotional ones and ***invites*** the child to be analytical of their own situation, without insisting on the point:

"I notice you hesitated a little there..."

"I notice you seemed to squirm a little as you said that,"

"I notice that football went interestingly close to the living room window..."

"I notice you say 'maybe' and 'perhaps' quite a lot,"

"I notice that seems to have created a lot of energy in you,"

It may well be that the child whose actions, emotions and behaviours we are 'noticing' refutes our observation, e.g. **"No, I don't think I'm agitated at all,"** in which case our catch-all 'detachment statement' can be employed: **"That's fine, I'm not really attached to that observation; so tell me, what are you experiencing then?"**

We can form questions using "notice" too:

"Am I noticing a little reluctance here?"

"If you were in my shoes, listening to this, what would you be noticing about your language?"

"I want to understand, but can you be specific about what it is I should be noticing about this?"

Of course we can use any kind of 'noticing' - we can use words like **perceive, detect, note, sense, see, hear, observe** and so on. The key is to ***remain outside the content of the conversation,*** by just facilitating the dialogue with observations. However, as often happens, when we appear detached from the content, the child, who has been hoping for some guidance or advice or intervention, may then accuse us of being too remote and not caring enough. So, another good catch-all stock riposte is our 'belief-demonstration' statement, i.e.

remain outside the content of the conversation with simple observations

"It's not that I don't care about this; on the contrary, I care deeply. However, I totally believe you can work it out in the way that works best for you. So rather than me find a solution for you, which you may not like or want, I'm just going to ask you questions to help your mind to focus on how it wants to do it."

15.

Encourage Magnificent Mistakes

In the delightful film, The Odd Life of Timothy Green, Cindy and Jim are trying to convince the adoption panel that they are suitable to be allowed to adopt. I won't reveal any more in case you have not seen it.

Cindy: "I had made a mistake"
Jim: "We made lots of mistakes"
Cindy: "We made mistakes trying to fix our mistakes"
Jim: "Isn't that how you know you're a parent?"
Adoption Panel Chairperson: "You seem to have forgotten what the object is here? You need to persuade us. What would you do differently?"
Cindy: "Make better mistakes"
Adoption Panel Chairperson: "Better?"
Cindy: "Definit..."
Jim: "...Not the same"
Cindy: "...No, new..."
Jim: "...Make new mistakes"
Cindy: "That's what we'd do"
Jim: "Yeah"

As parents, we flock to talks and workshops about how to talk and listen to our children. We are hungry for tips, hints, advice and shared experiences. We so want to do the right thing, of course we do. I regularly encounter parents who report that they have ***never*** thought about these Coaching-for-Parents techniques. How often I hear parents say wistfully, even after twenty years or more of parenting, "I wish I'd known this twenty years ago."

If this is the case, (and it often is), then how can they expect to have imparted (and, more to the point, ***modelled***) respectful communication for their children to mimic? The good news is it's never too late to start building those communication channels. Let's give ourselves a break from too much pointless retrospection.

Let me regale you with another of my audacious acronyms: let's create a '***SMILE***' wherever we can. Just in case we had any illusions about this coaching journey being straightforward and simple, let me extend an invitation to enter the ***Safe, Mistake-Inherent, Learning***

Environment. This vast experiential zone is essential to the coaching process - we cannot fully learn without mistakes, and yet we seek to make the least possible.

There's only one way not to ***ever*** make a mistake. And that's to ***Not Try Anything New***. Then life is an unending series of continued and imaginary successes. Hooray for us. But if we want to join the mass majority who feel driven to participate in new experiences from time to time, we will, we ***must*** make mistakes. Hooray for us a second time.

we cannot fully learn without mistakes, and yet we seek to make the least possible

The road to heaven is paved with good participation. We can't go wrong if we fully participate because, on one hand, if we achieve what we tried for, great learning ensues and with it, a warm sense of achievement. That's success, in most people's book. If we didn't achieve what we tried for, and we screwed up royally - great learning ensues about what not to do next time. Success again. Win-Win.

The Roman playwright, Terence, wrote ***"humani nihil a me alienum puto' -*** "[I consider] nothing that is human is alien to me," indicating a profound empathy with his peers' ability to test the boundaries of social acceptability. Hands up who has made mistakes in their lives? Hands up who has told lies? Used bad language? Kept secrets? Stolen from a shop? Been ill from over-imbibing alcohol? Tried drugs? Hands up if we're not putting our hands up because we still haven't even told our partners of certain indiscretions? Or simply that we're concerned other people may judge us?

And yet we cannot possibly ***KNOW*** what other people's reaction to us and our secret or misdemeanour is until we, ***WE***, have done that action, or something pretty similar. Nor how our relationship with that person will change as a result. Nor how our relationship with ourselves might change. And if we ***have*** been open, what are the lessons we learned there? How else could we have learned those lessons? What did we hide from our parents because we feared a punishment rather than an understanding? And what are our kids hiding from us because they fear the same thing?

open questions, open minds, open conversations

Don't know? So let's ask! Let's go home tonight and ask our children exactly this:

"What sort of things do you hide from me because you are nervous of my reaction?"

Let's pay attention to the phrasing - let's ask it ***precisely*** like that - as an open question, not:

"Is there anything you want to tell me?"

Open questions, open minds, open conversations.

So as of now we are going to make some fabulous mistakes as we start to coach our children, so we may as well accept the notion now and get comfortable with it. Let's give ourselves permission to luxuriate a while there. Our children will balance our errors with some humdingers of their own, never fear. So if we're happy to provide a SMILE in our household, let's remember to be happy that it gets well used.

Under the banner of ***'insightful observations'*** earlier, I offered this - a favourite catchphrase at home: ***"Of COURSE you're going to screw up from time to time – that's your job – that's what teenagers are meant to do – and it's great that you're fabulous at it."*** True it backfires from time to time as I get hit broadside with the insinuation that it is, apparently ***me*** who is accountable for some of their more excruciating howlers, i.e.

"But Dad, you are always telling us to look for the learning in a crisis, so we thought you'd be pleased when we talked that instructor into taking us down those out-of-bounds off-piste slopes. It turned out to be the perfect opportunity to see how to deal first-hand with real avalanches ..."

Moving on swiftly...

How many of us grew up with parents who had fixed, uncompromising ideas about how things should get done? How many of us are now intent on continuing that tradition, come hell or high water, with our own children? How many of us have worked for managers who micro-managed everything we did, believing they were sure to be able to find something that didn't come up to scratch? How did (do) we feel about that? How many of us insist on checking our children's homework and household tasks, just to find the things they have done poorly? How might this negative scrutiny be making our children feel?

The chances are they would feel stifled, suppressed, uncertain, less confident, perhaps resentful. Essentially this sort of behaviour leaves them scared to make a mistake. They put limitations on their own abilities, because we have conditioned them to check in with us for every decision. What happens to their creativity or initiative or spontaneity now?

Sir Ken Robinson is an expert in the field of creativity and innovation in business and education. He told two stories during a popular talk he gave to a TED Conference. The first describes how his four year old son had been chosen to play Joseph in the school nativity play – he didn't get to speak in the play but he had to receive the gifts from the three wise men.

They didn't get a lot of rehearsal time and at the performance, things must have got a little out of sequence and the first wise man comes in on cue, with the inevitable tea towel on his head, and says "I bring you gold." The third one came in second and, obviously improvising rapidly, says "I bring you 'mare.' " The boy who was due to come in second now had little choice but to follow on last, and he entered the stage, took a big breath, an even bigger guess and announced, "and Frank sent this!"

That's creative thinking. That's spontaneity, and the delighted reaction from the audience no doubt bolstered his confidence to just improvise many more times in his life. (It could also be argued that this story illustrates that the children hadn't had the story explained to them properly and were imitating the words without understanding them, but I prefer the first interpretation.)

Where's the fulfilment from existing in a state of continuous consensual appeasement?

His second story describes an eight year old girl who was absorbed in drawing a picture at home one day. Her mother approached her and asked what she was drawing, and the girl replied "It's a picture of God." The mother, (showing rather a weary naivety in my opinion), said, "but nobody knows what God looks like," to which her daughter responded casually, without looking up, "Well, they will in a minute!"

So his point is: children will take a chance - they'll have a go – and that's great. They are demonstrating that they are not afraid to be wrong. And open to the learning that inevitably results. How many of us parents can still lay claim to this willingness? Which parent is still up for taking a few risks, particularly when there is the weighty issue of our children's health and personal development at stake?

Who can deny that there is a certain frisson of excitement to be had from occasionally visiting that compulsive space known as "wrong"?

Where's the fulfilment from existing in a state of continuous consensual appeasement? Who can deny that there is a certain frisson of excitement to be had, ***for us parents too,*** from occasionally visiting that compulsive space known as "wrong"?

Sir Ken's belief is that creativity is as important as literacy, [and let's add as important as numeracy too]. Now I'm not saying that creativity is the same as being wrong. Merely that if we don't ever go out on a limb with the possibility of being fabulously wrong, we may well never come up with anything particularly innovative. Nor deliciously wicked for that matter. Let alone arrive at an understanding of those who do. Our kids for starters. And even if we have long ago crossed over from experimenting with 'the dark side", and can honestly claim never to have set foot there again, even once, it doesn't change the fact that our kids are only experimenting there, as did we, and will grow from the experience in time, as did we also.

The reason I say this – rather tongue in cheek perhaps, but truthfully none the less is because I believe today's teenagers know deep down, just as we knew as teenagers, what is likely to be of significance to them later in life – and what isn't.

I have always had a bit of a block with maths. I can do the basic SMAD stuff - subtraction, multiplication, addition, division, and I am pretty sure that I knew, at age fifteen after taking my high school maths exam a year earlier than most, that continuing to take a further exam in advanced maths would serve no purpose whatsoever in my later life. So, against my teacher's advice I dropped it like a stone.

making mistakes, is an amazing and necessary step in the learning process – it is essential to let children make some howlers.

And from that date to this, that teenage intuitive decision has proved to be wholly dependable. I cannot think of a single moment in my later life where advanced maths might have helped me make a decision, a choice, or take an action that might have provided me with a better life than the one I have. And likewise, there are undoubtedly millions of youngsters who do choose to persevere with their maths, knowing deep down that they ***will*** live by it daily, decades later.

So for me it's maths, for others it may well be other subjects or disciplines – geography, sports, art, music, languages, history, religious studies. The point is we ***know***. Even at a young age, if a voice inside us speaks loudly enough - we must learn to listen and parent-coaches can help with that.

Making mistakes, whether intentionally or unintentionally, is an amazing and necessary step in the learning process – it is essential to let children make some howlers. Let's face it; we adults continue the practice frequently. There is no more empowering learning tool. ***A parent's role at this point is to guide the child towards its learning of the consequences.*** By the time most children become adults – i.e. by the time they have completed the prescribed exams and tasks set them by their local education system - many of them have sadly lost this ability to be carefree about mistakes.

Suppose they had allowed themselves the luxury of getting things wrong on many occasions? Mistakes give us the opportunities to get perspectives on the implications of not thinking things through. As teachers are fond of telling their classes, some of the world's greatest products and inventions have been created AFTER things went very wrong, and the alert minds of their inventors were able to see new and wonderful possibilities from the "mistakes." And yet we, teachers and parents, have real difficulties giving youngsters enough creative freedom to make mistakes themselves.

How about awarding school prizes at end-of-year assemblies for more innovative categories? For instance:

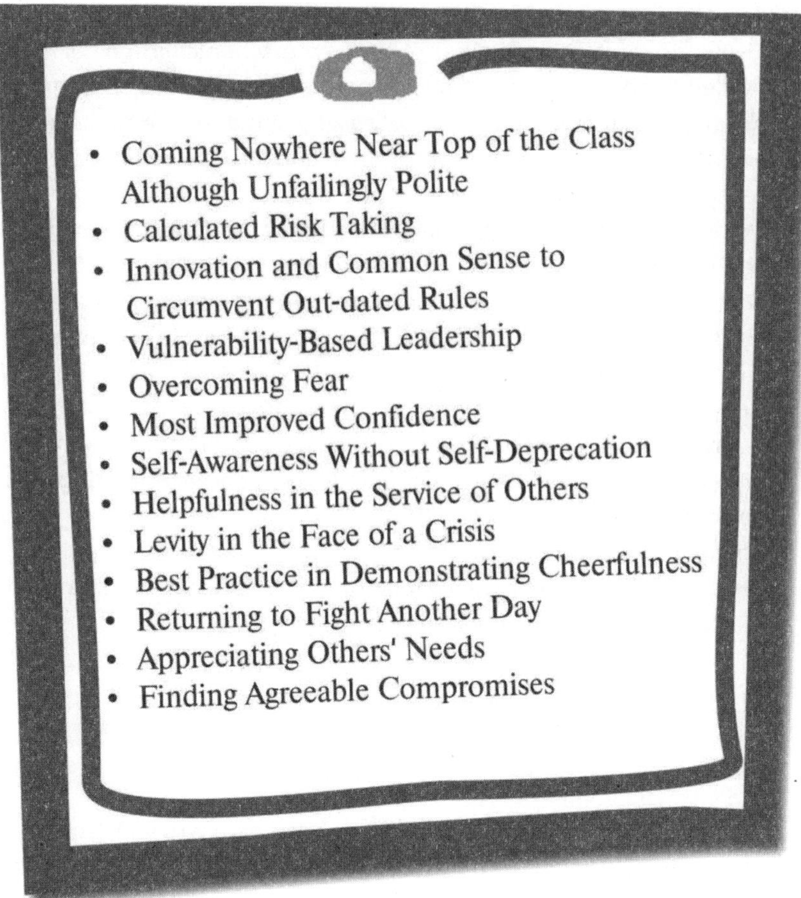
- Coming Nowhere Near Top of the Class Although Unfailingly Polite
- Calculated Risk Taking
- Innovation and Common Sense to Circumvent Out-dated Rules
- Vulnerability-Based Leadership
- Overcoming Fear
- Most Improved Confidence
- Self-Awareness Without Self-Deprecation
- Helpfulness in the Service of Others
- Levity in the Face of a Crisis
- Best Practice in Demonstrating Cheerfulness
- Returning to Fight Another Day
- Appreciating Others' Needs
- Finding Agreeable Compromises

We can surely think of more. And while we are in a hypothesising frame of mind, let me introduce a new raft of "What if?" questions.

how might schools design and develop the concept of ***family homeworks*** based around respectful communication skills?

What if we were to introduce a couple of new high school exams for teenagers? How would an exam in Cordial and Creative Communication look? Why not introduce a whole syllabus of Emotionally Intelligent literacy? How might society look if children were conditioned to understand self-awareness and responsibility? If they understood that every mood and state they exhibit was of their own choosing? That it was able to be modified at will? How it was consequential to their immediate and wider environment?

Suppose every child at school had mandatory Talking, Listening, Questioning and Thinking modules to learn and practice every week from the age of four? So as to be ready for their exam which would be staged a couple of years earlier than their general academic subjects, say at the age of 12 and 13? Therefore ready to be competent and respectful communicators ***before*** their teenage turbulence kicked in?

How would it be if we were to educate schoolchildren for an exam module within a Creative Thinking component, in which children are set tasks singly and in groups that ostensibly shouldn't be achievable, but which then offers marks for imaginative and structured applications and attentive thinking?

making a career out of a passion is the only truly fulfilling and sustainable path open to anyone

What messages might be gleaned by schoolchildren from an extended modular approach that rewarded listening, questioning and respectful feedback skills? How might parents be able to assist them with (and most likely learn from?) their homework tasks? Indeed, how might schools design and develop the concept of family homeworks based around respectful communication skills? How might that benefit the awareness of how well or how poorly their families are communicating at home - a singularly common gripe among teachers who notice the after-effects of 'difficult' familial relationships every day in their classrooms?

Has it been a 'mistake' to ignore this foundation stone of our education for the last fifty years? If so, there's no blame implied here, let's just label it a 'monumental awareness gap,' which we can start to fill as of now.

* * *

My stated aim as a teenager was to become a writer. It sounded like a cushy life although I was totally ignorant of the disciplines and skills involved at that age. I also wanted to be a PE Teacher. Sports too, have always been a passion. At the age of seventeen, in the summer holidays before I was to take my 'A' (Advanced) level school exams, I announced to my parents I was going to quit studying English. Inexplicably, they didn't fight my decision, although I was moderately talented, and I returned to school in the autumn for my final year with a twenty-five percent reduced workload, gaps in my calendar with nothing else to fill them, and a heady, if admittedly fragile, confidence in my ability to control my own destiny.

Why my parents acquiesced I couldn't imagine. My mum even *taught* English for goodness sake. I chose in its place to do Economics, a subject I couldn't have been less suited to. My decision had been based on laziness - I can admit it now; we were required to write an extended essay over the summer holiday, and, put simply, I couldn't be bothered. Easier to dump the whole thing. This is the same person who has now ended up writing books nearly forty years later.

My parents have since told me they allowed my decision because:

a) sometimes one has to let people take the consequence of their actions, good and bad (a little fanciful and worthy methinks - easy to say after the event),

b) there was no reasoning with me at that age, apparently.

It's fair to say b) sounds more probable.

Could they have coached me through that period? Might that have changed anything? It might - it's difficult to know for sure now. Maybe they did. I can't really remember. But what space would their questions have come from? Whose agenda would they have been working towards? Was this a mistake on their part? Or on mine for being a lazy hothead?

Probably the only time my parents did offer me straight counsel me on a life-decision was when they persuaded me, a year later, to put aside my sports ambitions for "something more academic" when I was considering university options. On reflection that was both good and bad counsel.

Bad, in that it didn't come particularly from a place of wisdom - more from a place of their own sense of their own worlds and an unwillingness to understand the basis of mine. And bad too, because I was later to return to full-time sports for twelve expansive and edifying teaching years (after floundering aimlessly in and out of various yuppie business jobs throughout my twenties).

It was good counsel too though, insofar as by taking their advice and studying languages, I gained an undeniably tolerant and inquisitive outlook when country-hopping over the next decades of my life. On my courses, I naturally also met many wonderfully linguistically-minded people and and kept friendships with them for the next thirty years (and counting). Good counsel too in that it brought me to an unshakeable belief that making a career out of a passion is the only truly fulfilling and sustainable path open to anyone.

those who never made any mistakes, never made anything

And having studied languages, I am acutely aware that in today's global family It has become impossible for anyone (at least, for anyone inclined and able to read a book like this), ***not*** to personally know people whose lives originated in countries, cultures, customs and languages different from their own. The world is too small for that kind of isolation now. Accessibility is now just too, well, accessible.

My choices made since then, over more than three decades, have been governed daily by that good/bad counsel from 1977. Regardless of what work I have involved myself in since, I have cultivated an inescapable awareness and belief that world citizens with an ability to converse in at least one, if not several languages other than their native tongue, are hugely more tolerant and innately wiser than mono-linguists, mono-culturalists and xenophobes can ever be.

What's more, I have been able to make the association with the microcosm family too - mine, our neighbours', other peoples'. If we are unable or unwilling to speak or attempt to understand the language of our children, then our families will be all the more intolerant of children; fractured and joyless until a common ground is reinstated and embraced.

So my parents' counsel has had far-reaching consequences in many directions. As is the nature of counsel. Parents, let's be prudent with what we insist on. But equally, let's remember that even if we are potentially making a mistake, there is huge learning available there too. We'll never know either way if we don't try ***something***.

Those who never made any mistakes, never made anything.

16.

Being Right Or Wrong - Who Cares?

Here are a few easy maths questions for us to keep our brains ticking over:

You are participating in a race. You overtake the second person. What position are you in?

Answer: If you answered that you are first, then you are absolutely wrong. If you overtake the second person and you take his place, you are second.

Answer the second question in even less time than you took for the first question.

If you overtake the last person in that race, then you are now...?

Answer: If you answered that you are second to last, or if you even spent time considering what position you ***might*** be in, then you are wrong again. Tell me, how can you overtake the LAST person?

OK so I'm just reflecting on how important it was for me to be able to catch someone out. And which of us is feeling smug because we answered one or both questions "correctly"? I bet many of us are already thinking who we can repeat the riddles to, in order to catch them out.

And who really cares anyway - at least all these people are keeping fit.

Another question – very tricky maths. Read this out loud to someone for the best effect. This must be done in ***our heads only***. Ready?

Take 1000 and add 40 to it.
Now add another 1000.
Now add 30.
Add another 1000.
Now add 20.
Now add another 1000.
Now add 10.
What is the total?
Who said '5000'? Nearly everyone to whom we read it out will also.

The correct answer is actually 4100. Don't believe it? Work it through on paper.

Maths, eh? Over-rated if you ask me. Although not many people do.

Following on from our previous chapter, if we choose to allow being wrong to become stigmatised, the education system, and we as parents, must take our share of the responsibility for creating an environment where mistakes are the worst thing a child can make. If mistakes equal progress and learning, fun and laughter, why on earth would we want to stigmatise them?

for children and young people, being right and wrong is a learned behaviour which becomes a currency of importance

For children and young people, being right and wrong is a learned behaviour which becomes a currency of importance. The more often they can be right, and be SEEN TO BE RIGHT the richer they believe they become. They also believe they can get rich by highlighting other people's 'wrongness'. Why might this be? Could it possibly be because we adults model it for them, perhaps?

How might it be if we could promote the idea that true riches are to be had from being ***grateful*** for the courage of those who seek to make as many mistakes as they can? After a while, only constructive solutions would be left lying around for us to find, and make our own. Rich pickings indeed.

one of the huge delights of being a coach is that coaches don't have to KNOW anything about anything

Professor Anders Eriksson has compiled and edited a wonderful book called Non Campus Mentis, containing actual prose submitted in papers and exams in the USA and Canada. Non Campus Mentis, already a beautiful example of a typical student mishearing of 'non ***compos*** mentis,' [meaning: not of sound mind], illustrates the ingenious and often comical ways we all attempt to make sense of information we can't understand because we have no context or frame of reference for it.

Sir Ken Robinson's son's classmates made fabulous attempts, so did the girl drawing God. Here are just a few magnificent attempts at understanding world history from Eriksson's collection:

Bonapartism was the way of people who wanted Napoleon back to rule even though he was dead.

The founder of the new Italy was Cavour, an intelligent Sardine from the North.

Military technology progressed with ideas such as guns which would shoot generally straight.

So let's talk about this being right and being wrong thing. One of the huge delights of being a coach is that coaches don't have to KNOW anything about anything. All we do is listen, really listen, (and we will look at some different levels of listening later in this book), and ask insightful questions. We will give many examples of these too.

In many situations, isn't this idea of being right and wrong simply contextual – simply OUR experience of what a good idea might look like? In 'pure' coaching, parent-coaches won't 'need to know' anything about anything; we don't really bother ourselves with what ***might be*** right or ***might be*** wrong. We trust that the child will know it, or come to know it through our questions. Parent-coaches focus on what appears 'right' or 'wrong' from our children's points of view, and ask them what they might want to do about it.

As parents, however, (divesting ourselves of the 'coaching hat' for a moment), we might regularly need to make the difference between 'sensible' and 'not sensible.' There is a place for didacticism - parents will naturally tell (yes tell!) their children that it's 'wrong' to hurt others, it's not 'clever' to cheat, bullying isn't 'just a bit of fun' and so on. And at some point parents have to cover grey areas like the 'white lie' too. A large part of parenting is the intention and responsibility to teach, particularly where moral instruction is an ulterior motive.

We shouldn't overlook the humour inherent in mistakes either, especially other people's. By way of a reframe, (that well-worn technique kept in every coach's top drawer), if we find it refreshing and, dare I say, amusing, when ***someone else's children*** are causing mischief and mayhem, (come on, yes we do) - is it just possible that other people might be enjoying the predicaments our children present to us? Look at it this way - we are all providing great theatre and the tickets are free.

In 2012, Andreas Müller, a famous and highly paid footballer, was asked where he might be interested in playing when he moved on from his current team. "Oh I don't mind really," he replied, "Madrid, Milan... so long as it's in Italy." This comment made international headlines, attempting to highlight his ignorance, and by association the alleged low level of education of footballers in general. Come on! We've all been guilty of similar *faux pas.* Andreas Müller is a highly gifted footballer, an entertainer. He's brilliant at what he does, and what he's paid for. It's too easy to vilify him for an unguarded comment, particularly when all his public words are required often to be highly spontaneous and scrutinised.

What would we do if we were this police officer, pulling over this motorcycle (overleaf)?

Or that young woman's parents, for that matter, when the incident was brought to their attention? Or simply anonymous witnesses to someone else's drama? I challenge all of us not to pull at least a wry smile. So in the big scheme of things, might it be possible to scale down the outrage, the irritation, the impatience within our own families and just laugh at ourselves a little more?

An article appeared in a British newspaper claiming that one in every seven people is considered 'socially dysfunctional' to some degree. Which would indicate that in most extended families, there are likely to be one or more such culprits. So before pointing the finger at others for dysfunctionality, let me take a long, hard look at those around me. If I can't see anyone around me that fits the bill, let me pause a moment before congratulating myself and directing the blame game at other families. After all, just maybe that one person in seven... ***is me.***

* * *

Educationalists are currently (in 2013) piloting schemes where pupils are allowed to take their computers into exams. They can use the internet too - unheard of even five years ago. Exam questions are being written to test the pupils' abilities to source and access relevant information and then distil it into rational, cohesive trains of thought.

This allows pupils to examine received knowledge from several, varied angles and find their own way through it, to reach a conclusion that is theirs. Sourcing information, processing it, using it, or discarding it - who cares that their conclusion isn't the same as ours? The child is learning the essence of learning and we must trust in their intelligence to relate this to their own model of their world as they see it.

Whatever we may think of this idea, the concept of phrasing open exam questions, where there is no set answer, is compelling at many levels. Surely it rescues all of us parents of the responsibilities of having to know and provide the 'only,' 'right,' 'acceptable,' answers? What a relief.

So here is another place where we can make a contribution to the child's learning environment. Have we created a predominantly stable, consistent, playful, relaxed, blame-free, open, searching environment? Or does it somehow lapse into impatience, tension, fault-finding, closed-mindedness, irritation...?

is the grow-zone we have created for our children, a listening or a telling one?

In short, is the grow-zone we have created for our children, a listening or a telling one?

We've said it already: children will take a chance, they'll have a go, and that's splendid. If they are still demonstrating that they are not afraid to be wrong, let's encourage that. Which of us would not admit to being our own toughest critic? And which of us finds ourselves transferring that culture of criticism towards our children? How long will our children continue to trust their own initiatives and build their own confidence if we continually find fault? Here's more from Non Campus Mentis:

> **Israel was founded despite the protests of local Arabs known as Zionists. There would not be all these problems if the West Bank would lend more money to the Arabs and if the Palaced Indians were not so troublesome.**

As I see it, a major part of our job as parent-coaches is to embrace mistakes whenever they decide to pay us a visit. Embrace them as heartily as the biblical father embraced his prodigal son. Embrace all 'mistakes,' as platforms for progress and learning, whether they be our children's, our partner's, our friends' or our own. Especially our own.

Let's bring a SMILE back into our family homes. In that Safe Mistake-Inherent Learning Environment live unfettered creativity and initiative. They are the perfect landlords for confidence and self-belief.

Let's create a SMILE and protect it with everything we've got!

17.

Shared Agendas

Now here, it is perhaps the right moment to make a fundamental point that any experienced coaches reading this may be anxious to hear. It is a pivotal coaching point and concerns '***agenda***.' It goes hand in hand with the principle of detachment, which we covered earlier under the Principles of Coaching.

'pure' coaching cannot happen where our shared agenda is allowed to influence the child's thinking

Agenda is one of those words which wreaks havoc with newbie coaches. It deals with the situations where coaches may share a path, knowledge or a desired outcome with their coachees. Where parents are coaching their children, this shared experience and attachment is practically inevitable.

For example, if someone's daughter says, during parent-coaching, that she wants to learn horse-riding and muck out and work out the horses at a stables five miles away, it may be difficult for her parents to ask her 'pure' coaching questions while keeping schtum about fees, early mornings wake-ups, driving responsibilities and so on. They very much have a stake in her needs; they are inextricably tied up with their own, i.e. finances, time management etc. In coaching terms this is known as a ***shared agenda***.

So, 'pure' coaching cannot happen where our shared agenda is allowed to influence the child's thinking. Questions emanating from this space of shared agenda will likely become advice, suggestion, leading, judgmental, instruction, direction. ***None of these can be coaching questions.*** 'Pure' coaching would entail asking ***unconcerned questions*** around the daughter's goals (horse-riding), her current situation (homework, friends, piano lessons, school-runs), setting herself actions (time management, financing, transport), and ***all without comment, opinion or judgment from the parent.***

As a parent hearing all this, (we who have our own busy lives, stretched budgets, concerns about our children's school-work and believe we deserve a lie-in as often as possible), how might we be able to ask coaching questions with no bias as to the outcome? How tricky will we find this?

So, once again, openness must be addressed. We are not only bringing it to the conversation, we are modelling it for the children to notice and copy. If we were parents of the girl who wanted to ride horses, we may find ourselves needing to be very open about how far our 'pure' coaching might be able to go, and when we might not be able to resist bringing in our own agenda.

Similarly, hundreds of managers who train with me to become coaches in their organisations worldwide, balk at the mechanics of coaching their employees, particularly those who report directly to them, for the very same reason: the employee's goals matter to the manager too. There is a joint interest in the outcome.

So what to do? Can a parent learn to be a 'pure' coach, and work with goals where there is a shared agenda? Do we, indeed, *wish* to become text-book examples of coaches, or just good parents? Carol Wilson wisely counsels,

"We must acknowledge that when we are coaching someone close, our child or good friend, or indeed, colleague or employee at work, it can still be useful although it will never be 'baggage-free' coaching. And where it can't be baggage-free, there is always going to be a third agenda - where the coachee is probably going to be consciously or subconsciously holding things back in a way that they might not do with a detached coach, regardless of how 'clean' and neutral we try to be. We shouldn't feel that we have failed because of this - it's fine so long as we don't pretend it doesn't exist."

Putting our own agenda to one side is to fully detach ourselves from our child's thinking processes, mistakes and stated desired outcomes. True parent-coaches would need to be comfortable allowing their child's desired outcome to be too ambitious, too modest, too unlikely, too unstructured. True parent-coaches can keep their advice and suggestions to themselves, at the very least until their children have listed a high number of options for themselves. True parent-coaches can keep their judgement, blame and accusations under wraps and ask challenging, open questions. True parent-coaches can stay out of the dramas that unfold.

If our mirror reflects back this person next time we look, we can call ourselves True Parent-Coaches. Good for us. Reality suggests, however, that once a shared agenda is identified, which, let's face it, is going to be most of the time, we will probably have to content ourselves with slightly 'impure' coaching. So let's pursue the relationship with bags of openness, sensitivity and awareness of the responsibilities of accommodating our child's designs on its own life.

18.

Confidentiality

'pure' coaching cannot work if any part of the content leaks

Coaching, 'pure' coaching, cannot work if any part of the content leaks. At the first hint that their confidences are being shared with others without permission, the children's minds will start to censor what they will explore in front of the coach, and the deep thinking will be compromised. Or, knowing that certain facts may be shared, the young brain may strategise as to what it may reasonably expect to be conveyed to any given audience on its behalf. So instead of being a coach we have become a messenger. And instead of growing the young brain, we are encouraging it to shrivel.

If we feel we are too close, or too entangled in the outcome of the coaching, we can always ask another coach-trained parent or trusted friend to coach our child on those issues. And if we are that person who has been asked to be this coach - no small responsibility - we must be open from the outset, to both the child and the parents that we will undertake to keep the coaching conversations confidential, unless we receive permission from the child to divulge their content.

Of course, to protect ourselves too, when acting *in loco parentis,* we must make it absolutely clear to all parties that certain issues ***will*** be relayed either to the child's parents or appropriate authorities if any concerns should surface regarding the child's safety, neglect or criminal activity. We may also decide to draw the line at drug-taking, gambling or other addictive behaviour, and bullying, for example. We must tell our young coachees that (if they are legally minors) we have a duty of care to report certain issues, but that we will discuss it as fully as possible before we report any part of the conversation to an appropriate audience.

Most parents and all teachers are pretty clued-in on paths to take should issues like these arise, so I'll leave this *caveat* section here.

19.

Filters

We all look at life through unique filters. Our personal filters may be cultural, financial, emotional, violent, humane, prejudiced, humorous, inclusivist, ageist and so on and on and on. Two similar people can and regularly do look at exactly the same event and interpret it in completely different ways.

as coaches we can only regard the person in front of us as a Terrific, Outstanding Person Capable of Astonishing Things

What stories do our eyes convey to our brains? Or our brains to our eyes for that matter? On the subject of eyes and eye contact, for many it represents trust. For others it is painful. One man at a workshop told the group he became anxious when people held his gaze while talking to him or when they asked him to look at them while they were talking to him. He told us it reminded him that, as a child, his dad ***only*** ever held his gaze when he was going to beat him. Through his filter, eye contact represented violence. What a catastrophically debilitating burden for a child to carry.

As coaches we can only regard the person in front of us as a Terrific, Outstanding Person Capable of Astonishing Things. A TOPCAT no less. (I couldn't resist another acronym). By all means, substitute any number and variety of different superlatives: **t**remendously **i**nspirational **p**eople **c**apable of **p**henomenal **a**chievements, **t**horoughly **e**xceptional **p**eople **c**apable of **a**mazing **c**reativity - all related to TOPCATs, even if their acronyms are less satisfying. Whichever way one looks at it, we are all scarily special, every one of us.

coaches cannot and will not see other than that infinite potential - why would we? Why would anyone?

Coaches cannot and will not see other than that infinite potential - why would we? Why would anyone?

Coaches have no limiting beliefs that TOPCATs may not be able to achieve what they profess to aspire to – we have no agenda for them and we try to remain detached from their successes and failures. Our job is to ask them searching questions and allow them to find their own paths, their own reasons for doing or not doing things, and allow them to face their own fears and mistakes.

Now it's an easy direction to give - not always so easy to carry out. Particularly the bit about being detached and having no agenda for our children. We have looked at the reality of holding a shared agenda in Chapter seventeen, and it's definitely a major challenge to pure coaching practice. The obvious difference to a professional coach/coachee relationship is that of course we parents almost can't help BUT have an agenda for our children.

So what do we often do? We manipulate. Yes we do. Subtly or less than subtly, sometimes our interactions with our children are down to nothing less than self-interest. Parents deserve an easy life too, right? We are biologically conditioned to be involved and engaged to lesser or greater degrees with them. It's true that some attachments appear to have remained almost umbilical, during and even after childhood. That umbilical cord seems to be lengthening too, with our children staying at home longer and longer. Many of our children seem to be far more attached and dependent than we were to our parents, so we may be talking about twenty-something's and thirty-something's here too, not just school-aged children.

Create a filter of amazingness and tremendous admiration and see the children through it. It becomes far easier to 'catch our children doing something right' rather than the opposite

So in these circumstances parents with a day to day involvement with their 'grown-up' children may find coaching even more daunting than otherwise. However, typically our motives are honest and well-meaning; our intentions are to make personally sure that our children get the most positive experiences out of their early lives.

The way we approach people and situations is always determined by the filters through which we view them. While it is difficult to "switch off" our emotions and judgements, it is possible to work hard on our self-awareness, and to gradually remind ourselves to modify the context and viewpoints we may be harbouring, so that we can be as open and accommodating as we can to the situation before us.

Let me ask you to turn back to Chapter One for a moment and refresh your minds with the words of "I am the square root of infinite potential." They seem to me to be an appropriate way to start a book like this - from the child's-eye view. If we are looking for inspiration for some filters to adopt, we could do worse than closely regard our children through some, maybe even all, of those points.

And, remember Annie from our Prologue at the beginning of this book? Annie was a woman who looked into the eyes of a young man, Ajay, who to most other people was wretched, pitiful, stupid, ugly. But she chose to create a permanent filter of beauty and respect and saw her world through it.

As parent-coaches, indeed simply as parents too, if we continue to create a filter of amazingness and tremendous admiration, it becomes far easier to catch our children doing something right, rather than the opposite. Let's look through that filter, right into their eyes, while we tell them sincerely how pleased it makes us feel that they have achieved something – anything – today. If we've neglected to create any kind of empowering filter last time we interacted with our children, let's try this next time and see how we feel differently towards them – or indeed, them towards us.

Let's hold warm eye contact the whole time and say silently to ourselves, this is a **t**otally **o**utstanding **p**erson **c**apable of **a**mazing **t**hings, who is on the learning journey of life, has challenges and obstacles to overcome, and is doing the best possible job with what's available. (Just as we are, incidentally).

20.

Coachable Moments Vs. Coaching Series

Professional coaches know that to work with someone towards achieving something life-changing takes many months and many sessions. Each session is highly structured, although skilled coaches make it seem like a natural conversation to the coachee. There are many books and training courses available to learn how to structure regular formal coaching sessions. If we want to go that route then we can research the internet and choose the one that suits us best. This book is not going to cover the ins and outs of formal structured coaching sessions because as parent-coaches we've got enough on our plates already just to master the art of the ...

...Coachable Moment!

Not the... Coachable Moment! Yes! The Coachable Moment.

No-one expects the... Coachable Moment!

OK. So apologies to Monty Python and their Spanish Inquisition sketch, but it's true. Coachable Moments crop up all the time - typically several times a day and nearly always without warning or fanfare. I also call it Lightning Coaching - compared to a formal coaching series, it's over in a flash.

It is as much of a challenge when starting our coaching just to be able to spot a Coachable Moment when it pops up, let alone know how to deal with it. However, as our coaching competence and awareness increases we will notice them popping up everywhere.

21.

Interested Or Useful?

One of the things that never fails to make a mark at workshops is a simple (and yes, relatively audacious) acronym that I call my coaching I.O.U. No, it's not the amount of money I need to pay in lawsuits from disgruntled coachees following bad advice dished out while coaching them. As if.

What it is, is a very straightforward and very memorable reflection that all coaches would do well to keep front-of-mind at all times. It is this: ask ourselves at any moment, are we being Interested Or Useful? That's it. I said it would be simple. However, like all things that appear to be simple, there's a lot more to this little acronym.

If one considers coaching in terms of its bare essentials, one has just structure and content. The first is the responsibility of the coach, the second is determined by the coachee. As far as is possible, they should be kept separate. It is very possible, probable even that most coaches will regularly find some common ground with the scenarios brought by their coachees. For parent-coaches who are coaching their children, even more so, because of the shared agendas that exist in families.

Our children have hundreds of stories which we, as parents, can readily identify with and become attached to. But ***only if we allow ourselves*** to become attached. The moment we find ourselves becoming 'interested' in their story we will struggle to remain in pure coaching mode. By stepping across the line from structure into content, and deciding to help, share, advise, sympathise or otherwise contribute to the child's story and its denouement we lose the ability to remain detached, one of our core coaching principles.

It may well be that our intervention and 'interest' is of help to the child insofar as we introduce some new thoughts, emotions and energies into the mix. However, by then we are no longer 'coaching.' It's one of the hardest and most counterintuitive things to fully grasp about parent-coaching. I see parents in workshops struggling with this concept every week. By the end of their practice over several weeks or months, however, they nearly always report that the I.O.U. has become one of their biggest insights into coaching, and that it is an incredibly liberating experience.

So next time we find ourselves with a choice between becoming 'Useful' i.e. detached and trusting, rather than 'Interested', i.e. helpful and involved, with all that this entails, let's choose 'Useful', and free ourselves up from the need to continually contribute to others' thinking. Given space, time and far fewer well-intentioned interventions from others, we can all dust off the less well-used parts of our brains and learn to polish them brightly again.

22.

Never Ask A Child 'Why..?'

I gave this little nugget out spontaneously in reply to a question from a parent at a Coaching for Parents workshop and was amazed at the immediate reaction from the entire group. They all became very animated and restless and were turning to one another and whispering little anecdotes of how true this was. We turned it into an impromptu exercise and everybody's stories were similar: children (i.e. anyone under twenty-five) seem to have very little ability to rationalise a 'Why' Question.

When we boiled it down to the basic ingredients we discovered that while there are infinite situations where 'Why?' can be employed, there are only two categories of 'Why?' Questions one can ask. The first category of 'Why?' Questions is simply informational: "Why does the moon orbit the sun?" or "Why does a human pregnancy take nine months?" We can use these as often as we feel we need to, although generally the sort of information that is useful in a coaching conversation is more explorational than factual.

The second is always interpreted as accusatory at some level: "Why have you done (or not done) this?" This always receives defensive, evasive or non-committal replies: "Because..." "He made me..." "No-one told me..." "She wouldn't let me..." "I don't know."

That's it.

Recognise scenarios like this?

Mum: "Olly, why have you eaten Charlie's birthday chocolates? You know she was keeping them for later."

Olly (13 years old): "Oh. I didn't know they were hers."

Mum: "Well you knew they weren't yours so why didn't you check with her? You'll have to buy her some more now."

Olly (13 years old): "That's not fair! How was I to know they were hers? They didn't have her name on them!"

Result: Impasse with immediate blood pressure increase all round.

Whatever the truth of this situation it is unlikely to ever become apparent for several years. If Mum is likely to get justice for Charlie anytime soon, she might do slightly better to take a different tack without using 'Why?' Questions. Although this is still potentially precarious:

Mum: "Olly. Charlie says she left her chocolates in the living room and now they are missing and you've been the only person in the room all afternoon."

Olly (13 years old): "Well I did have a couple but I thought they were for everyone."

Mum: "Well, they are all gone now, and she says she hasn't eaten any."

Olly (13 years old): "So maybe she's not telling the truth. I told you I only had two. Or maybe three. Why do you always blame me for everything?"

Result: Impasse with slightly slower blood pressure increase all round. (And Olly ricochets a 'Why?' Question for good measure).

These 'Why?' Questions demonstrably don't serve any useful purpose before the age of about twenty-five. That's when the brain should have fully developed its social cognition capabilities (re-read Why Teenage Brains Don't Behave As We Want Them To, from Chapter five) and the brain owner has acquired confidence and perspective. Oh, and probably money too. Give it a few years and re-visit the scenario:

Mum: "Olly, why have you eaten your Charlie's birthday chocolates? You know she was keeping them for later."

Olly (25 years old): "Yeah, sorry. I couldn't resist them. I got a bit peckish and there was nothing in the fridge. Sorry, Charlie, I'll buy you some more this afternoon I promise."

Result: Peaceful and gracious restitution.

So unless we are prepared to wait several years for a more appropriate resolution, let's not waste our breath or our energies using 'Why?' Questions with youngsters. In fact, while coaching people of any age, we'll not get much more joy from these 'Why?' Questions. Find better questions. Chapter 31 in Part Three will help here.

Incidentally, there is a further dimension of 'Why?' Questions in that same chapter under the 'What makes a good coaching question?' section, which we can work through at our leisure too, if we have the inclination. Frankly though, my candid opinion is that I wouldn't recommend that we spend too much time with the 'Why?' questions from there either - there are so many better and more imaginative questions for ambitious coaches to cut their teeth on.

ARE WE NEARLY THERE YET?

You're possibly thinking, "When are we actually going to get some coaching started? Enough of this setting-up-a-coaching-space already, I want to get going."

Well, it's true a few of the remaining groundwork chapters may be (temporarily) dispensable, particularly if you're not big into theory-based learning, and of course, there is nothing to stop you from jumping forward to Chapter 27 but you're doing so well and being so diligent, I'd love to recommend that you stick with it.

Already you'll have made such a difference to your understanding of the respectful conversations you'll soon be having at home. Stay with it if you can - not long to go now.

23.

Treating All People Equally

Transaction Analysis refers to the social interactions, or 'transactions', that take place between people, and was conceived by psychologist Eric Berne, famous for his 1960s best seller, 'Games People Play.' When two or more people encounter each other, Berne said, sooner or later one of them will speak, or give some other indication of acknowledging the presence of the others. He called this 'transactional stimulus.' Another person will then say or do something which is in some way related to the stimulus which he called the 'transactional response.'

During the course of working with hundreds of patients in the 1950s, Berne noticed a familiar pattern occurring: most of his patients tended to be in any one of three co-existing 'states', which he defined as Parent, Child and Adult. I find these very useful when coaching children - they help to ascertain how I am, (or the child is) 'transacting;' i.e. with which voice and with what behaviour.

Berne's ***'Parent'*** state occurs when we are reproducing language, behaviours or attitudes which we have absorbed from our own parents and early role models. Babies are programmed to learn by reproducing what they see and experience from the people around them. Some of the patterns absorbed are useful in later life and others the opposite.

If we have ever heard ourselves speak, or noticed ourselves react to something, and then thought (perhaps with horror) 'that's what my mother/father used to say/do,' then we were probably having an Eric Berne 'Parent' moment. Reproduced 'Parent' transactions may be positive and useful in providing discipline, boundaries and responsibility, while on the other hand, the negative outcomes can be that we become controlling, bullying, didactic, critical, judgmental and wag our forefingers a lot.

The ***'Child'*** state is a reproduction of the stimuli and responses we had with our own parents. Berne saw that babies *require* transactions with other humans from birth, in order to develop. My colleague, Carol Wilson, calls these interactions 'strokes,' and notes that ideally, where babies and young children are concerned, these strokes will take positive form, e.g. affection, close attention, feeding, playing games, etc.

However, if those strokes are not forthcoming, or are completely absent, the children will create strokes by other means, perhaps by being naughty, because they are still likely to receive the attention and acceptance they crave. The behaviours exhibited in 'Child' transactions might be sadness, over-excitability, moodiness, despair, throwing temper tantrums, giggling or simply speaking in baby-talk. Even if their behaviour means they get punished, they still receive strokes - a negative stroke is better than no stroke at all.

Some children seem to cultivate the habit of 'shooting themselves in the foot' in this way, and continue it well into later life by exhibiting self-destructive and childish behaviour. Incidentally, being in a 'Child' state is not exclusively reserved for children by any means. We older humans manage to bypass the chronology to inhabit this state quite frequently too - who's noticed?

This is probably the reason why negative behaviours are assimilated as much, if not more so, than positive ones. Psychologists talk about the area for negative 'real estate' in the brain being five times greater than that available for positivity. It seems therefore that this would contribute heavily to the fact that children appear to access the negative aspects of a given situation so readily. If no strokes are received from a parent in relation to their children's positive behaviour, there is a strong probability that the children will automatically access the larger 'bank' of negativity, kept in reserve for precisely these occasions. The 'Child' is resourceful when searching for its strokes.

the language of coaching encourages children to take responsibility, discard learned prejudices and view each situation from a clean slate instead

This is the strongest case I can find for giving acknowledgement and praise for any and every little milestone passed by our children. Reward and acknowledge the easy things, every time; then there is no further incentive for the 'Child' to materialise to chase attention by dipping into its negative equity account. Parent-coaches can ***always*** look for and find positivity in our children.

What might be possible, I wonder, if we parent-coaches, with our permanent access to the children, could effect a 'coaching rewire' on their private cerebral real estate and create a larger field for positivity at an earlier age?

The ***'Adult'*** state is the label Berne gave to the times when we are interacting 'in the moment' without repeating a pattern from the past. This is the healthy way of transacting; free from the baggage of past prejudices, 'knee-jerk' reactions while exercising rationality over painful memories. These types of transactions are straightforward, attentive, non-threatening and non-threatened, using tempered language like "I see," (rather than a contradiction), "Possibly," (rather than "Never,") "Probably" (not "Definitely,") "Disappointing," (not "Devastating,") "I think you are..." and "I feel..." (thereby taking responsibility, instead of "You are," "It always," "It never...")

The language of coaching strives to exhibit all of these 'Adult' qualities and encourages children to take responsibility, discard learned prejudices and view each situation from a clean slate instead of falling back on previous behaviour patterns.

Human beings, whether babies or children, are capable of absorbing and reproducing ***all*** of the transactions we experience. As we grow older, we can make choices between which behaviours we want to reproduce, although it is not always easy to differentiate a pattern of behaviour set in place by childhood experience from one which is not.

our behaviour patterns are not innate character traits, they are simply learned habits that, once identified, can be mastered and reprogrammed

Ancient patterns sometimes seem bewildering to us and to those around us, when reviewed in later life. An example of such a pattern is a limiting belief statement like, "People always leave me, eventually" which sets up an unconscious pattern of choosing only those partners or acquaintances who will leave. This behaviour serves to validate the original belief, which can then transmute into an even more destructive belief; "I'm not worth being around." Another might be, "I never do anything right," which results in people sabotaging their own success.

The most useful aspect of Transactional Analysis in terms of coaching's solution-focused approach is its underlying philosophy that everyone has the ability to change. Our behaviour patterns are not innate character traits. They are simply learned habits that, once identified, can be mastered and reprogrammed. Parent-coaches can help the child identify these, and coach them through to a re-frame.

24.

The OK Corral

Berne's original work has since been developed by a number of psychologists, in particular Frankl Ernst and Thomas Harris MD. Harris wrote a best-seller 'I'm OK, You're OK' in the 1960s. Taking Berne's three transactional states a stage further, Franklyn Ernst devised a neat quadrant he called the OK Matrix, now commonly nicknamed the OK Corral (after the famous 1881 Tombstone shootout between the Earps and the Clantons). Ernst identified four 'Life Positions' we meet in our relationships with each other, which can result in effective or ineffective communication.

The ideas set out below can be enormously productive when used in coaching and in talks about mature dialogue with young people. Explaining the squares in the quadrant to our frustrated youngsters and asking them to place where they stand in different situations and with different people is often revelatory. Let's make time to take a look at the diagram below with our children - they really understand the positions and can relate to them.

We can explain that the model represents how people see themselves and their thoughts, alongside other people and their thoughts. Children may be helped by looking at the quadrants and becoming aware of which they see themselves operating in at different times in their various relationships, particularly with their siblings, parents and teachers. Of course, to some extent we move around all the quadrants at various times and situations, but most people tend to have one particular quadrant that they act on most of the time.

I'm OK – You're OK:

This is where both people in the transaction are in Berne's 'Adult' state. Both take responsibility and make mature effort. When I consider myself OK and also frame others as OK, then there is no position for me or any of us to be inferior or superior. Each of us might be expressing "I am capable and confident," or "I believe you are capable and confident," or "We will achieve great things together." This is the peer to peer stance of implicit equality - an essential foundation for productive coaching.

This is, in many ways, an ideal position, as both people are comfortable with other people and with themselves. They are confident, happy and get on with others even when there may be points of disagreement. They both feel they will add value to any situation.

I'm not OK – You're OK:

When I think I'm not OK but you are OK, then I am putting myself in an inferior position with respect to you. This is Berne's Child state, when one person feels 'small.' Children starting high school might feel overawed, or might find that they become tongue tied when speaking to older children or authoritarian teachers. Grown-ups too can demonstrate this 'Child' state by being overly deferential to teachers or police officers, particularly when in front of children.

This position may come from being belittled as a child, perhaps from dominant parents or maybe careless teachers or bullying peers. People in this position have a particularly low self-esteem and will put others before themselves. There is a culture of dependence. Their state of mind and behaviour is consciously adopted by those witnessing it and can result in frustrations, tantrums or simply not achieving very much through fear and refusal to take responsibility.

They may thus experience a strong drive to please others. 'Pleasing Others' is one of the drivers originally identified in the field of Transactional Analysis by Taibi Kahler. There are some simple and useful notes on the components of Kahler's relationship drivers in the following chapter.

I'm OK – You're not OK:

People in this position feel themselves superior in some way to others, whom they see as inferior and not OK. As a result, they may be contemptuous and quick to become angry. Their talk about others will be smug and supercilious, contrasting their own relative perfection with the limitations of others. This state of mind can produce bullying and overbearing behaviour, at home or at school.

It is the equivalent of Berne's 'Parent' state. For a parent it might mean claiming too much responsibility for the child's achievements, 'helping' too much with home-works, sports instruction or music lessons. Any of the 'master-pupil' types of relationship in fact - all of which are anathema to the coaching way of thinking. Taking this position is a trap into which many managers, parents and others in authority can fall, assuming that their given position makes them superior and, by implication, others are therefore not OK. People in this position may also relate strongly with Kahler's 'Be Perfect' driver, below, and their personal striving makes others seem less perfect.

There is a pervasive attitude of "I know best," and "You've got it wrong."

I'm not OK - You're not OK:

This is, fortunately, a relatively rare position to witness or experience, and can occur where people unconsciously try to project their unease onto others around them. As a result, they feel bad in themselves whilst also perceiving others as bad. This is the worst possible state when people are behaving from either or both of Berne's 'Parent' and 'Child' states. Both parties squabble, can be disloyal and give up easily.

This position could also be a result of relationships with dominant others where the other people are viewed through filters of inconsistency, betrayal and retribution. This may later have the effect of normalising other dysfunctional people (e.g. bullies, overbearing parents), and projecting that normalised *persona* onto everybody they encounter.

We might hear expressions like, "This is hopeless," "She goes or I go," "We'll never get anywhere." The equivalent phrases expressed during childhood might have been "I'm not playing any more," from the child or "The conversation is closed," from a parent. It becomes the easiest, and often most dramatic, way out of a difficult situation and always the least productive for everyone concerned.

If we have ever witnessed a Monopoly board game tossed into the air, scattering all the pieces because the game wasn't going well for one player, or the golf club thrown down the fairway for the same reason, we have met people taking this position. (Just as an aside, how many adults can we name who still seem to 'dine out' on stories of their dysfunctional behaviour as youngsters, as though it is somehow a badge of pride...? And then wonder why their kids resolve their difficult issues in similar ways?)

* * *

All in all, this is a super chapter for creating discussion with our children about, well...creating discussion! Remember way back in chapter 7 where our exasperated parents are asking plaintively how they can get their children to hold any kind of meaningful conversation with them at all? Well here's another opportunity. We have to try everything, right? Ask the children for their observations about how some combinations work together. For example, where one person has the position of 'I'm OK - You're not OK' and the other person has 'I'm not OK - You're OK'. Or when positions do not fit, particularly when both people are 'I'm OK - You're not OK'; this can be a recipe for conflict or confusion. Talk it through together - it can be exceedingly insightful.

There's a lot of learning in that. Perhaps we can encourage them to say where they frame themselves and their friends in the various quadrants in various situations. Where do they position us on the quadrants in certain situations? What are their thoughts about these observations? And what are our thoughts about their observations about us?

25.

Relationship Drivers

Taibi Kahler identified five common drivers in the field of Transactional Analysis that motivate us. Any of these may be rooted in early admonishment from teachers and parents who were most likely intending to help the child become socially functional. Typically, Kahler suggests, they perhaps did not offer sufficient guidance and praise for adequate behaviour, thus leaving the child overdoing things.

In reasonable quantities, these drivers are effective in creating functioning and successful adults, although when people, (children particularly) do not know when to stop, then dysfunctional behaviour can set in. He offers some useful pointers for coaching 'treatments' at the end of each one too, in the event that we might recognise any 'overplayed' drivers in any young people we may know...

Best of all, invite the children to read through them and ask them for their thoughts. Awareness is such a big part of coaching.

There are certainly overlaps with the OK Corral too and I reproduce his drivers here, without further comment or examination.

1) Pleasing Others

Imperative

- I must make other people happy. I know that I've done this when they acknowledge and praise me.
- Only others can tell me when I have done well. If they do not, I have failed.
- Other people's happiness is more important than mine.

Identification

- Ingratiating behavior, always seeking to please.
- Always testing that people are happy and satisfied.
- Smiling and friendly expression.
- Frames everything as a question that invites approval.
- Apologetic. Will say 'sorry' for almost anything and even just to fill space.

Benefits

- Comfortable working with other people. Often well-liked and good company.
- Sympathetic and concerned about others.

Problems

- Anxious around others. Worrying too much as to how they are being perceived.
- Seeking approval. Finds positions of authority difficult.
- Unable to say 'no' to any request.
- Finds criticism particularly difficult when it implies they have not pleased others.
- Worried when ignored. Easily offended (but unlikely to mention it).
- Can get locked in mutual hugging patterns or competitive pleasing with other pleasers.

Treatment

- Make pleasing themselves a criteria for pleasing you. Be happy when they are happy (but beware of getting in a mutual pleasing competition).
- Help them accept criticism without feeling put down or a failure. Do not get angry with them.
- Help them to see when pleasing others turns into dysfunctional subservience.
- Encourage them to become self-sufficient and praise themselves.
- Get them to indulge themselves now and again. Separate out some 'space for just me.'

2) Being Perfect

Imperative

- I must be perfect, wonderful, correct in every way.
- I must succeed in everything I do.
- I must get top marks and win.

Identification

- Exact language, including qualification when they are not sure, such as 'probably', and absolutes when they are, such as 'absolutely.'
- Always neat and well-groomed.
- Never completely satisfied with what they do.

Benefits

- Hardworking, with excellent quality output.
- May achieve great things.

Problems

- Fears of failure and losing control, and subsequent overcompensation.
- Overwork. Not finishing things for fear of criticism.
- Expecting others to be perfect too.

Treatment

- Laughter.
- Praise, including for less-than-perfect work.
- Reframing of what 'perfect' really means to 'good enough'.
- Be very specific with criticism (and praise).

3) Hard

Imperative

- I cannot refuse requests. I must at least try.
- I must improve and always get better.
- Wherever I am is not good enough.

Identification

- Not satisfied with what has been done.
- Language that uses the verb 'try' (rather than 'will').
- Tense and anxious in appearance.
- Will often side with the underdog, seeking to right wrongs.
- May well not achieve goals (although these are often high).

Benefits

- They always give of their utmost in all situations.
- Persistence in difficult and time-consuming situations.
- Helping others.
- Working toward noble causes.

Problems

- Craving praise, but never satisfied when it is given.
- Find criticism very hurtful, especially for not trying enough or not considering others.
- Effort of trying leads to physical burnout.
- Lots of 'trying' but no real result.
- Fear of completion (run out of things to try).
- Expecting others to try harder.

Treatment

- Use their need to improve to help them to not try too hard.
- Praise for completion of specific items. Do not praise just for effort.
- Help them move from 'trying' to 'succeeding.' Start with the language they use.
- Stop them moving to another task before the first is complete.
- Help them distinguish between that which is achievable and that which is not realistically possible.

4) Being Strong

Imperative

- I must be invulnerable at all times. I must not cry or show any weakness.
- I cannot express emotions. I must help others but not myself (I do not need help).

Identification

- Aggressive or assertive attitude, demonstrating strength in attitude.
- Objective language, distancing themselves from their feelings. Avoids 'I' language and any talk about emotions.
- Frozen face and body, hiding emotions.
- Will take on all tasks without complaint.

Benefits

- Good for getting things done, especially in a crisis.
- Does not take things personally or get sucked into emotional situations.
- Generous, always helping others before self.

Problems

- Withdrawn under stress as they hold emotions in. Refusal to acknowledge they are stressed.
- Bottled-up emotions that may explode outwards onto others or be held in and do internal damage.
- Can get into 'who is the strongest' competitions with others, especially those who also have powerful 'be strong' drivers.
- Expecting others to be strong. Contempt for the weak.

Treatment

- Praise for consideration of the feelings of others.
- Put them in slightly vulnerable situations and praise their handling and exposure of emotions. Only make them as vulnerable as they can handle without going into fight or flight...
- Be considerate about their emotions. Show that you recognize them and that it is OK for them to have feelings
- Show them that they are not to blame for things, including their own internal issues.
- Help them receive with good grace as well as give to others.
- Help them see where their strength appears as a threat to others.

5) Hurrying Up

Imperative

- Go faster. Whatever I am doing, it's not being done quickly enough.
- So much to do, so little time.

Identification

- Enthusiastic and action-oriented.
- Many things on the go at once. Often juggling several quite different activities.
- Time language, using words like 'now,' 'schedule,' 'timely' and so on.
- Complaints that there is not enough time.
- Talking quickly and checking the clock frequently.
- Impatient (watch for tapping fingers and huffing).
- May explode into anger if held up.

Benefits

- When given work delivers it quickly.
- Good focus on output and delivery (when not combined with **'try hard').**

Problems

- Fretting over having 'nothing to do.'
- Speed over accuracy.
- Taking on too much and then complaining
- Hassling others to do things before they are ready.

Treatment

- Thank them for their time.
- Ensure they think before they act.
- Help them to 'be' without 'doing.'
- Get them to sit quietly and appreciate a single moment.

26.

Taprooting

It is difficult to find analogies more commonly used in personal development books than those about acorns and oak trees. Understandably so, perhaps, since it is quite astonishing that something so utterly immense should be able to be contained in something so minute and seemingly unremarkable. Yet an acorn is certainly the opposite of unremarkable. How can something so tiny contain all this 'oaktreeness' inside it? Of course it's perhaps ***because*** we humans also originate from microscopic beginnings, that we have come to be able to accept this and other illogically amazing feats of nature relatively easily.

humans have come to be able to accept illogically amazing feats of nature relatively easily

Sir John Whitmore in *Coaching for Performance, GROWing human potential and purpose* offers another aspect of the analogy too:

"Oak saplings, growing from acorns in the wild, quickly develop a single, hair-thin taproot to seek out water. This may extend downwards as far as a metre while the sapling is still only 30 cm tall.

"When grown commercially in a nursery, the taproot tends to coil in the bottom of the pot and is broken off when the sapling is transplanted back, setting back its development severely while a replacement grows. Insufficient time is taken to preserve the taproot and most growers do not even know of its existence or purpose.

"The wise gardener, when transplanting a sapling, will uncoil the tender taproot, weight its tip, and carefully thread it down a long vertical hole driven deep into the earth with a metal bar. The small amount of time invested in this process so early in the tree's life ensures its survival and allows it to develop faster and become stronger than its commercially grown siblings."

The taproot, then, becomes yet another organism to be granted pride of place on the shelves of personal growth analogies. Extending that parallel to the subject of this book - creating opportunities for our children to develop - this new aspect of an old analogy lends itself well. I'm going to call it "***taprooting"*** from now on.

So, a well-informed gardening taprooter wishes to give each acorn its best possible chance of accessing its full 'oaktreeness' potential, thereby creating a vertical, nutritious cocoon to accommodate and feed every centimetre of its long taproot. The taproot can then establish itself confidently, safely, without undue setback and over time becomes strong, steadfast and resilient as a magnificent oak tree.

Likewise, well-intentioned parent-taprooters create around their child a similar nutritious cocoon, in the form of a pervasive environment of praise, choices, responsibility, self-directed learning, listening, attentiveness, mistakes (safe ones - riskier ones can come all in good time). The child can then establish itself confidently, safely, without undue setback and over time becomes strong, steadfast and resilient as an amazing adult human.

Malcolm Gladwell, storyteller supreme, picks up the acorn theme too in his book *'Outliers - the story of success',* and continues this theme of a privileged growing environment. His view is,

"The tallest oak in the forest is the tallest not just because it grew from the hardiest acorn; it is the tallest also because no other trees blocked its sunlight, the soil around it was deep and rich, no rabbit chewed through its bark as a sapling and no lumberjack cut it down before it matured."

This implies that the old belief that we are simply born as empty containers waiting to be filled with the random behaviours our guardians deem appropriate has definitely had its chips. And the idea that it's enough just to have grown from strong genes holds little truth either, any longer. Furthermore, I believe we should be wary of the notion that humans are born into competition with one another. It's a powerful school of thought, understandably espoused by those who have chosen to fight for their place in their societies, compared to those who have been unquestioningly embraced despite little or no effort to achieve acceptance.

Whether we humans have been raised with or without the skills that poverty teaches us, I don't believe we were designed as part of a survival competition. To need to be the most important, the strongest, the richest, the most acclaimed could be seen, in evolutionary terms, as an affliction of insecurity which is not central to personal growth and development. I believe these acorn-taproot-environment-oaktree analogies above, highlight a different purpose for humanity, namely that we are born of community and connectedness, to assimilate the lessons of community and connectedness. By exploring our emerging emotional intelligence (that allows us to be aware of the significance of community and connectedness) we are able to take responsibility for our relationships with other beings and environments.

It's considered unlikely that other living creatures imagine the notion of having a purpose, as we humans do, although, not being able to fully communicate with them, it's hard to be 100% sure.

Is it allowed to partly disagree with Darwin's theory that we have evolved to be fit enough to survive ***over another***? I believe we have evolved in such a way as to understand that we are fit enough to be the same, to be equal, to complement one another. Knowing this, surely enables many more of us to survive, in a perfectly balanced way, than otherwise.

To paraphrase, and entirely decimate the metre of the immortal John Lennon song, isn't it time to give connectedness a chance?

Oft-repeated (and oft-embellished) stories of taprooters abound in business and sport. Many become deservedly the stuff of legend. Sadly the beleaguered educationalist and parent taprooters don't seem somehow to receive the same coverage or adulation, (or salaries). Leadership, teamwork, management are words that are naturally associated with sports, commerce and industry. We know they associate just as naturally with families, households and schools, except there they are known as teaching and parenting and somehow seem to have become comparatively invisible.

If you can see any ***differences*** in the skill-sets required between growing young minds or growing older minds, let me know would you? Because I can't.

to partly disagree with Darwin's theory, is to believe we have evolved in such a way as to understand that we are ***fit enough*** to be the same, to be equal and to complement one another

Knowing this, surely enables many more of us to survive, in a perfectly balanced way, than otherwise

RIGHT. THAT'S IT. WE'VE ARRIVED!

Small fanfare please. I can't think of any more stakes that might need to be in place. Our coaching perimeter is adequately ring-fenced. It's time at last to move on to the practicalities of actually coaching.

PART THREE
COACHING LADDERS

COACHING FOR REAL
- BEING THERE AND DOING IT
CREATING CORDIAL COMMUNICATIONS

"Stand together, yet not too near together:
For the pillars of the temple stand apart,
And the oak tree and the cypress grow not in each other's shadow."

Khalil Gibran, The Prophet

FOUNDATION SKILLS, TECHNIQUES AND TOOLS

27.

The First Ladder - Emotional Intelligence

EQ explained

A wonderful training workshop exercise, introduced to me by Sir John Whitmore, involves asking participants to think of a favourite leader of theirs; someone who has had a very real and personal influence on their growing up. The leader might be a teacher, an aunt, a scout leader, a grandparent, a manager - not forgetting of course, a parent! - but in every case, it should be someone who is known to the participant and not a distant figurehead from the world of politics, or sport or music or business.

The participants are then asked to discuss with a few others the things that favourite leader ***did*** that they liked so much. It is a very energised icebreaker and everyone always has someone to share thoughts about. Then after a few more minutes, they are asked to pinpoint exactly what that leader made them ***feel***, when they were doing those things. A quick *résumé* and capture of their response provides two columns of highly commendable actions, behaviours and feelings on a flip-chart. The trainer then reveals the next slide of the PowerPoint presentation which contains almost identical actions, behaviours and feelings to those that have been captured on the flip-chart.

Psychic? Uncanny? Not really. But it does happen ***every time*** without fail. It seems that when one asks a group of people, any group of any people, to answer these two questions, they collectively assemble identical, universal viewpoints of leadership.

I have presented this exercise hundreds of times in dozens of countries, many different cultures and continents. The result is the same. I note to the group that it's interesting to observe the things that they haven't mentioned too. Things, in fact, that are ***almost never mentioned*** during the exercise.

For example just occasionally someone mentions qualities like 'charismatic,' 'strong public-speaking,' although rarely 'good advice-giver' or 'great supervisory skills.' Occasionally, too, people might report that their leader left them feeling 'protected,' (although they do often say 'safe,' or 'secure,' which are slightly different). The columns invariably contain a huge selection of the following:

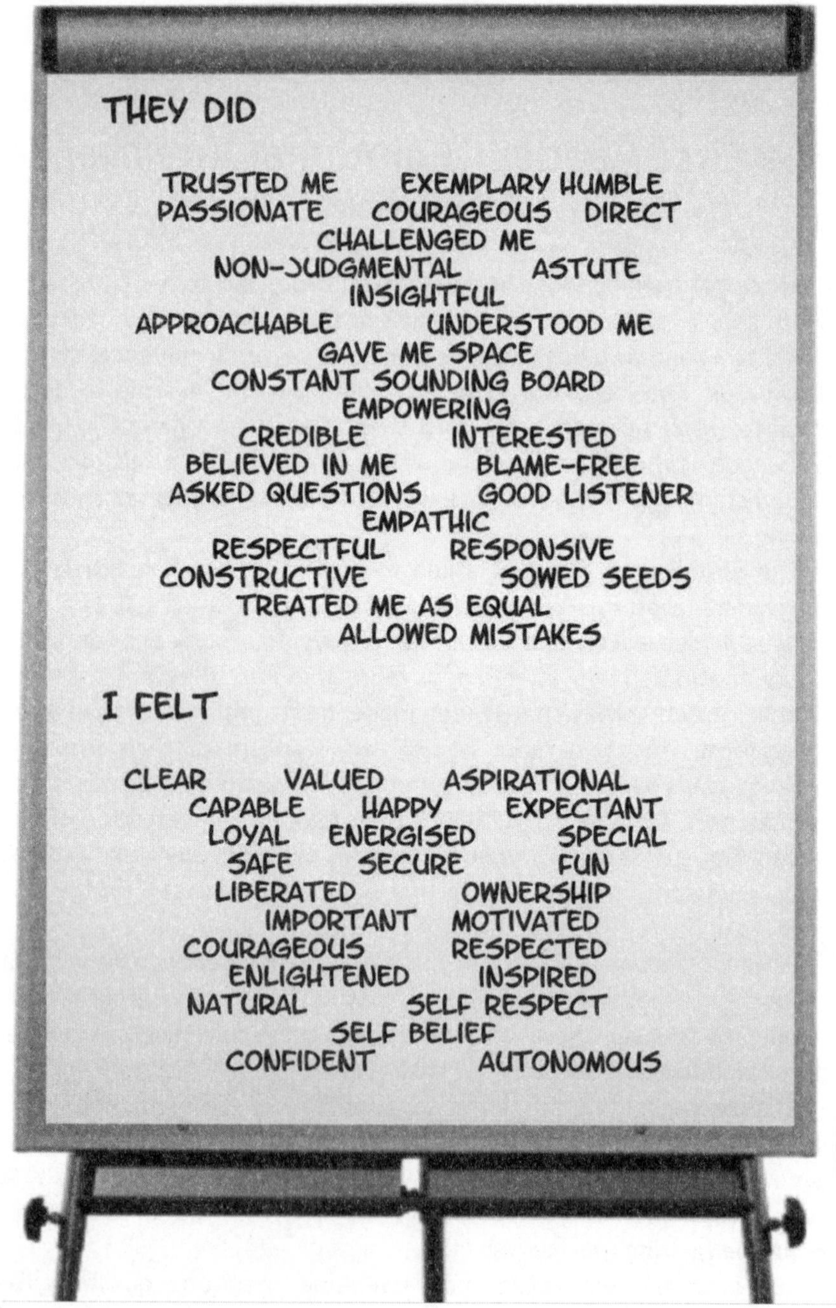

THEY DID

TRUSTED ME EXEMPLARY HUMBLE
PASSIONATE COURAGEOUS DIRECT
CHALLENGED ME
NON-JUDGMENTAL ASTUTE
INSIGHTFUL
APPROACHABLE UNDERSTOOD ME
GAVE ME SPACE
CONSTANT SOUNDING BOARD
EMPOWERING
CREDIBLE INTERESTED
BELIEVED IN ME BLAME-FREE
ASKED QUESTIONS GOOD LISTENER
EMPATHIC
RESPECTFUL RESPONSIVE
CONSTRUCTIVE SOWED SEEDS
TREATED ME AS EQUAL
ALLOWED MISTAKES

I FELT

CLEAR VALUED ASPIRATIONAL
CAPABLE HAPPY EXPECTANT
LOYAL ENERGISED SPECIAL
SAFE SECURE FUN
LIBERATED OWNERSHIP
IMPORTANT MOTIVATED
COURAGEOUS RESPECTED
ENLIGHTENED INSPIRED
NATURAL SELF RESPECT
SELF BELIEF
CONFIDENT AUTONOMOUS

Next, I ask,

"Who can do these things?"

Answer: "Anyone."

"So who can be a (favourite) leader to others?"

Answer: "Anyone."

Here are a few follow-on questions we might find insightful:

"Which of us feels that our family (school) is full of people behaving like this, all the time?"

"Which of us works around people behaving like this, all the time?"

"Who feels the feelings we have listed above, all the time, because of the people around us?"

And if *'all the time'* is too extreme, ask:

"How about some of the time?"

And, more personal questions:

"Which of us feels that we might actually be that leader for other people (our children, spouse, partner, pupil, colleague) all the time?"

"Some of the time?"

"What would our home environment be like if it was always like that?"

"Some, or more, of the time?"

"How would our relationships be?"

For us to remember those people that we cherish as our own favourite leaders is a huge compliment to them and what they represented to us even after all this time. I'm sure every one of us could talk at length and with some animation about the immense impact that these people had and probably continue to have, whenever we think about them.

So by extension, wouldn't it have been a life lived well to be talked of in this way by the people closest to us of all – our own children? A parenting job well done indeed.

Perhaps, by understanding the nature of doing and being these things with other people, accepting that these qualities, actions and behaviours reside in our own DNA and are visible to others, just *perhaps* are we creating the same leader relationships around ourselves too? We should keep an eye out behind us from time to time - who is hanging on to our coat-tails?

These qualities and behaviours have come to be known as Emotional Intelligence, or EQ. EQ, as previously noted in Chapter Three, embraces all that is positive, respectful, challenging and confidence-building in ourselves and others. EQ is distinct from IQ, which embraces what we know, our ability to analyse, compute and inform our areas of experience.

History shows that IQ has been consistently rewarded with

promotions, money, respect and awe. And that's unlikely to change too much in the future I daresay. However, EQ is snapping at the heels of IQ, whose popularity in the polls, as a leadership pre-requisite, has taken a heavy knock since research by Daniel Goleman (mentioned earlier in this book) was published.

Goleman carried out surveys and researched hundreds of books about management and discovered that when people described the leaders they most admired, they would mostly talk about EQ skills, such as those in our 'Favourite Leader' columns above, rather than IQ criteria like knowledge, skills, facts, statistics and experience.

Statistically, his conclusions show that EQ is considered to be twice as important as IQ in the workplace in general, and nearly 6 times as important in leadership jobs. And if we were to transfer that research to parents, we could justifiably argue that knowing things, being right and parenting our children from that standpoint would be not nearly as highly appreciated by our youngsters as if we were to ask them questions. Maybe someone will tackle that research. Maybe I will. It would certainly make for fascinating insights.

Let's take a look at how emotional intelligence and coaching really fit together, and how we might apply them to the tricky job of parenting. After all, aren't we already doing the best we can, with skills and rationale that we decide are best for each moment? What should we do differently, that we don't do now? Some of us discuss parenting with other parents, some of us work on instinct and our version of common sense. Some of us believe in a strict boundaries formula, or try and replicate what our own parents did with us; some of us believe in letting the child find its own rules.

And unless we are maliciously dysfunctional and neglectful in our parenting attempts, most children eventually reach a 'socially sustainable and functional adulthood,' don't they? (Just like we have, patently...) Let's ask ourselves: ***"When did we 'turn our corner?' At what age? And what were the circumstances that allowed us to feel we had reached that 'socially sustainable and functional adulthood?'"***

For me personally, I was around thirty years old when I 'turned that corner.' Some people tell me they knew they had turned it at ten years old. There is no norm, if my research and experience is anything to go by. Allow me to describe the tipping point as it occurred for me, by way of illustration.

I allowed myself to be guided by my parents into taking a languages degree at university when my instincts were telling me that I wanted to do a sports degree and be a PE Teacher. The man that always comes to mind for me when I present that 'Favourite Leader' exercise is Richie Gledhill, my sports teacher at Ernest Bevin Comprehensive School, in

Tooting Bec, a modest, moderately chaotic sprawl in South West London.

There were many typical inner-city problems apparent amongst the boys at my school, and I still hold close the way he managed and inspired me. He immediately created successes at National and Regional level for our Judo, Volleyball and Swimming teams, which barely existed before he came along and undoubtedly, many of the qualities we have outlined above connected with, apply to him too. Thanks, Richie.

For my parents though, sport was and remains to this day a complete mystery, and they advised me to "do a *REAL* subject at university, keep sports for a hobby." But inside, I knew I would have to give attention to the quiet, insistent voices within, and would fulfil the sporting and teaching destinies eventually. And so it proved to be.

Despite my languages degree (or perhaps, subconsciously, to spite it) I left a short-lived career with a translation agency and spent a number of years during my twenties selling mobile cellular phones, at the time a revolutionary concept in communication. I was promoted to manage the sales teams for a short while until our company was acquired by a more ambitious competitor and we were all made redundant. I found other jobs selling advertising space in random magazines with titles something like Hydraulic Engineering Monthly (I can't remember exactly what they were called) and finally ended up with a particularly soulless company which brokered bespoke lists of names for direct marketing purposes.

While playing golf with an old school friend on my twenty-ninth birthday I must have mentioned one too many times that I was fed up with my boss for changing the sales deadlines, as it was going to seriously impact my time in America over that summer of 1990. I was by then in the habit of coaching summer volleyball camps in the USA for as many weeks and days as I could fit in with my annual leave.

Fed up with my whining he just asked me simply, "Look, why don't you tell him to stick his job and go and live in America then, if it's so important to you?"

More a command than a question, on the face of it, and relatively aggressive and leading as coaching questions go, but this wasn't a seasoned coach by any means. This was a friend who knew me well, and he definitely was attached to the outcome; i.e. that I should stop "yanking his chain" as he put it, and ***just do something*** instead of repeating the same old miseries.

So with no particular science behind it, that raw question taken at face value hit me broadsides and I resolved in the instant to do exactly that.

I called my boss immediately I arrived home from the golf game, and quit my sales manager post over the phone there and then. My boss was not best pleased and I received the 'silent treatment' from all of my colleagues the following Monday as I was chaperoned around the office while I cleared my desk. A few whirlwind weeks later I had rented out my flat and flown to America to seek my fortunes in volleyball.

I was so excited to begin this new direction that I arrived at the University of Hartford on the say-so of a young sophomore I'd met at a camp that summer, who 'believed' that the Men's Varsity team at her University were looking for a coach.

Which, indeed proved to be true, although in my haste I had omitted to consider that I would need to interview first with the University Athletics Director. So, after introducing myself to the team and running a couple of *ad hoc* sessions, my presence filtered through to the aforementioned Director's attention and I was summoned to his office where he demanded to know who the hell I was and what I thought I was doing.

Twenty minutes later I was being escorted out of the University. Hmmm, I was starting to make a habit of being ejected from organisations. A day or two's research followed, which uncovered a junior elite girls' volleyball programme just outside Chicago that were looking for coaches. A few phone calls with the Director, Rick Butler, revealed that they were building the country's first Volleyball-only facility from the ground up and might be able to accommodate me as a coach, although it would be impossible to pay me without a Green Card. (Ah yes, I had overlooked that detail too).

We worked out a plan where I would work with his Sports Performance Club, one of the most ambitious and successful junior club teams in the USA at that time, and they would find me six months' accommodation with the family of one of the players and her father, to whom I am indebted. I had fully intended to stay in the USA and climb the potentially lucrative ladder of university athletics coaching. My parents and family had all thought now I was living there that I would permanently emigrate too.

However, I re-met a charismatic and no-nonsense coach from Glasgow, Scotland at one of many camps that summer of 1991, this one in upstate New York. Tommy Dowens persuaded me to leave the American Dream to come and work alongside him and his Men's teams in Glasgow. So I returned there with him and met the new Great Britain National Team Coach, Ralph Hippolyte. My apprenticeship with these two sporting and philosophical gurus continued in Glasgow and later in Leeds, where I was to spend the next fifteen years. (Incidentally, I was still largely unpaid by the way; despite being one of the top five participant sports in most countries ***in the world***, volleyball stubbornly manages to wedge itself well down the pecking order in Britain).

I picked up in the world of Academia again, much to my Dad's approval, to study for a Master's degree, even though it was in the field of Sports and Exercise Science to support my coaching credentials. To make enough money to get by, I began to lecture in sports psychology and coaching at Leeds Metropolitan University, and created a volleyball development post in the Yorkshire region for three years. Soon I was also asked to work with the England National Volleyball Team where I stayed coaching until 2002. That was unremunerated too.

So, despite having eschewed sports for languages at my parents' suggestion some twelve years earlier, I think I can safely say a huge number of the important things in my ongoing quest for personal fulfilment and evolution were learnt while involved in a full time sporting environment of one sort or another. I felt at home, finally, and ***I*** had made all the difficult decisions. ***Myself.*** I had returned to sport, against the advice of my parents because in that period it was the only thing that made any sense ***to ME.***

all of us know intrinsically, and from a very young age, where our innate strengths lie

And of course in 2002, I made more strong decisions after becoming aware of the (then relatively new) concept of Life and Business Coaching, While continuing to nurture my need to teach and to feel useful to others, I spent a further decade studying and developing this form of coaching with luminaries I have mentioned earlier.

My own personal measure of the depth of fulfilment I experience doing work that is so ultimately compelling to me is that ***I have not missed one single day of work, one single training session, one single talk or workshop in over twenty years.*** To be able to do what I feel completely at home with has meant that I have managed my health, my time and my values as meticulously as I could, so as not to miss even one, single opportunity to bring my passions to their audience. I think that this is when one knows that one has 'turned the corner.'

My highest value after *health* is definitely *connection*. So creating coaching cultures everywhere has now eclipsed my formative passion to teach sport and physical performance. Now I reach myriad audiences; private, public and third sectors all over the world, including the most precious people of all - parents, schoolteachers and children.

I hope I have not come across as too self-indulgent by biographing those years of my life here. My own story is intended, like all the other stories in this book, merely to serve to illustrate a concept. The concept being, in this case, that I believe ***all of us know intrinsically, and from a very young age, where our innate strengths lie***, and that there is huge fulfilment in chasing them, often against huge odds. Ask anyone who claims to have achieved this and they will tell us they have no real regrets and have grown exponentially from the experience.

So those questions from earlier; may I put them out there for our reflection once more?

"When did we 'turn our corner?' "

"At what age?"

"And what were the circumstances that allowed us to feel we had reached that 'socially sustainable and functional adulthood?' "

And here's a new one:

"When did we finally understand the hugeness of what our parents have been undertaking with us, and begin to make steps to build from that process with our own children?"

When we have some authentic answers ***of ourselves*** to questions like these, we may well find our questions to our children come via new filters. Filters of empathy, understanding and acceptance. Children crave these things, especially acceptance.

I have asked this ***"When did we 'turn our corner?' "*** question of many hundreds of people in many dozens of workshops. Most people seem to be able to recall a particular time, and the age they were, when 'Life Made Sense.' They describe that 'Sense' in various ways, but boiled down to its essence it seems their understanding of it was about living alongside others in a passably tolerant and reciprocal way. Interestingly, the qualities and behaviours we are now calling EQ are the same adjectives they depict in their eureka moments and I would say a majority have related their breakthrough to parenting scenarios. Here's a representative selection:

"I 'turned my corner' when ...

- I saw how he'd been allowing me to make all those mistakes so I could own the new learning
- I realised how much my mum had been sacrificing for me
- I accepted how they had been showing me they believed in me when I was always doubting myself
- I recognised I had had so many special moments although I didn't appreciate them at the time
- I used to create beautiful descriptive stories about everyday things from a very young age for my mum who is blind. She really loved listening to me. Now I see beauty everywhere and in everyone."

Just as interestingly though, the participants report probably as many negative angles on similar themes too that enabled them to turn their corners:

- "They never insisted we eat round the table, so we just had TV dinners: [insight] *so I promised myself that **my** kids would make a* *social event of dinner times as often as possible*."

- My parents didn't like me having friends round to our house so I spent more time at my friends' houses than I did at home: [insight] *so now my kids are my best friends, and we love their friends to come over. Life's about company and talking."*
- My parents talked openly when we were young, probably too openly about some things. Other parents kept secrets from their kids: [insight] *so although it was embarrassing sometimes, I realised later that I was really well equipped to understand the value of making my own views and decisions*."

So what does all this prove? A number of things really. It seems to point to the fact that ***most of us make sense of life sooner or later.*** So that's surely a good thing. We can ask whether there is an advantage to making sense of life sooner, ***rather*** than later? Do positively angled parenting efforts create eureka moments ***earlier*** in a child's life? Or stronger, more sustainable ones, perhaps? Do parents' 'flaws' and 'mistakes' hamper their children's development to relate well to the world? Or merely provide them with a ***different*** model from which to draw their learnings?

young people's current perceptions of life will almost certainly change every six months as their sense of reason and observation develops

I don't believe I'm qualified to answer those questions on anyone's behalf, so apologies to those who were looking for a *de facto* 'truth.' In true coaching fashion, we will probably finish reading this book with far more questions than answers.

As with all coaching the real question is, "What do ***you*** think?" And just as importantly, "What do ***our children*** think?" In the name of openness, lay out this entire chapter in front of them and ask them what they think. Ask them what they appreciate about our parenting. And ask them too what embarrasses them, relaxes them, saddens them, frustrates them, infuriates them, 'tickles' them. Get them in touch with their understanding of EQ as early as possible. Ask them about their own favourite leaders; what those people do that they like and how they feel around those people. And let's not show too much disappointment when they name people other than us! It's fine for children to think expansively. Our chance for recognition will come.

In doing so, ask them *open* questions, i.e. those to which we are ready to listen to any and all answers without judgment or blame... or derision. Especially without that. Ask them about how they currently see their world and their place in it. And accept their current perceptions - don't try to change them or colour them or prejudice them. We don't need to, because they will almost certainly change them every six months as their sense of reason and observation develops anyway. Watch them grow in confidence from not being contradicted and from being really 'heard.'

So with all this in mind, let's pose another fairly straightforward question:

"What exactly is coaching, then?"

we all grow in confidence from not being contradicted and from being really 'heard'

It's best to really get a handle on this I feel, because we probably all know parents who ask more than they tell, listen more than they talk but still have difficulty building and maintaining relationships, particularly as their youngsters grow older and their needs become ever more complex and adult. My belief is that if we are operating from an emotionally intelligent space, naturally and consistently offering respect and building confidence in our children, partners and friends, we will be a long way down the coaching road without ever needing to do a coaching course.

If we find ourselves short of a fascinating and moving book to read, we won't do much better than to pick up "Banker to the Poor," an incredible true story by Muhammad Yunus. He founded the Grameen Bank and the whole concept of micro-credit in Bangladesh. This bank is lending miniscule amounts of money to poverty-stricken families in Bangladesh, and now all around the world; families to whom the only source of money was previously from money lenders charging horrendously inflated interest rates, and virtually enslaving the families via accumulative debt.

our children have unfathomable opportunities awaiting them

He talks of his own favourite leader, a man named Quazi Sirajul Huq, his assistant headmaster from when he was thirteen years old, who he said electrified his imagination and became his friend, philosopher and guide for life. Yunus talks about the sublime moral influence Huq had on all those in his care, and how he taught them always to aim high, channelling their passions and their restlessness.

Yunus couldn't possibly have known as a small boy growing up in Bangladeshi poverty, that in his thirties he would be confronting the President of the World Bank and turning down a $300 million loan on the principle that this would be in effect enslaving his own bank to the World Bank. I suspect though, it wouldn't have surprised Quazi Sirajul Huq.

Coaches are never surprised by the achievements of their coachees. Can we parents say the same of our children?

Our children have unfathomable opportunities awaiting them. I believe EQ is already built into all of our DNAs so we have simply to learn to listen with confidence to our heartfelt values and passions. We have simply to learn to make life decisions from that space, even when it conflicts with apparently unfavourable financial comparisons and others' well-meaning, though un-informed, advice. We have simply to model these messages for our children.

I use the word 'simply' a lot there - can it really be 'simple'? Well, let's reflect that when our children are confident enough to make and hold to decisions that fly in the face of our earlier 'advice' for them, they will also be wise enough to recognise they were misled. Let's start trusting that confidence and wisdom now, today, at whatever age they are. It's a two-part process:
1) We just ask them questions, like ***"What do you think about this?"***
2) We don't contradict whatever it is they reply.

our sole purpose for parenting our children is to prepare for letting them go

At the time of writing (2013) it is being said that our children will leave education and enter a world where we can't possibly predict what amazing lives they will eventually build for themselves, and the impact they will have on the world. But if we can't predict what amazing things they'll be doing, we can choose how we ***SUPPORT*** them as they make that transition. Our sole purpose for parenting our children is to prepare for letting them go. Khalil Gibran reminds us of this in his poem, The Prophet:

> **"You are the bows from which your children as living arrows are sent forth [...] Your children are not your children. They are the sons and daughters of life's longing to itself. They come through you but not from you. And though they are with you yet they belong not to you."**

EQ is the intention behind our coaching words. The quality of our EQ will determine the quality of our children's responses to us

I don't see how coaching can truly exist where EQ is not present. EQ is the intention behind our coaching words and will determine the quality of the child's response to us.

Good leaders are necessarily self-aware and responsible. If we truly know ourselves, and act on what we know then we can grow others far more effortlessly than might otherwise be the case. At all and any levels. In my personal dictionary, a great leader is not defined as someone who creates followers, but rather as someone who creates a new generation of leaders.

So isn't that what we are here to do as enlightened parents? Create a new generation of enlightened parents? I'm not recommending that we should get them to become new parents just yet, but you get the drift. (However if they do, I can always edit this into a Coaching for Grandparents book).

there's little point in searching for more things to 'know.' Any knowledge we may still need will always find us

I've come to the realisation that knowledge for its own sake isn't so interesting to me anymore. There's little point in searching for more things to 'know.' Any knowledge we may still need will always find us. Wisdom on the other hand is more gratifying. Because in wisdom is emotional intelligence. In complete wisdom is the certainty that, regardless of the situation presented to me, I would react according to what I personally aspire to as my own emotional intelligence; kindness, non-judgmental, playful, inspirational, challenging, aware, responsible. Now ***that*** certainty I would consider to be the aspiration of a wise parent-coach.

My intellectual intelligence can trudge behind, a distant also-ran for all I care.

28.

The Second Ladder - Openness And Transparency

How to create the right moments for coaching to occur

And so we arrive at the first rung of the Second Ladder, preparing to build the ground floor of our Coach Chateau - the floor where all our relationship building takes place. We might be forgiven for thinking that this far into a book on coaching our children, we ought to be relatively practised at it by now. Maybe we are, although if we have really immersed ourselves in creating the backdrop to productive, effective, relaxed coaching of our children, we will be that much more sure of their response when we start consciously exercising our coaching muscles.

The groundwork has now been at least covered, if not yet mastered, in Part Two. The coaching 'stakes' are now firmly embedded, creating a conducive coaching enclosure within which to safely practice. Already, even if we read no further about the actual exercise of day to day coaching at home, we will already be so much further on in our understanding of how to communicate with the young minds we meet, every single day.

As a parallel to the ways we can practice creating openness at home, let me illustrate how the initial 'open' connections in some of my workshops occasionally unfold.

I ask the participants to introduce themselves without stating their job titles, in other words without saying what they do. Rather, I encourage them to say a few words about who they are and how they feel about beginning quite a demanding, lengthy coach training course. I introduce myself by way of a demonstration, to encourage them to follow suit and open themselves up a little.

"Hi, everyone. I'm James, I'm quite friendly and approachable, I value kindness and playfulness, really enjoy being around people who are generally upbeat and positive, have a can-do attitude, although I can be a bit intolerant around moaners, it's true. I'm working on that. I have two fun teenage boys and love to see them working through the tricky stuff I went through at that age.

"I'm not very good at ironing as you can see from my shirt and I have just finally given in to the necessity of wearing glasses and am coming to

terms with how they affect my image. I appreciate all sorts of sports and competition, live music and, in fact, all forms of performance and I really enjoy finding out how to get coaching to create new connections of all sorts.

"That's me. So who would like to go next?"

It is quite usual for there to be a significant pause in the room at this point while people decide how to present themselves. Many people ask for a couple of minutes to scribble down some notes, in order to be able to make the impact they are searching for when they speak.

it is far easier, and more anonymous, to introduce oneself as what one does, rather than who one is

In most workshops, I must say, the openness is generally quite forthcoming and relaxed. However, it is still not uncommon to hear from these participants that although they are perfectly happy to reveal a little about themselves in a workshop environment amongst other adults or even colleagues, they had never really considered the option or impact of being similarly open at home with their children. It was genuinely a revelation to them to think of doing so.

Most people are entirely comfortable introducing themselves as a Marketing Director, a Chef, a Head of Plant Security, a Delivery Van Driver, a Learning and Development Officer, a Chief Superintendent, an HR Manager, a Business Owner, etc. (Parents, incidentally, are somehow all these job titles rolled into one. And more besides).

The purpose of asking for participants to identify and share personal information, insights and perhaps values too, is to allow relationships to develop based on human aspects rather than status and job titles. It is far easier, and more anonymous, to introduce oneself as what one does, rather than who one is. So this exercise doesn't always go smoothly. In one European workshop (where the majority of participants happened to be male), a father eventually volunteered to start like this (names changed):

"OK. So I start. My name is George and... I think I can say I am an introvert."

I waited for more. He sat down, very much proving his identity statement to be accurate. Another pause.

ME: "Thank you George. Very succinct. Who would like to go next?"

Another man stands up.

"So, my name is Bill. I too am probably quite introvert."

He sits down.

ME: "Er...thank you Bill. Perhaps the next person might like to expand a little; say a bit more on who you are?"

Another man stands up.

"My name is Jon. Like the others I would say I am an introvert and... I like fishing."

He sat down, complete and satisfied with his extended proclamation.

And so it went with several of the others. This was a course where I was able to enjoy very little down time as the participants relentlessly approached me in the breaks and lunchtimes with individual questions that they hadn't felt comfortable asking in front of the others for fear of being perceived as inadequate. The fear of losing face was huge while the propensity for risk-taking was tiny. The nervousness around revealing personal information was almost palpable.

Defining ourselves by what we do permits us to define ourselves to our audience as part of a recognised hierarchy. Conversely, working alongside someone knowing only their personal tastes, stated values, likes and dislikes, hobbies, family situation and so forth, i.e. who they are, is often very confronting and challenging. Though liberating too.

One parent was particularly tight-lipped to begin with. Although initially forceful and forbidding when he did speak up on day one of the course, he returned several weeks later on the final day of the series of workshops and unexpectedly announced in front of the group that he understood now why he had never really attracted very many friends and how his family and children were very closed around him.

He told us he was known at home, (and as it transpired, at work also) for his intolerance to small talk. He never asked questions to which he didn't anticipate a particular answer and never asked about others' feelings at work or even those of his own family. He preferred to tell people what he perceived they ought to be feeling, and always from his own sense of the high ground. He even bossed his parents, he said.

Just to acknowledge this to begin with was a huge shift for him and he stated in front of the group that having decided now to become a 'coaching father and husband' he was changing his whole relationship with his family; his wife, his children, his parents, and, most importantly he attested, starting with himself.

When another participant challenged him to put that insight in just a few words as a new identity statement, he thought for a moment and then said simply "I'm my new best friend." What an empowering thing to be able to say. How many of us can say truthfully "I'm my own best friend"? And when we can, what impact does that have on our ability to be best friends with our children?

So all this is to highlight that we MUST create the environment where the children are attentive, expectant and open, BEFORE we can hope to engage them in meaningful dialogue. And if that means we have to model it, to volunteer some of our personal lives, to expose ourselves a little first, then so be it. Let's take a deep breath and open ourselves up.

Only then can we really hope to commence the level of coaching we feel is appropriate. The essence of coaching is, as we now know, self-directed learning. It's a good idea to remember always to inform our children of our intentions and reasons and motivations. We can model that responsibility by allowing our children to process their decisions fully, just by putting them in possession of all relevant facts.

coaches must have tools, perceptions and insights that are accessible to others

Let's be open with our children. Totally open. Being open is a skill in itself. It needs practice and courage. Be bold and be generous - expose ourselves first. It's so liberating when we do. Our children are far, far wiser than we might expect them to be.

Here's just one example, if we are deep down scared that we are losing the habit or ability to converse with our son or daughter - let them know exactly that: e.g.

"I really want to be able to have the talks we used to have when you were younger. I loved those chats and I miss them. I'm scared that we will drift apart for good if we don't reconnect again soon. What do you feel you would be OK to talk about with me?"

As we read this book we will encounter some techniques and ideas that we feel we can try with our children. So let's tell them about what we are encountering, and why we want to introduce them to our conversations: e.g.

"I've seen this interesting model of listening in a coaching book I've been reading and it highlights a number of situations I feel we experience all the time in this family. I'd like to talk about it over dinner tonight. Would that be OK? I think it could help us to be more patient with one another when we are all together."

My view is that one needn't be afraid of being quite open with a child about the mechanics of coaching. Every child has an amazing capacity for common sense and wisdom. Often, many novice coachees who have seldom experienced coaching believe that a secret process is going to be "done" on them. Regardless of whether the coachee is known to us - children, pupils, friends, colleagues; or less familiar to us - associates, business colleagues - many, typically, are wary of the initial meetings. For this reason I really encourage us all to share our own insights and understandings of coaching as much as possible, and particularly, early on in our children's lives. Let them grow up with coaching phrases and responsibilities as their norm.

Openness at home means telling our children what we are going to be doing, what outcomes are possible, what sort of questions we are asking them, giving parallel relevant situations, assuring them regularly of confidentiality and that they do not have to answer questions that make them feel uncomfortable or awkward. Openness means letting them know that we believe fully in them, we are not going to judge, or steer or advise. And that if we have suggestions that we feel may be helpful, we will hold back from offering them until the children have come up with as many front-of-mind ideas of their own first.

a child that is well-informed and well-prepared for coaching is infinitely more coachable than one who isn't

Let's start and continue with the intention of being as open and see-through as possible. One part of being a coach is to have tools, perceptions and insights that are accessible to others. A good coach is not secretive about these things and wishes as many people as possible to know as much as possible about coaching and how it can work best. A child that is well-informed and well-prepared for coaching is infinitely more coachable than one who isn't.

Coaching starts with attention. If no attention is apparent up front, point it out immediately. Always get buy-in before beginning deep coaching. Let's look at how to do that; e.g. we might say,

"I'd like to ask you some questions – are you OK with that? Would you just pause your X-box game for a few minutes while we talk, please?"

always get buy-in before beginning deep coaching

Here's another true-life scenario; (throughout the book I've used true-life illustrations as far as possible to give weight to the learning).

A mother had attended an evening workshop I ran for the parents of boys at a school in London. The subject that evening had been Insightful Questioning, and "homework" exercises were given to the attending parents based on practising the styles of questions at home with their children. The following week I asked how they had fared.

One mother volunteered to start and said; "It was a nightmare! Hopeless. I tried to engage my teenage son with some open questions about his day at school and his homework, and without looking up he just said; "Oh God, I suppose you're gonna try to get me to open up with your new coaching stuff." I told him, yes, that is what I wanted to happen, and tried again, and this time he just mumbled, "It's not going to work you know," and slouched off to his room."

Many of the parents were sympathetic and experienced similar reactions, although certainly not all. So I asked her;

"What happened next?"

"I went after him, and told him this wasn't what I wanted, and he just told me to leave him alone as he was tired."

"And then what?"

"So I told him that I would leave him alone, but that I would really like to address and improve our ability to properly talk. As I was leaving his room I asked him if I could talk to him a bit later when he was less tired. He said he "supposed so." And I went back downstairs."

"So what happened later?"

"Well, later, while we were eating dinner, I again asked him if I could talk to him. He nodded. I told him I wanted to organise the next couple of weeks because his father would be going away on a business trip for some of the time and he, my son, was due to go away with the school. He surprised me by asking me what I needed to know, (he asked me a question!) and waited for me to reply. I told him I wanted exact dates and times put into the family diary, and who would need to drive him, and any friends, to and from the pick-up points. I also asked if I could check in with him about when his homeworks were likely to be set and expected in, so that we could plan some sort of schedule for that time and he sort of agreed, (although I have to admit he was by now going 'off the boil' a little with the effort of such a 'protracted' conversation!")

from a coach's-eye view, each and every turning point and insight is a major event

I turned the focus to the rest of the group and asked them what they noticed. They were very complimentary and told this mother she had handled that first structured coaching conversation beautifully. They noticed her staying calm, avoiding irritation, asking permission to talk at a later time, and using what coaches call 'placement' phrases in telling her son that she wanted their relationship to improve, and asking when would be a good time to chat. (A 'placement phrase' is often just a signpost for something we wish to happen later, e.g. "would it be OK to discuss this when you come home?" or "I'd like us to be able to fully concentrate on this, can we agree a time to chat it through sometime tomorrow?") They noticed that she hadn't judged or blamed him for his moodiness and that she had reached some sort of agreement.

The other parents were impressed. She merely felt that it had only been a very minor victory, since she felt their verbal relationship had deteriorated over the years to a sullen, monotone battle, just to elicit information and make things happen. (Remember how we have already highlighted our innate tendencies to be overly critical of ourselves?)

What this exercise had illustrated was, in fact, a simple, but important, breakthrough for this mother and her son. I pointed out that from a coach's-eye view, each and every turning point and insight is a major event and to be celebrated. This mother said she would try to notice them as they arose and pat herself on the back.

Make no bones about this - if we have practised becoming wary of our children's withdrawal and lack of enthusiasm for adult dialogue over a number of weeks, months or even years in some cases, then small concessions like this, made after a couple of heartfelt attempts by a parent, where a young man agrees to make time to discuss something, and even asks helpful questions of his mother - these are major coaching wins!

Vulnerability is a difficult thing to equate with leadership, but it's an essential component nonetheless

The other parents shared their experiences from week to week. Some had been rocky, some smooth, but as our training evenings went on, all were encouraged that there seemed to be a structure emerging that was within their grasp, and that if they could stay true to it and remain open about their intentions, the victories would (and did) materialise.

Some parents of course, noted that they already felt they had very equal and mature relationships with their children, younger and older, and were finding little need to preface conversations with placement phrases. That is always wonderful to hear, and reinforces the point I made earlier about us choosing our own starting points with these foundation skills. We are the best judge of where we want to pitch in.

So back to openness and transparency.

I've mentioned that in many of the corporations I work with, where my brief is to help instil a coaching culture throughout the organisation, many managers and team leaders report real concerns about how their team members and direct reports may perceive them as weak leaders if they ask questions instead of giving directions. They believe the same perception to be true were they to expose their genuine, personal feelings about a situation, particularly if the feeling they exposed could be construed by their teams as negative, i.e. degrees of helplessness, overwhelm, uncertainty, indecisiveness.

If this is true of them as managers dealing with adults, it is not a big leap to imagine them having similar concerns as parents dealing with their children. Vulnerability is a difficult thing to equate with leadership, but it's an essential component nonetheless.

Happily however, after several weeks and months of practising and embedding the coaching ethos into their everyday conversations, it is commonplace for them to report significant, positive shifts in their relationships with these same employees and colleagues, and, by extension, their families too. The employees, far from seeing their managers as weak for introducing emotionally intelligent questioning into conversations or for asking them their opinions on how projects should be managed, saw them as stronger leaders, and were more motivated and productive as a result. And at home, far from seeing them as overbearing, intransigent parents, their children (and spouses) saw them as more approachable, more engaged and in many cases, more fun and relaxed.

So, to continue the parallel, if this were to be true of us as adults responding to a purer coaching approach in our workplaces and then our families, it is a similarly small leap to imagine our children responding positively, and indeed gratefully, to our attempts at spending more time listening and understanding their worlds, and sharing more of our own.

we humans thrive on being valued and respected so let's model this for our children. If this becomes their norm while young it stands to reason they will proliferate the model as they become the next generation of parents

We humans thrive on being valued and respected. So let's model this for our children. If this becomes their norm while young it stands to reason they will proliferate the model as they become the next generation of parents. And leaders in life too. This starts with modelling openness and self-awareness, and it is striking how many adults find this difficult, particularly in front of peers and colleagues at work, and of course in front of their children.

If we can encapsulate even one of the elements of this framework for coaching each time we create dialogue with our children, we will be making small, but oh-so-important steps towards responsible, cordial conversations. If we can encapsulate several elements - or even EVERY element of it - into EVERY communication we EVER have with our children, (in fact with ANYBODY AT ALL) we will surely be making a giant leap for respectful, harmonious and empowering communication.

PRACTICAL COACHING SKILLS, TECHNIQUES AND TOOLS

29.

The Third Ladder – Permission "Would It Be Ok If...?"

The benefits of asking respectful permission when exploring children's lives

Nowadays, most parents recognize the importance and respect involved in knocking on our children's bedroom door and waiting outside until we are invited to enter, before turning the door-handle. We expect it of them too. These are private spaces we are entering. Their own bedroom may be the only private space children can find where they can gather their thoughts, explore their developing tastes, make sense of them and be alone with them.

In that bedroom, the arrangement of the furniture and colour schemes have probably been decided by the child. The posters and photos on the walls are of their choosing and match their current phase and mood-moment. The music played is personal and significant and the accumulated possessions, cluttered or otherwise, are comforting. This space is where their individuality can blossom and parents, generally, understand and respect its sanctity. There is little positive to be gained from blindly blundering in.

as a coaching technique, Permission is hugely underestimated and under-used

A young mind is another such bedroom, except vast and amorphous, although every bit as personal. A space filled with billions of 'bytes' of information that make sense of their here-and-now. Why would we not 'knock' at this door and wait to be invited in, in the same way? Why would we waltz in to this space without invitation, re-arranging the furniture and decor willy nilly? Where is the benefit to the child of our advising and dictating how this space should be organised from an adult point of view? Of overlaying our own adult model of what a young brain should and shouldn't be considering? Of making no attempt to find out what this young brain is already aware of and working on?

Wouldn't this maybe be just a little presumptuous on our part? Isn't it a little like a forty year old saying to an eight [and nine and ten and...] year old,

"Come on, do it like me, it's quicker and more efficient and you too can be thinking like a forty-year-old in no time at all. Forget being eight, [and nine and ten and...] you can be grown up immediately, I can save you a generation of mistakes and experience!"

Permission is respectful and respect is the door-key here. Parent-coaches must use Permission to gain admission and respect. As a coaching technique, Permission is hugely underestimated and under-used.

Imagine you have met me for the first time and you have kindly invited me back to your house for a cup of tea. (Very British.) You invite me in, offer me a seat on the sofa in your living room while you disappear into the kitchen to put the kettle on and prepare the tea. Imagine you come back into the living room with a tray of tea (and biscuits too) to find I am no longer on your sofa. In fact I am no longer in your living room.

YOU: "Here is the tea...James? James??!!"

ME: "Oh hi, I'm upstairs, just taking a look around - very interesting things you keep in your cupboards."

How might you be feeling? Awkward? Intruded on? Angry perhaps?

Let's rewind a few moments.

Imagine you come back into the living room with a tray of tea and biscuits, to find me still on your sofa, where I have been given permission to be.

YOU: "Here's the tea, James."

ME: "Thanks. Lovely house you have. I can see you must have spent a lot of time designing and creating this space. It's impressive."

YOU: "Thanks. Yes, I love to be creative - my home space is very special to me and my family."

ME: "Would you mind showing me around? I'd love to see what you've done."

So at this point I have respectfully acknowledged the personal space we are in together, and asked whether I may move, with you, ***to a new level*** in that personal environment. And then I must ***wait for your answer*** to my request. Likewise, in a coaching conversation, when I decide to preface any question with the permission to ask it, I must always wait for that request to be answered.

It may well be that you grant permission and show me around, but just as possible that you feel uncomfortable showing me upstairs in your house since you prefer to keep some spaces private. In which case you may decline my request. You may, too, demur till another time, explaining that since it was a spontaneous invitation and you weren't expecting to invite anyone back to your home that day, that I could come to visit another time when it is tidy and looking its best, and you might then be happy to show me around.

Continuing the analogy, parent-coaches must recognise that, in order to foster and maintain high levels of respect and trust, an appropriate degree of permission must be sought when moving to new, unvisited areas of the child's private thoughts.

CULTURES OF PERMISSION

I conform to a fairly simple coaching tenet - ***coach only with a person's permission.*** I am careful to not even start coaching someone without first asking, and being granted, permission. As parent-coaches we will quickly tune into dozens of potential dilemmas or 'coachable moments,' daily. There's little more irritating, when a youngster merely notes that a friend was starting to get on his nerves a bit, than his over-zealous parent-coach asking, ***"...and what might be some of the possible consequences of that?"*** or ***"and how is that affecting other aspects of your life...?"***.

permission must be sought when moving to new, unvisited areas of the child's private thoughts

We simply have to ask youngsters whether we may ask coaching questions at a certain time, and they will let us know whether they are receptive, or not. It's not as easy as we might think to "stealth-coach" an intelligent youngster who has not agreed to the process. If they are not receptive at that moment, we can always persist with, ***"When would be a good time?"***

Coaches don't ask questions out of interest or curiosity, as we have seen earlier. Certainly not deep, probing questions. Coaches ask questions to be useful. New, unvisited areas may well turn into coaching hotspots requiring respectful permission. These areas typically centre around relationships, money, family matters, sex, health, politics, faith, confidence, values and belief systems and as such, may be especially difficult or emotional for children (and parents) to confront.

coaches don't ask questions out of interest or curiosity - coaches ask questions to be useful

I have worked in many different countries and cultures delivering coaching talks and trainings. Some families seem to be very hierarchical, where it is simply not expected, for example, that a parent will ask permission of their children to explain themselves or to ask them to carry out a chore. The parent will simply instruct, direct or advise and expect compliance.

Some parents I worked with in Romania tell me (with some pride) that permission is not needed regardless of the depth of information I may be seeking. They inform me that in their culture, permission is not always necessary - I can just ask straightforward questions and they will give me whatever information I need to know, regardless how personal I might deem it to be. Friendships, families, money, marriage happiness, opinions, politics, religion - very little appears to be 'off limits' in Romania, with or without permission.

In Finland it seems, it is not necessary to even *ask* how much someone earns - it is all documented on the internet for anyone to research should they feel a need. Finns I have met seem to pride themselves on their open, transparent and responsible approach to community. At polar opposites to this, one Chinese employer in Beijing told me he decides how much to pay each of his workers, and they are forbidden to discuss their salaries with anyone else - if they did he would sack them.

In the Northern Americas, I have found I am generally *expected* to make myself at home when invited to stay. Take a beer from the fridge, make a sandwich, watch TV; all spontaneously and without specific permission. Simply being invited to stay carries with it an implicit invitation to treat their homes as if it were my own. This hasn't always been my experience in Britain, where there seems to be an expectation that I should wait to be offered things in someone else's home, or ask for things I may want, rather than helping myself.

Of course, it's not accurate or always appropriate to generalise. It's easy to blithely list a number of cultures we perceive to be different from our own and proclaim that they fall into this or that 'category.' Can we really list *all* British or American or Middle Eastern or African families into cultural 'categories' also? Do we talk about *all* Asians as though two billion people on the planet can be identified by a common cultural thread? Or indeed, *all* Romanians, or *all* Finns? Can we differentiate *all* Asian families from *all* eastern Europeans, *all* northern Italians from *all* southern, *all* children from *all* adults by a single common denominator? Are those denominators really that homogenous and simple to spot?

One easy-to-spot cultural custom can be found In Bulgaria where the people nod when they mean 'no' and shake their heads when they mean 'yes'. This is confusing to get used to for most other Europeans, who do the opposite, but it is fairly easy to notice, nonetheless. Problems with coaching can arise however, where these differing values and customs are less easy to spot, and indeed, less easy still to accept than a simple nod or a shake of the head. By being unaware or unobservant of such values and customs, or by generalising one experience across a whole population we may easily appear timid, rude, brash, prejudicial or offensive to our hosts without realising it.

So it's probably fair to say that there are myriad customs that one can encounter as one travels the world. And they are nowhere more intense and diverse than in families. Families in the same street may grow up respecting the same national flag, the same religion, regional culture and educational background, but may likely still embrace very different values and customs to the families next door. All arising from their individual experiences in life. One family may have a repressed and secretive culture at home while their next-door neighbours may be explicit and extrovert. Some families shout at each other and think little about it, others never do and are shocked when confronted by loud voices. Even individuals *in the same family* often relate to vastly different codes of behaviour.

All this is to illustrate how tricky it can be to relate to another person at a level that complements perfectly our own outlook on life. Permission is therefore one of the most useful tools in coaching (and parenting). It is effective at *so many levels* (see Carol Wilson's Permission Protocol below) and respects the boundaries we cannot see, like showing our passports at the border of another country. We are effectively asking, ***"Can I enter?"*** True, not every question needs to be preceded by a permission request, but it softens the exchange to ask permission, from time to time and in particular circumstances, thereby creating rapport and making people feel comfortable.

asking, "May I ask you a question?" is often interpreted by the child as an alert that the parent wants to give an opinion or advice

My experiences of different cultures may or may not tally with your experiences. However, I am convinced that permission respects and unites all of them. I've been weaned on permission, and regardless of cultural norms and expectations, I'm sticking with what I know works.

it can be tricky to relate to another person at the level that complements perfectly our

SPRINGBOARDS AND SIGNPOSTS

Sometimes we think we are asking permission when we're not. Or, if we are, it may have been asked in a way that doesn't inspire acquiescence. For example, asking, ***"May I ask you a question?"*** is often interpreted by the child as an alert that the parent wants to give an opinion or advice; i.e. ***"May I ask you a question [so that I can then tell you what I think]?"*** Asking permission like this is not as effective as when we can ***qualify the area we wish to investigate***. Create signposts whenever possible, as an alert to the child that we would like to explore more deeply. To highlight this, let's create a scenario of a teenager with a 'new relationship.' For sure, a tricky subject at the best of times.

QUITE A GOOD ATTEMPT:

First of all, remember to frame the ***area*** we want to tackle and then ask the permission ***before*** asking our eventual question and ***wait*** for a response before continuing, e.g.

"I notice that you have been a little more private when you have been sending texts recently. Would it be OK to ask you about that?"

I call this a 'springboard' question - a question designed to ***prepare*** to launch into the deep end. Note I have not included the eventual object of my concern in the springboard question. I have merely signposted it by asking whether I may ask further questions. They are very respectful, sensitive questions and create tremendous trust when used consistently.

NOT QUITE SUCH A GOOD ATTEMPT:

It is all too common, and very awkward, when permission is mentioned ***but assumed to be granted*** by effectively including the personal question at the same time; e.g.

"Would it be alright to ask, if that's OK with you, about this boy you're seeing?"

This question may be interpreted by the young person almost as a statement, i.e. "You're going to give me a lecture about boys." There is permission implicit in the sentence (***"if that's OK with you,"***) but it seems to the young person as though the parent has an expectation that it is indeed "OK." And in effect the tricky question is now already asked. Young people may understandably feel a little 'cornered' and 'clam up' because it seems expected that they should open up to the adult, regardless of whether they feel comfortable.

Let's expand this same scenario with three possible outcomes; one where a teenager grants permission, one where permission is declined and one where the options are left open for further consideration:

'Yes' - permission granted.

Parent: "I notice that you have been a little more private when you have been sending texts recently. Would it be OK to ask you about that?"
Teenager: "Well, there's nothing to tell really, but OK."
Parent: "Thanks. I like it that we can talk about grown up things together. Do you mind talking about personal things like this?"
Teenager: "No, it's OK. What do you want to talk about?"
Parent: "Well I was wondering whether you might have met someone special, and you weren't sure how to tell me?"
Teenager: "Well, actually, there's this boy, and..."

So here the teenager was given the opportunity to consider a response to the request for a more in-depth chat and decided to agree. Notice permission was asked twice, in different ways, to preface the real subject of discussion, which can then be asked directly.

'No' – permission declined.

In the same situation, if the teenager decides he/she is not comfortable to give that permission, and declines, the conversation may go something like this:

Parent: "I notice that you have been a little more private when you have been sending texts recently. Would it be OK to ask you about that?"
Teenager: "Well, not really, there's nothing to tell really."
Parent: "OK, that's fine. I like it that we can talk about grown up things together from time to time. Do you mind talking about personal things like this?"
Teenager: "It depends. Not really. What sort of things do you mean?"
Parent: "Well I was wondering whether you might have met someone special, and you weren't sure how or whether to tell me?"
Teenager: "No... there's nothing like that."
Parent: "OK, well anytime you feel like you want to chat stuff through, I'm a good listener."
Teenager: "Yeah, thanks..."

In this way, full respect is given to the teenager's reluctance to reveal or explore information he/she is not ready to provide. It doesn't necessarily mean that discussing this information will ***never*** be permitted, just ***not yet***. We might also chance our arm with a question like **"...So what *would* you like to talk about then?"** to try to open up a different dialogue. While it is a very positive and open question, and ostensibly gives control to the teenager, it might be interpreted as, ***"You're being very unresponsive and you should really talk to your parents when they ask about things."*** So tread carefully with that one.

However, this question does highlight a very useful coaching precept; remember our earlier coaching tenet: in case of doubt and indecision, ***ask our child what to do.*** This strengthens and reinforces the underlying assumption that our children are the experts in their own affairs, at no matter what age, and that they will know best what is relevant to explore at any given stage of the coaching conversation.

'Maybe' – permission under consideration.
Parent: "I notice that you have been a little more private when you have been sending texts recently. Would it be OK to ask you about that?"
Teenager: "Well, I'm not sure, I suppose so, but I'm not that comfortable..."
Parent: "I notice a little reluctance. Are you OK if I ask you more questions?"
Teenager: "Well, it's just... it's embarrassing."
Parent: "So there's a bit of embarrassment. What would make it less embarrassing?"
Teenager: "If we didn't talk about it!"

Parent: "I know. I like it that we can talk about grown up things together though, even if they might seem embarrassing at first. Are you sure you don't mind talking about personal things like this with me?"
Teenager: "No, it's OK. What do you want us to talk about?"
Parent: "Well I was wondering whether you might have met someone special, and you weren't sure how or whether to tell me?"
Teenager: "Can we talk about this another time?"
Parent: "Of course we can - you know I'm here when you need me."

In all three scenarios, the teenagers are treated with respect and their responses are heard and respected. Be patient and sensitive - they will talk, when they feel they will be listened to and not judged.

Unlike most coaching questions, which are open, asking permission is in essence a closed one. Its power is in the fact that people can say 'no' although this is rarely the result. Of course, one has to be prepared to accept a 'no' if that is the reply and find another way to invite learning, i.e. "...So what ***can*** we talk about then?" However, the reason this is unlikely to happen is because what we are giving the person is control, and control is a fundamental human need.

In modern times we have come to recognise an opportunity for control and an increased sense of safety and trust when people ask our permission. The safer our children feel in the home, in terms of a blame-free and supportive environment, the more confident they will feel, the more they will feel comfortable with risk and mistakes and the higher their sense of self-awareness and responsibility will be.

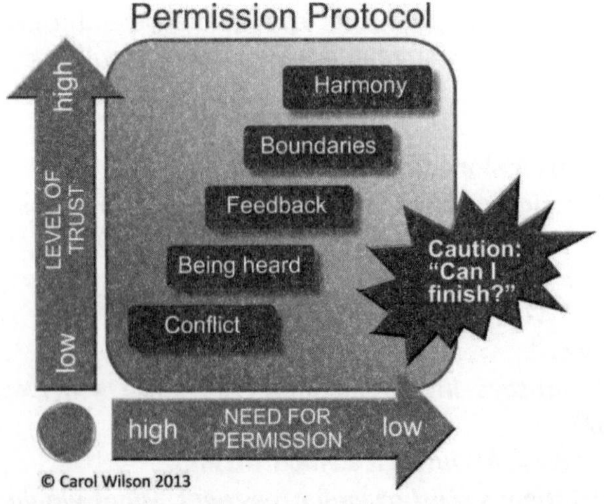

The diagram above shows how the need to ask permission is related to trust. Let's explore these briefly:

CAROL WILSON'S PERMISSION PROTOCOL

1. Resolving conflict: "Would it be okay if ...?"

Permission is the unsung hero of conflict resolution. Think of the person or event that consistently provokes irritation in us, the person who effortlessly 'pushes our buttons' and we find ourselves feeling a strong need to defend or assert ourselves - verbally or physically. Is this 'someone' in our family perhaps? Or a particular situation within the family? We may well have vowed before encountering that person or event that we will be ultra-polite or friendly or cheerful in order to avoid the usual conflict. Yet, when the moment arrives, the person or situation creates just as much upset as ever.

"Permission is the unsung hero of conflict resolution" - Carol Wilson

What is missing here is almost certainly the use of permission, whether spoken or implied by our body language. "What I think we should do is..." or worse, "What you should do is..." however politely spoken, are phrases that will only pour oil onto the fire. If we can grit our teeth and rephrase it to, "Would it be OK if I say what I think we should do?" and similar phrases, the barriers will start to crumble and rapport will grow. Note the use of the word 'say' rather than 'tell you' too.

Again, by demonstrating strong Attentive Listening, (more on this phenomenon in the 5 Levels of Listening model in Chapter 30) and 'softer' phrasing, an astute parent can move the conversation away from the initial sources of the conflict where that might be beneficial to the situation, e.g.

"I notice you seem to be," is less conflictual than ***"You are obviously..."***

"Might it be useful if...?" is more respectful than ***"Why don't you...?"***

In this way tangential issues can be explored too, deflecting the tensions while emotions stabilise. Such conflicts, frictions and tensions often arise purely because trust has broken down or has not been properly established, so if in any doubt, be prepared to pepper our conversations with bags of permission just to be on the safe side.

2. Being heard: "Can I add something to that?"

'Can I add something...?' carries the message that we have heard and understood what has been said and found it so valuable that we want to expand the topic instead of introducing a new one. Other people will then have a sense of hearing more about their own ideas rather than ours. It validates what they have said.

In a situation where one or more people are 'talking over' us and not making it easy for our contribution, try the phrase, ***"Can I add something to what Georgia has said?"*** People will stop talking and listen to us, because we are respecting what has just been said. Use it at the dinner table when everyone is animated and giving their own sides of a story all at the same time, and often contradicting each other.

Of course, once we have the ears of those around the dinner table, we may actually want to give a point of view that is entirely at odds with the person's idea that we are 'adding to,' i.e. ***"I like what Georgia has said although I think that there's another side to her point of view too..."*** The difference is that we *respectfully* created a space for our own ideas to be heard, using permission.

This is a very different different approach to ***"Yes, but..."*** or ***"No, that's complete rubbish, the truth is actually..."*** both of which imply dismissal not only of everything that has been said before, but of the people who said it, laying a ripe foundation for resentment.

NOT QUITE SUCH A GOOD ATTEMPT:

An elderly parent, now a retired merchant, mentioned that he was trying to become more of a coaching Dad to his grown-up daughter who was starting up a business (you see, one is never too old to start coaching the kids!) and was trying to be more 'useful' than 'helpful' by asking questions rather than giving her his advice, which she resented.

it is SO important to children to feel they have the mantle of control

It turned out that his questions ran more along the lines of ***"Yes, but I'm sure you could charge a higher day-rate than that, couldn't you?"*** where she was intending to begin with (to his way of thinking) modest charges, and ***"Where would be a better place to rent your first office?"*** in response to her proud declaration that she had found a low-rent business unit on an industrial estate out of town.

A BETTER ATTEMPT:

A simple twist to his well-intentioned, though leading and somewhat judgmental questions, was to recommend a little more permission and a little less interference. There was evidently trust at some levels between father and daughter, but in the arena of business-building, in which he considered himself to be somewhat of an expert, the trust was fading as she felt he was trying to bamboozle her into making decisions based on his ideas. The excitement and fun of building her business was becoming diluted, along with the trust that her father really understood her.

He agreed to preface all his on-going coaching questions with...

a) validation; "You've worked really hard to put this all together,"

b) ***praise; "I'm so proud of you for getting to this point,"***
c) ***permission; "May I just add something you may have considered anyway, and I'm not attached to it if it's something you don't feel is right for you?"***

...and so on. A week later, with all the emotionally intelligent backdrop in place he reported that she had really appreciated the new-look questions, and had listened more openly to his (slimmed-down) suggestions, and decided [to allow herself to believe that] perhaps he had a point with a couple of them, that she 'might' build in to her business plan. (Note she said 'might' - it is SO important to children to feel they have the mantle of control).

3. Giving feedback: "Can I share something I have noticed?"

Every one of us can identify a number of times when we feel a desire to comment on someone's work, appearance, performance, speech or effort. In a majority of cases we probably intend the comments as a gift - something to be helpful or of use to the other person. There is an entire Chapter (32) in this book dedicated to 'Coaching Feedback,' so we don't need to dwell too long on feedback here.

However, when we decide we want to give an opinion to someone, it is either going to be a positive comment or a message intended to allow the person to see their situation from another angle. Both opinions are ours, typically, and both are essentially judgments that are received more smoothly if prefaced with permission. Even the positive ones.

It is not that people don't want positive feedback, it's just that by asking, ***"Would it be OK if I tell you what I see when I look at your work?"*** we will almost certainly be granted permission, *and* we have got their undivided attention, so they can hear the full effect and energy of our comment; i.e. ***"I think you have made an incredible use of colours in your painting, it is so bright and fun, it looks like you have really put a lot of thought and effort into it - good for you!"*** So that's a double bonus.

suggestions and advice can be given as part of a coaching etiquette, only after the children have come up with as many of their own options, thoughts and ideas first

On the other side of the coin, the term 'negative' feedback is sparingly used these days. People now diplomatically refer to critical comments as 'learning' or 'constructive' or 'building' feedback, and are generally more aligned with asking permission to give it.

"Can I tell you what comes into my mind when I see this?" or just, ***"Would you like some feedback?"*** are both acceptable springboard permission questions, although they generally produce a 'negative-alert' state in the other person. Since we are conditioned to expect criticism of some degree when we hear the word 'feedback,' asking permission to do so seems to soften the blow and relax us, so that we will be more ready to listen and cooperate with the comment.

May I make a suggestion here? I may? Thanks. Here it is :

Please be patient, ***don't*** turn to Chapter 32 and read the wonderful Section 2 - 'Emotionally Intelligent Feedback. The Way Forward' ***just yet.*** There are plenty of foundation skills still to be learned, practised and embedded first.

For now, just be content knowing that giving feedback is an important component of the Permission Protocol model. It sits some way up the Trust axis but nonetheless there are many situations when it may be necessary to be more direct with our comments. Permission will ease those situations.

4. Creating boundaries: "Can I make a suggestion?"

As we know by now, coaching is about enabling self-discovery. It's about asking people to manifest their own solutions that are appropriate to their own sense of the stage they currently occupy. However if we, as parents or teachers have some useful information or experience, or our intuition is flagging up a message, it would be churlish not to pass it on. Suggestions and advice can be given as part of a coaching etiquette, although of course, only after the children have come up with as many of their own options, thoughts and ideas as they can first.

if our suggestion or advice does not appeal to the children, we must detach from it

I always add a disclaimer to my suggestions or advice. I say,

"May I offer a suggestion/some advice at this point, although I'm not attached to it in any way - feel free to use it however you choose, or ignore it altogether if it doesn't fit for you."

With our parent-coach 'hats' on we ***must endeavour not to attach to the outcome***; if our suggestion or advice does not appeal to the children, we must detach from it and set it aside sufficiently to allow the children to re-connect with their own ideas. (The question of risk does mitigate this point again here - if our teenage daughter has fallen for a handsome, three-times divorced, smooth-talking would-be popstar of fifty, we may not be so keen to fully detach from our "suggestion" to dump him. Remember of course, we may switch 'hats' and become a concerned, experienced parent any time we choose.)

Equally important is that if I am offering a suggestion or advice, I must give exactly that and NOT ***an instruction in disguise,*** e.g.

"I must strongly suggest that you take this advice if you want to see a real improvement."

A general rule of thumb is to offer suggestions no more than 20% of the time and only after the child's own ideas have genuinely been exhausted.

With our children in these cases, it is likely that there exists a fairly high trust anyway. So by continuing the practice of asking permission to give suggestions or advice, we are highlighting the fact that we are aware of the boundary between eliciting information from the child's mind - which the child is getting used to giving by now - and lending our own mind to its situation, albeit temporarily. The presence of permission in conversation eliminates intrusion and hierarchy ***and turns our contribution into a gift which can be used if helpful, or discarded without any awkwardness if not.***

the presence of permission in conversation eliminates intrusion and hierarchy

It is exceptionally useful to remember to observe boundaries by employing permission questions when the whole family is present, or when the children's friends are with us. We are now demonstrating respect, collective trust and the fact that in our family, people are willing to listen and take account of each other's views.

permission respects, permission unites

Don't be surprised if our children's friends were to start to gravitate more and more often towards our house to be treated as equals in this way, particularly where they are not experiencing it in their own homes.

I said it earlier and it's worth saying it again here:

Permission respects, permission unites.

Fundamentally, permission is the tool that creates and respects the non-aggressive types of boundaries essential for harmony in relationships. The importance of positive boundaries has been recognised for centuries in different cultures all over the world, and the proverb ***"Good fences make good neighbours"*** exists almost identically in Western Europe, Scandinavia, Japan, India, Russia and doubtless several other countries too. My own favourite is found in Medieval Latin; imagine wise old men in beards and robes giving counsel with phrases like ***"Bonum est erigere dumos cum vicinis" ("It is good to erect hedges with the neighbours.")*** Nothing like a classy bit of topiary to keep the peace.

5. Harmony

When trust is at its highest, permission is much less important. Think of an exchange with our husband or wife or best friend; the actual words of permission are probably rarely used because permission is inherent in the relationship. It will however be evident in voice tone and body language. ***"Lend me £20.00 till tonight, I've come out without my wallet,"*** or ***"Turn the music down a little, I'm on the telephone."***

When our children are relaxed, playful and trusting, it's easy to just direct, with no need for permission. We might say***, "That was great fun.***

OK, toys away, time for bed now," and the child will happily comply. Catch the same child at a bad moment (tired, hungry, too long glued to the X-Box, etc), and all the rules of permission in conflict apply once again; e.g. cartloads of permission, ***"Would it be alright if we start to pack away the toys in 5 minutes? We will need to start thinking about getting to bed, are you OK with that?"***

Careful - When is permission not permission?

We have all heard politicians say, "Would you please let me finish?" when interrupted by an interviewer or opponent. This is an example of a question that, on the surface, appears to comply with all the coaching criteria of asking permission yet which provokes conflict. This is because of the lack of generosity in the intention behind the question, and probably the lack of respectful tonality too; there is implied criticism and the question is presented as an attempt to wrest back control rather than the true objective of permission which is to offer control to the other person.

Additionally, such a question is inherently rhetorical, assumes a 'yes' answer and is less a request, and more a demand coupled with exasperation; a coaching cocktail that has yet to make its first appearance in the foundation skills chapter of any How To Be A Useful Coach manual I've come across.

Once again, it is essential to keep in mind that coaching is a mindset and attitude rather than a set of tools; our underlying intentions as parent-coaches must be aligned with coaching values and EQ which as we now know are all about building respect, confidence, trust and responsibility.

30.

The Fourth Ladder – 5 Levels Of Listening

Understanding how we can listen more effectively as parents

So, now we have broached the concept of offering control to the child, in communication at least, let's broaden the child's experience and perception of that control as we move on to the minefield that is genuine listening. Who, reading this, has been told they are a good listener? Who has been told they are a terrible one for that matter? What does it really mean to be a great listener? Who has ever considered that there may be different levels at which we listen, and that these may drastically affect the rapport we are creating?

One thing is certain. Being a good listener does not always mean just staying quiet while our children talk, although many of us could do a lot more of just that part alone. Being a good listener is, listening, showing that we are engaged, processing what we hear and formulating an effective response that allows the child to develop its thinking. All of that is wrapped up in being a good listener.

This chapter, and the next one on asking effective questions should help us make sense of these skills, so that our children see us modelling exquisite communication skills and know they have a voice that is valued and respected by adults. Once again, I am indebted to Carol Wilson, this time for her inspirational '5 Levels of Listening' model, to which I have applied my trusty CASE principle.

Let's investigate.

LEVEL ONE: INTERRUPTING

How many times have we been hearing younger members of our family drone on (oops, for sure I meant to write 'cheerfully chatting') about something that obviously has some importance to them but our minds are on something altogether more momentous, like getting vegetables prepared ready for the evening meal, for example?

Billy: "...and then Jack rolled up this paper and made like a springboard with his ruler on the desk and he fired this paper ball and it hit the desk where the teacher was sitting instead of the boy in front and the teacher..."

Pre-occupied Dad: "Get me some broccoli out of the fridge would you, Billy? And the chopping knife from next to the bread bin too if you could?"

Billy: "Er, OK then."

Rate this Dad on a scale of 1-10 for listening. 1? 2? Zero perhaps? I'd go with 1 or 2 probably - there was actually some listening going on. Dad was listening for Billy ***to finish talking***, and since Billy showed no sign of doing so, decided to muscle in and issue some orders to keep the evening meal schedule on track.

This is Level 1 Listening - we'll call it Interrupting. Dad has moved the conversation on to his own agenda and there is no real attempt to acknowledge either Billy or his lively mind. Instead Dad effectively *gives himself permission* to re-direct the conversation to suit himself. And talking of permission, listening at this lowly level isn't really improved when permission is employed either. Rewind that conversation:

Billy: " ...and then Jack rolled up this paper and made like a springboard with his ruler on the desk and he fired this paper ball and it hit the desk where the teacher was sitting instead of the boy in front and the teacher..."

Pre-occupied Dad: "Excuse me, Billy would you mind just focussing on the job in hand for a moment? I'm sorry, we've got dinner to prepare. Get me some broccoli out of the fridge would you? And the chopping knife from next to the bread bin too, if you could?"

Billy: "Er, OK then."

So now Billy has still been interrupted, albeit using permission, and been asked (told) to switch his attention. Dad has missed three opportunities here with Billy. Firstly, he has not shown full respect for Billy's enthusiasm, and secondly he is inhibiting Billy's expectation that it is normal behaviour to initiate and maintain conversations with his Dad at the end of his school day. Lastly, he is shutting down opportunities for learning to pop up - he will now never know where that conversation may have led.

We may sympathise with the Dad to some degree, but if this scenario is repeated dozens of times whenever Dad is focused on achieving a domestic outcome and Billy is focused on processing some recent thoughts, very soon Billy learns to shut down and keep his thoughts inside. And a few years later, Dad wonders why he can't hold an easy conversation with Billy.

NOTE - In the name of covering all the bases we shouldn't neglect to mention that there is a subversive LEVEL minus 1 too, heartily enjoyed by all kids, and known as Selective Listening. To be observed especially when the children are asked to stack the dishwasher, vacuum the stairs or tidy their rooms, this level involves them sticking a forefinger in each ear and chanting annoyingly, ***"Can't hear you, la la la la!"***

But let's gloss over that one.

LEVEL TWO: HIJACKING

Moving on to a new scenario. Two sisters are talking:

Sally: "I'd really like to sing with the school choir at the concert this summer but it clashes with my softball tournament. I don't know what to do."

Janet: "I just love singing. They asked me to sing a solo last year but I decided not to, but I just sing any chance I get. I think I'm going to ask my singing teacher about recording a few tracks again, because I did that a few years ago when I was twelve. Do you remember that? Maybe I could even make an album this time."

Sally: "Right..."

Whose agenda are we on now? Who is helping Sally make sense of her dilemma? What has happened is that her sister, Janet, has latched on to the theme of singing and is now letting Sally know her own story. Almost inevitably, Janet's story, certainly when compared with the dilemma of Sally's, turns out to be a wonderful adventure and leaves Sally feeling caught between trying to retrieve the opportunity to explore her own dilemma, and supporting her sister's.

We call this Level Two Listening - Hijacking. Now, of course ***we personally*** would never do this, although we probably know a number of people who do...

Another example: It might be we are deliberating with a friend as to whether we can afford to take the family to America to see relatives. This triggers, in our friend, spontaneous memories of her own, ***fabulous*** back-packing holiday as a student, starting in New York and taking the Greyhound bus across to Chicago and then the Grand Canyon, blah, blah.

The outcome is that although we initially were wanting a bit of space to explore the possibility of an American holiday for our own family, our friend has hijacked the theme and now we find ourselves listening to ***her*** American Dream. Which '***naturally***' was '***far more exciting***' than she can imagine ours ever being so there's little point in her asking us any more about our American Dream really, is there?

Or here's another scenario. We mention we are thinking of buying a second-hand piano for the kids' lessons. Rather than ask us about our choices our friend announces she knows someone who just bought a baby grand from e-Bay for next to nothing. And his kids are thinking about giving free lunchtime recitals at the municipal theatre as they are just ***SO*** talented...

Get the picture? Indeed, when we notice it happening, hijacking can be intensely irritating. The difficulty is that Level Two Listening is so prevalent that it often passes unnoticed in our conversations, and the person whose story carries the most energy on the day generally gets to recount it most out of all those present.

After many years of practice, I am now fully tuned in to how people are listening to me, and am able to confront potential hijackers with some well-practised light phrases, like ***"Hmmm, I don't remember giving you permission to hijack my dilemma and replace it with your fairy-tale successes,"*** and other such attempts at irony. It generally works though, and usually my theme is returned to me with an apology along the lines of "Oh, sorry! Go on then, you were saying..." However, by the time I have generally twigged that I am unlikely to get much of an opportunity to explore my predicament in any real depth with this person anyway, I pass, and ask them to continue; ***"No, no, don't worry,"*** I say,generously, ***"Tell me more about your friend and his baby grand, it sounds like a great bargain."***

So back to the Listen-O-Meter. What do Janet and our other hijacking friends score? 2? 3? 4 at a push? At least we are on the same subject and there's a chance I can learn something more about cheap pianos.

HiJacK !

Hijack? **I'll show you a hijack! This is a hijack!** So you've decided to talk about listening to us have you? So, if you really meant it, listen to this. We do have something to say.

To all you parents "out there" - you want to find out how to bring us up? Try this for a reframe up front. **Just suppose it was the law of the universe that us kids get to choose to be born into the family of our choice.** Ask yourselves, now we've picked you, what might have been our reasons for that? And what do you suppose we felt we could best learn about development and education from you, that we couldn't get from another family?

And suppose we chose you because we had spotted something in you that needed attention, that we were uniquely qualified to fix for you. You're always telling us how ungrateful we are. Maybe now it should be you who ought to be grateful to us for **choosing** to live with you now, **right?**

In a nutshell, **parenting is all about communicating** really. Show me the rule that says it only works from old towards young, or from more experienced towards less or from adult to child? You just have to know how to **make us think**. In fact, what's to know? Just *stop* telling *us to do stuff* and we'll think perfectly. When was the last time you gave us "a thoroughly good listening to?"

None of you sets out to be a bad parent on purpose. Well, virtually none. So, **every family is a unique and shining example** of the millions of tactical approaches to our education. Oh, and to **minimising conflict**.

Isn't that what parents are all **REALLY** looking to achieve? A harmonious, fun and peaceful environment? Makes it so much easier to practise your parenting skills, right? You probably think there's little wrong with your parenting when everything is calm and we are doing what we are told – ever noticed that? Sometimes it seems like it's just **when we have the cheek to think and speak out for ourselves** that it all starts going **pear-shaped.**

Harsh? Maybe. Maybe not. Deal with it either way. Everyone knows parents are hard-working, well-meaning and generous (because you tell us so often) and you probably hear all too seldom what a magnificent contribution you are making, every day of your lives, to us younger people. **So, fine. You're doing the best you can too.**

You act like you think we're going to be really **resistant to this coaching malarkey**. Like we just wish that people would leave us alone for several years with our **childish insecurities and hormones.** So here's a shocker for you; we **do** see the power in it. We do. We want so much more than you just harping on about us behaving better and trying to fix us. Really. **Our brains are smart and hungry** - of course they are - just not always when you want them to be. So pick your moments, OK?

Often, **all we want is simply space** in which to make our transformations. Read that again. In fact I'll write it **again**. We just need some space to explore our transformation opportunities. So if that's all your coaching is – just creating and holding a safe space for people to explore themselves – then we all want some of that. No question. Who wouldn't?

Let's see if by exploring this coaching together we can create that harmonious, fun, peaceful space you're so fond of. And shed some of the tension and stresses that seem to accompany so many family moments while we're at it. *We learn so much slower when there's tension.* Doesn't everybody? If you get nothing else, at least get that.

So first let's all be grateful, shall we? We are all investing every single day into each other's **education.** It's not just you investing into us. It's us into you too, if only you'd get off that high horse every now and then **and see it as we see it.**

You want a bit of acknowledgement from time to time for the job you do for us? Then send a little our way sometime for the s p a c e we create and hold w i d e open for you to explore yourselves too. Quid pro quo. kid pro quo. This will allow us **all to** evolve and **grow.**

Continually. End of. Right, back to you.

- N.E. Jung-Pursson

LEVEL THREE: ADVISING

So, er... well, good for you for getting that off your chest. Thank you.

In my workshops, I might ask people to think of a real dilemma, of current significance in their lives along the lines of

"I would like to [..........] but [............]"

For example,

"I would like to [get my daughter into the local nursery] ***but*** [it's so expensive]."

"I would like to [find more time to go cycling with my kids] ***but*** [we're understaffed at work and I'm having to go in to the office on weekends at the moment]."

Each person thinks of his or her own dilemmas and then I ask individuals to volunteer them for me to "listen" to, at each one of the Five Levels. They can then rate me out of ten, with 1 being 'not good listening at all' and 10 being 'superb, empowering listening.'

What then generally transpires is that everyone squirms a little bit as they recognise themselves as perpetrators of the first three levels of listening, certainly in social situations, and often in more formal, professional environments too. So let's take a look at Level Three Listening.

It's a recurring theme at my workshops that a third dilemma is sometimes more difficult to obtain from the participants, since they have now seen how brutally the first two volunteers have been treated. But eventually one brave soul might raise a hand and offer another situation, hoping for some valuable, pro bono professional coaching, only to have his hopes cruelly dashed as I 'fix' his sensitive dilemma in seconds flat. This one is real:

Brave soul: "I'd like to... be able to talk to my daughter more about her friends and their interests ***but...*** she just ignores me, even when I'm driving her to one of her many sleepovers."

Me, aka Mr Fixit: "Just let her talk to her mum. Be happy she talks to at least one of you. She'll talk to you when she's ready."

Bam! Sorted. Why on earth couldn't he see it for himself? I'm good at this advice game. Give me more dilemmas, I'll provide solutions. People just need to air their dilemmas within earshot and my agile mind will unravel and decipher all. Let's face it, world peace suddenly doesn't seem so unachievable after all.

Level Three Listening. Simple as blinking. Do you perhaps know people who are ready with instant solutions on whatever subject crops up? In the example above, was the Brave Soul actually asking for my advice? Am I qualified to give this advice, after hearing one short sentence?

I ask the workshop participants how they rate me on my listening and I hear, "4, maybe 5 out of 10." It seems that at least I have remained on the subject, 'heard' the real dilemma, and it's just possible that a number of people feel my advice may be useful. This dilemma (above) was raised by a real Brave Soul in one workshop and I actually received an '8 out of 10' score from him when he said he saw sense in my advice and would have a chat with his wife about it that evening. (So; useful after all - on that occasion I struck lucky!)

John Gray has written a must-read classic: Men are from Mars, Women are from Venus. It highlights and embraces the differences between men and women. We are fundamentally different and thank goodness for that.

One principal difference he has highlighted between the sexes is in the way we process information - women process by talking, men process by thinking. And where the woman has arrived home first to be confronted by youngsters, she is keen for some adult company with whom to make sense of her day. The man, on the other hand, is keen for some 'cave-time.' When he arrives home after a day full of testing situations, his inclination is for quiet, non-significant activity, like reading the paper, watching the Simpsons on TV or just reclining on a sofa and letting the kids crawl over him.

His wife, whether she is aware of his need for his 'cave-time' or not is compelled by his arrival to start processing her own thoughts and challenges, using him as a sounding board. And the 'cave-man' is caught in a quandary. Whether to pay token gestures towards her verbal unburdening, and nod and grunt in her general direction; whether to stay in his 'cave' where he feels he has a right to be for half an hour or so, and ignore her, at the risk of appearing rude; whether to assert himself and 'solve' her problem quickly so there is no more problem (from his point of view).

adults model communication templates which the children are very likely to emulate

A typical outcome is that he tries to achieve all of these together and often succeeds, (where 'success' is defined as his wife shutting down, having realised after a few minutes that she is not being listened to as attentively as she considers is appropriate). Most definitely a win-lose sort of success though. Or alternatively, he fails, (where 'failure' is defined as his wife doing precisely the opposite of shutting down; instead opening up (both barrels) and firing angry broadsides against his insensitivity and accusing him of not caring). And that's most definitely a lose-lose.

In whichever way the scene might play out, what is certain is that the adults are modelling a sort of communication template which the children are very likely to emulate, now and later in life.

Consider this Level Three scenario between a Dad and his daughter, Teri:

Dad: "Hi, everyone. I'm home!"

Teri: "Hello, Dad. Good day today?"

Dad: "Pretty good, thanks. You?"

Teri: "OK, I suppose. Well, actually, if I'm honest, a bit of a nightmare towards the end of the day. My boss has landed a whole lot more work on me. And you know how much I'm struggling with the work I already have. He says you should always give urgent stuff to a busy person, they get things done. So now I've got three projects on the go at once. It's crazy!"

Dad: "Uh - awful."

Teri: "You're not listening to a word I'm saying!"

Dad: "I am, of course I am. Wait...! So you're saying he's giving you even more work? Hold on, he can't do that, you've already got loads on."

WAIT – a handy acronym for all parent-coaches who find ourselves short on listening skills – ask "Why Am I Talking?"

Teri: "Yes, that's what I'm trying to tell you."

Dad: "He's got no business overloading you like that. You should tell him tomorrow that you can't take on any more. Say you've talked it through with me and it's going to mean you have to work even later than you do now. I'll back you up. He shouldn't be treating you like that. In fact maybe you should call him tonight - get it sorted immediately. Or do you want me to call him? I'm not letting him talk to my daughter like this. Where's his number?"

Teri: "No, wait..."

Now I want to point out, unequivocally, that listening at levels one, two and three is not ***wrong***. It's normal and natural to interrupt someone when our own story is so pressing and spontaneous that it just can't wait. (Level One). It's so tempting to pick up the theme of the moment and embellish another's experience with one's own. (Level Two).

And as for giving advice (Level Three) - well, we all like to feel helpful don't we? If we know where the German dictionary is and our daughter asks us where the German dictionary is, it would be vaguely perverse to ask her "How do you think you might find out where it could be?"

We all give advice. Some far more than others perhaps. I bet even the Dalai Lama gives unsolicited advice from time to time, so it can't be all bad. Here's another timely acronym which may help to know when to speak and when to listen. If in doubt - WAIT. There it is. WAIT - Why Am I Talking? A super question for parent-coaches to ask themselves many times a day. Succinct and to the point. Thanks again to Liz Macann for that one.

So while these first three levels of listening then are neither ***wrong*** nor ***bad listening***, they simply are ***not coaching listening.*** Certainly not so ***useful*** as Coaching Listening, which, under various aliases such as Attentive and Active, resides loftily on the Fourth and Fifth Levels.

The Five Levels of Listening

Attentive Listening 4 5 Active Listening

3 Advising

2 Hi-jacking!

1 Interrupting

Reproduced with kind permission of Carol Wilson

So how to achieve that elusive win-win? Aha. Inspired coaching question. Please read on - all will be revealed.

LEVEL FOUR: ATTENTIVE LISTENING

From numerous coaching workshops with parents it transpires that there are three words which men find most difficult to say to women. And more, in a marriage, many men agreed that these three words can mean the difference between domestic harmony and divorce. Alrighty then. Who is now wondering what they could possibly be?

"Is dinner ready?" Nope, that comes too easily.

"Where's the remote?" No again, most men seem [too] comfortable saying those words.

"How's your day?" Closer. But the chances are she may have already told him.

No, the three words that seem to cause hearts to beat faster and stick in the throats of many, many men, are:

i) Tell

ii) Me

iii) More

Coincidentally in that same order too. Because, of course, once that invitation has been made to her, there is, as one husband rather uncharitably put it, ***"...an overwhelming danger that she might do just that."*** So for the benefit of those that are, let's just say, unenlightened, let's explore what happens when these three words are uttered ***by a coach***.

we must no longer be trying to 'make sense' of our childrens' situations by organising their thoughts for them

This is Level Four listening; ***we are now moving into the realm of Listening Like A Coach. This requires a different sort of energy and care. Care with the words we choose, care with the content, care with the development and support of the person we are coaching.***

We will no longer be relating any conversations back to our own agenda, as we do at Levels One, Two and Three. We must no longer be trying to 'make sense' of our childrens' situations by organising their thoughts for them. What we are aiming to be doing now is to give the child the luxury of being listened to. This Level is called Attentive Listening, and it's not easy to do well. Most of us have spent a lifetime learning how to impose our opinions on others and being rewarded for that with either promotion or social respect – so it won't be a quick journey to unpick that. Don't expect that this will become an unconscious habit in just days. Patience!

give the child the luxury of being listened to

We start with those three difficult words, sometimes accompanied by permission, and then we just shut up and listen. For as long as needed. And it is very probably going to seem awkward and artificial too to begin with until both people are used to this process. Don't be fazed by this. It's normal, and can be overcome with openness and practice.

There are some rules to guide the parent-coach through this process.

Rule One: keep our eyes on (or definitely *in the direction of*) the speaker.

Rule Two: ask ONLY very neutral questions from the 'Permitted' list below that invite more reflection and externalising.

Permitted Level Four questions:

- **"Would you like to *tell me more* about that?"**
- **"What else?"**
- **"What more do you think, or know or want to say about that?"**

and questions to finish the conversation:

- **"What are your freshest thoughts now?"**
- **"What do you know now that you weren't aware of 15 minutes ago?"**
- **"What are you taking away from this conversation?"**

Rule Three: Leave silences - the coachee ***is*** processing.

Rule Four: Keep to a minimum, any noises and gestures of assent and understanding, nodding and unnecessary movements.

When we practice this in a workshop situation, as in real life too sometimes, the feedback usually centres around the observations that the coach seems actually ***disengaged***, and ***not*** providing any useful contribution to the learning. Sometimes the comments are directed at the words used by the coaches in their questions; they seem a bit stilted, brusque and distant. Perception is fact, in most situations, so we must take these observations seriously.

Parents have a difficulty with the idea of not nodding, or making noises of assent or understanding. They say it comes across as cold and uncaring. Which indeed it can, until practised often, and through a TOPCAT filter: remember this from Chapter 19?

"This child in front of me is a Tremendous, Outstanding Person, Capable of Astonishing Things."

Then the detachment feels natural and warm. Practise in different ways until it feels right again. It will soon enough.

Children will really learn to think more deeply when they know they won't be interrupted

Another thing - listen ***right to the end of every sentence*** the child speaks. We mustn't be tempted to finish a child's sentences with our own words, even if we can guess pretty accurately the remaining words or sense. Children will really learn to think more deeply when they know they won't be interrupted. Even an audible intake of breath as we prepare to reply or a lifting of our forefinger indicates to the children that we have decided they should stop speaking and let us take a turn. Try it - the child will stop speaking immediately we do these things. We are now back to listening at Level One - interrupting, or at the very least, ***listening for the child to finish so we can speak***.

So this is why we remain as neutral as we can at Level Four. Our challenge is to be warmly impassive, riveted while detached, neutral while fully engaged. I ask participants at workshops to practise listening at level four to their partners and children overnight between training days and bring their stories back to the training room the following day. The stories are always greeted with amusement, since typically, the person being listened to "rumbles" the would-be coach and asks questions like "Why are you being so weird?" or "Why aren't you telling me off like you usually do?" or "Have you been on a training course or something?"

One fun result occurred with a participant in a workshop in Hong Kong. He practised that evening with his wife; she allowed him to listen attentively for thirty minutes; he processed all her thoughts, and then when he asked her if she had noticed anything different, she informed him, "Well, I presume this is part of your workshop to become a real person at last!"

"Thanks very much," says he, a little miffed that she hadn't been more appreciative; "How did I do - will you give me marks out of ten for my listening?"

"Six out of ten," she replied, which he thought was a little harsh, and told her so.

"Well it could have been a nine," she told him, "...if you'd been giving me a foot massage at the same time."

There are so many aspects to exquisite listening that coaches have still to identify...

if parents model respectful and supportive communication whenever the kids and their friends are within earshot, the kids are likely to have a far better chance of picking it up too and becoming gracious communicators with their own kids

So what is the theory behind this form of Listening Like A Coach? Nancy Kline, is a complete master of this. She doesn't call coaches 'Coaches.' She calls them 'Listening Partners.' As in, ***"Would you be a Listening Partner for me for ten minutes or so, so I can hear myself think something through."***

So, my theory is, and call me old-fashioned, but if we can get the parents to be modelling respectful and supportive communication whenever the kids and their friends are within earshot, the kids are likely to have a far better chance of picking it up too and becoming gracious communicators with their own kids a generation later.

Let's re-draft the earlier conversation between Dad and Teri in a Level Four Listening style:

Enlightened Dad a.k.a. 'Listening Partner': "Hi, everybody. I'm home!"

(Equally enlightened) Teri: "Hello, Dad. Good day today?"

Dad: "Pretty good, thanks. You?"

Teri: "OK, I suppose. Well, actually, if I'm honest, a bit of a nightmare towards the end of the day. My boss has landed a whole lot more work on me. And you know how much I'm struggling with the work I already have. But, look, I know you need a bit of space to unwind when you get home, so how about we talk about it after dinner?"

Dad: "That's perfect, sweetie, thanks. Let me just catch up with your little brothers and slob in front of The Simpsons for a bit..."

[AFTER DINNER]

Dad: "Now then, it sounds like you've had a bit of a tough afternoon. Tell me more."

Teri: "Yes, I did. My boss has given me a ton more work. He justified it saying, "you should always give urgent stuff to a busy person, they get things done." So now I've got three projects on the go at once. It's crazy!"

Dad: "Go on..."

Teri: "Are you sure you want to listen to all this? It's probably not what you want to hear right now."

Dad: "Of course. What else is happening?"

Teri: "Well, I know he values what I do, because he often asks for my opinion on things, so now when Tilly's on maternity leave, he's schmoozed me into taking on her final launch project that she hadn't quite finished..."

Dad: ... [silent]

Teri: ... [reflects in the silence] "I mean, it's not a huge amount left to do, but it's still a big responsibility to get it finished in time. In other circumstances I might be flattered, but you know how much work I have already. OK, so that's all it is really."

Dad: "What other thoughts are in your mind about this?"

Teri: "Well, listening to myself rattle on, actually, what's just come to me is that it's actually quite an interesting project that Tilly was working on..."

Dad: .. [silent]

Teri: "...in fact, thinking about it, Jenny has offered to give me a hand with my other two projects in the past but I keep saying no. I suppose because I don't really know if she's up to speed with them ... or maybe just because I want to keep them close to my chest if I'm really honest..."

Dad: .. [silent]

Teri: "... I mean now would be a great time to see what she's made of really wouldn't it? What do you think? Shall I talk to her tomorrow and sound her out? She'll probably be fine, she's very capable under pressure generally. And... well... and what's coming through to me now is that really I'm quite excited about working on Tilly's project - I have been keeping a beady eye on it for some time. I think my panic earlier was just nerves really, because when he offered me the work, and I realised I had a chance to actually work on it, I immediately thought of all the details I could introduce to finish it really well, and I knew how much time I would need to spend on it. But if I delegate some of my stuff to Jenny, she'll be thrilled, and I can get stuck in to this new product and actually be the one to launch it."

Dad: "Sounds like a good plan then. So what's your freshest thinking now after processing it through?"

Teri: "Well, though I hate to admit it, I think my boss is probably a bit smarter than I gave him credit for. And he obviously seems to trust me, which is very reassuring."

Dad: "Glass of wine, hon?"

Teri: "Love one! And Dad?"

Dad: "Hm?"

Teri: "Thanks for listening!"

What do we notice about this?

Apart from them being a fantasy too-good-to-be-true pair that couldn't possibly exist in the real world, obviously.

Or could they? What ***actually*** happened in that conversation?

Point One: To begin with, Teri recognised that her Dad's listening abilities would be far more focused after he'd had a little down-time, a little 'cave-time' as we now understand it. They created a strong listening and thinking space (remember this from Part One?) That's not necessarily coaching *per se*, that's just astuteness. He then later opened the door with a generous "tell me more." And she gratefully accepted his invitation.

Point Two: She never asked for solutions, and wasn't given any. It has been said (on more than a few occasions) that males have a tendency to need to 'solve' things, perhaps in order to ***assert*** their usefulness. Here, Dad understands that he has an intelligent daughter, quite capable of making sense of her own life, and adroitly asks her a series of very succinct, very neutral, focused questions.

Point Three: All he then has to do is ***be there***. Close by, fully present, engaged. A still-life study of riveted, loving detachment. He is perfectly relaxed with staying out of the drama because he knows Teri just needs ***time to think.*** (Where have we heard that phrase before?) He recognises he best serves her cause by just being a sounding board for now. He understands that her questions to him and her pauses are, just aids to her own processing. He has enough confidence in his daughter to know he can remain silent.

one doesn't just pay attention; one bestows it

Point Four: And his questions are succinct, sparse and encouraging. He uses ten times fewer words than she does. Count them if you don't believe me. This is a good ratio at this Level of Listening. It's her dilemma, so it's appropriate that she should have ten times the space to develop her thoughts. Compare this with the same dilemma outlined in Level Three, where (not so enlightened) Dad manages to amass around sixty per cent of the words, so great is his need to wrest back control of the situation and assert himself.

At Level Four Listening we are becoming more conscious of our own presence and contribution in any given conversation. It's easy to occasionally (!) forget that other people, (especially youngsters) have wonderful creative brains that can fix and solve things too. Come on parent-coaches, let's give them that chance.

We think best when we know we will not be interrupted. It's empowering to be around people who know how to listen attentively. Attention is priceless. One doesn't just pay attention. One bestows it. Donate it liberally for birthdays from now on instead of buying clutter and fripperies. Our attentiveness will be valued and remembered for a lifetime.

LEVEL FIVE: ACTIVE LISTENING

We could be forgiven for thinking that this is as good as it gets when it comes to listening. Saying very little, and leaving thinking space for someone, believing in them enough to permit their own solutions to surface and not making them wrong by suggesting contrary advice. And we'd be more or less correct in many ways. It's difficult to get much closer to pure listening as a dictionary might define it. Listening - "Giving one's attention to a sound." Or something similar in our own dictionary.

Active Listening involves employing any and every foundation skill and every last gramme of EQ to elicit personal insight, breakthrough and learning

My dictionary neglected to mention anything about butting in with advice...

So where could we go from this apparent zenith then? How much better is it possible to be than Level Four? Well, rather than create comparisons for better or worse, let's instead consider another zenith. As we can see from the diagram, Level Five listening sits happily alongside Level Four. ***It's not a higher form of listening, it's just another form.*** The difference is it can be used to focus someone in on the 'energy phrases' they use. So it is, by its nature, a more interventional form of coaching listening. Coaches know it as Active Listening.

Active Listening is:

- ***listening to what might be behind the and between the words actually spoken;***
- ***creating expectant silences;***
- ***using intuition to sow seeds;***
- ***prompting exploration with purposeful questions;***
- ***clarifying exact meaning and reflecting back energised words and phrases for further examination;***
- ***asking permission to challenge at a deeper level;***
- ***facilitating self-directed learning and awareness;***
- ***and yes, even making additional suggestions (if there are still any appropriate ones to be made after the coachees have thoroughly explored and exhausted every last one of their own).***

In short – Active Listening involves employing any and every foundation skill and every last gram of EQ to elicit personal insight, breakthrough and learning.

Since we have been able to follow sample random dialogue for each of the previous four levels of listening, let's see if we can spot various of these elements by simply creating a separate, revised version of our exemplary Level Four conversation. Just to show another of the many ways cats can be relieved of their skins really.

Dad (With Active Listening Hat On): "Hey, Teri. You seem preoccupied. Wanna talk?"

Teri: "Yeah, I am a bit. Actually, if I'm honest, I had a bit of a nightmare towards the end of the day."

Dad: "A bit of a nightmare? Sounds ominous. Tell me more."

Teri: "Well at 3.30 this afternoon my boss landed a whole lot more work on me. And you know how much I'm struggling with the work I already have."

Dad: "Sure."

Teri: "I mean it's a ton more work. He justified it saying, you should always give urgent stuff to a busy person, they get things done."

Dad: "When you say, 'a ton more work,' break it down for me. What exactly have you been landed with?"

Teri: "Well you remember I told you Tilly was going on maternity leave in a few weeks' time? Well, she's been advised to leave a couple of weeks early by her doctor. So somehow my boss has 'schmoozed' me into taking on her final launch project that she hadn't quite finished..."

Dad: "So he 'schmoozed' you? Run that by me..."

Teri: "Well, I say 'schmoozed', I mean, I know he values what I do, because he often asks for my opinion on things, and he generally at least takes them on board even if he doesn't always implement them. He knows I have offered some thoughts on Tilly's project in the past, so somehow he's got me to take on her work too aswell as my own. So now I've got three projects on the go at once. It's crazy!"

Dad: "Sweetie, may I just play a couple of things back for a second?"

Teri: "OK."

Dad: "I'm hearing words like 'nightmare, ton of work, schmoozed, crazy!' What exactly is involved here?"

Teri: "OK so look, I mean, it's not a huge amount left to do, but it's still a big responsibility to get it finished in time. There's about a couple of weeks of before the launch so it's quite a tight deadline."

Dad: "So 'a ton' equals a couple of weeks extra work then, does it? Is that what you mean by 'quite a tight deadline?'"

Teri: "Yes. Put like that I suppose it doesn't sound all that much really, does it? I mean in other circumstances I might be flattered, but you know how much work I have already. Anyway, so... that's all it is really."

Dad: "Well, the fact remains you still have three projects on the go. What are your thoughts about that?"

Teri: "Well, listening to myself rattle on, what's just come to me is that it's actually quite an interesting project that Tilly was working on..."

Dad: ... [silent]

Teri: "...in fact, thinking about it, Jenny has offered to give me a hand with my other two projects in the past but I keep saying no. I suppose because I don't really know if she's up to speed with them ... or maybe just because I want to keep them close to my chest if I'm really honest..."

Dad: ... [silent]

Teri: "... I mean now would be a great time to see what she's made of really wouldn't it? What do you think?"

Dad: "More to the point, what do you think? I know you'll find the right solution for you, soon enough. You always do."

Teri: "Well I could talk to her tomorrow and sound her out. She'll probably be fine, she's very capable under pressure generally."

Dad: "So Jenny's capable under pressure. What else?"

Teri: "Yes she is. So that's a positive isn't it?"

Dad: "Sounds positive to me. Teri, can I tell you what I'm sensing here? I may be way off base, just tell me if you think I am, and I'm not attached to this thought really, it's just popped up while you've been talking..."

Teri: "Go for it..."

Dad: "Well, what's coming through to me now is that you seem to me to be really quite excited about working on Tilly's project - I know you have been keeping a beady eye on it for some time. And you mentioned about being flattered earlier..."

Teri: "Yes I did, didn't I? OK, so I think ...if I'm honest ...my panic earlier might have been just nerves really, because when he offered me the work, and I realised I had a chance to actually work on it, I immediately thought of all the details I could introduce to finish it really well, and I knew how much time I would need to spend on it. But I was excited. I am excited. You may have a good point there..."

Dad: "Great! So that's a start anyway. So what might you do when you get in to the office tomorrow?"

Teri: "Well the first thing I could do is just bite the bullet and talk to Jenny about delegating some of my stuff to her."

Dad: "OK, so talk to Jenny and delegate. Anything else?"

Teri: "So, after I've had her response to that, I could talk to my boss and discuss how to re-structure my job plan a little over the next few weeks."

Dad: "Right. So that will depend on Jenny's reaction, will it?"

Teri: "Yes, though she'll be thrilled, I know she will. And then I'll have to get stuck in to this new product straight away. Just think - I'll actually be the one to launch it now. That's pretty amazing!"

Dad: "Sounds like you're pretty enthused about it after all, now! So, is this right? Jenny first, then boss, then get stuck in."

Teri: "Exactly."

Dad: "So what's your freshest thinking now after processing it through?"

Teri: "Well, though I hate to admit it, I think my boss is probably a bit smarter than I gave him credit for. And he obviously seems to trust me, which is very reassuring."

Dad: "Good for you! I have to say your energy is ten times higher than ten minutes ago. Glass of wine to celebrate, Sweetie?"

Teri: "Love one! And Dad?"

Dad: "Hmm?"

Teri: "Thanks for making time for me!"

So there it is. A re-run of our earlier conversation, although this time using a far more *interventionist* approach to the outcome. And all those Active interventions (around twenty) contrived to arrive at a very similar state of understanding to the Attentive Listening conversation.

Twenty interventions, then. How many coaching techniques can we spot? It's good exercise for a coaching mind. See my table overleaf where I recognised seventeen, (but then I did write the conversation). Maybe you'll interpret some comments or questions in a different way. Sorry - there are no prizes other than an immense satisfaction at having reinforced all these techniques in our minds.

	Level Five Active Listening Techniques	Coaching Questions and Phrases Used
1	Reflected words and phrases	'nightmare,' ' ton more work,' 'schmoozed,' 'crazy!'
2	Dialogue openers	'tell me more,' 'what else?' 'anything else?'
3	Check for specifics	'run it by me...' 'break it down for me...'
4	Playback for clarity - hearing her words back	'So 'a ton' equals a couple of weeks extra work then, does it? Is that what you mean by 'quite a tight deadline?''
5	Silence for processing	...[silent]
6	Deflecting requests for advice	'more to the point, what do you think?'
7	Asking permission to present an intuition	'can I tell you what I'm sensing here?'
8	Using 'clean' words, i.e. exactly those used by the coachee	'quite a tight deadline'
9	Reading an energy shift and moving to action setting	'Great! So that's a start anyway. So what might you do...'
10	Checking the priorities of the actions	'So that will depend on Jenny's reaction, will it?'
11	Check understanding	'So, is this right? Jenny first, then boss, then get stuck in.'
12	Asking for more	'OK, so talk to Jenny and delegate. Anything else?'
13	Keeping it positively charged	'Good for you!' 'Sounds like you're pretty enthused about it after all, now!'
14	Looking for insights and takeaways	'So what's your freshest thinking now after processing it through?'
15	Validation and recognition	'I have to say your energy is ten times higher than ten minutes ago.'
16	Celebration	Glass of wine to celebrate, Sweetie?'
17	Appreciation	I know you'll find the right solution for you, soon enough. You always do.' [Teri] 'Thanks for making time for me!'

Wow! Seventeen different coaching techniques in around twenty interventions. That's a pretty intensive and purposeful exchange. That's Active Listening. Let's just compare Dad With Active Listening Hat On (DWALHO) to Enlightened Dad a.k.a. Listening Partner (EDakaLP) for a moment.

They are every bit as intensive and purposeful as each other. The only difference being that in Level Four, EDakaLP decides to allow Teri the space to ***explore her own mind*** to arrive at her freshest thoughts, whereas in Level Five, DWALHO chooses to ***participate and share in the denouement*** too.

That's why we place them **both at the same level of importance** - neither is necessarily more or less effective, and we can experiment with both. It may well be that, in conversation with one young person, a more patient Level Four suits better and for another, a more involved Level Five journey. Perhaps we might allow more space for Level Four at the beginning of a conversation to open up the subject and then introduce more Level Five interventions towards the end, to focus in on the finer points. It's flexible. We the parent-coaches, can choose, and ***with practice we'll probably mix the two together naturally and instinctively.***

when practising Active Listening every word from us has a purpose and an intention behind it

The idea to keep in mind when practising Active Listening is that every word from us has a purpose and an intention behind it. Otherwise it's just chat. And coaches, while working, don't chat. It's just not ***useful*** enough. So all the words in my Table contribute something to deepen the opportunity to explore Teri's dilemma. And every sentence has a coaching principle imbued in it; one might be encouraging responsibility or self-awareness, another might be challenging a belief with the option of a re-frame; one might be checking understanding in a blame-free way while another is a simple call to action. And so on. But ***it's rare that a coach allows a 'loose' question to stray into the fray.***

people generally air their dilemmas for one reason: as an entreaty to be listened to

The coachee would likely spot it immediately, having become used to a succession of high-level, *useful* questions. Imagine in the middle of this conversation, the DWALHO blurts out ***"Look, just make up your mind, either you want to do this project or you don't. Stop playing games and say what you really mean!"*** Phrases like that tend to shut down the other person's thinking immediately, and put them firmly on the defensive.

Some people generally think they are being useful by making snap decisions and giving solutions. (Do we know anyone that fits this description?) Other people generally air their dilemmas for one reason: ***as an entreaty to be listened to***. In that 'listened to' space, people process for themselves. Don't believe me? Ask them whether they want solutions or questions. Teri, above, isn't asking for solutions. She was not best pleased when in our earlier example her Dad began to truncate her thought-exploration opportunity through his impatience and need to assert his ego.

This emotionally intelligent listening applies to youngsters too. All youngsters have sharp brains. All youngsters love to see where their minds might lead them when they are not being interrupted by frazzled parents or needy siblings. How far can their minds go before they have need of ours? Where might their carefree patience lead them if it wasn't first overhauled by the tetchiness of our impatience?

We will find all these techniques discussed in various far-flung chapters of this book. Our challenge is to bring them all front-of-mind simultaneously and select the most useful for that particular nano-second of that coachable moment, not forgetting to then add only the most purposeful and well-considered words with an emotionally intelligent forethought. That's all there is to it really.

Oh, and manage to look serene and benign while doing it.

How wonderful to know how and when to give attentive, uninterrupted listening to one's family, knowing it will lead them towards embracing their own responsibilities. It's self-serving too by the way, as it creates us parent-coaches huge amounts of time to revisit our own too.

How gracious and far-sighted to model this kind of respectful listening for the whole family to observe. How could children of such parent-coaches fail to develop into wonderfully attentive parents themselves? How confident and courageous will all their children, our grand-children, be as a result?

Welcome to the wonderfully worthwhile world of Active Listening.

31.

The Fifth Ladder – Insightful Questioning

Open Questions, Open Minds

WHAT MAKES A GOOD COACHING QUESTION?

Good question. What do we know about a hierarchy of questions? What elevates a standard question into a 'loftier' coaching one? Well, one can't particularly compartmentalise questions precisely like that, although it is true that some questions have far greater impact than others. And that's the point, really. These are the crafts that parents can develop; using specific language techniques and an emotionally intelligent nature in order simply to ask searching, useful questions of the child; finding the right words, the right tonality, coupled with a strong intention to grow the child through insight and challenge and action.

what elevates a standard question into a 'loftier' coaching one?

Let's identify certain sorts of questions and then decide which might make the best coaching questions. First of all, most people understand the difference between **open** and **closed** questions. What they may not be so fluent with is ***how to select and construct*** open and closed questions to be most useful to a coaching conversation. I am going to give dozens of examples of what works and what doesn't and gradually we will notice a pattern emerging.

There are all sorts of 'types' of questions to choose from. We could call them **information** questions, **leading** questions, **judgmental** questions, **silences and pauses** (in themselves **tacit** questions), **'why'** questions, **multiple (stacked)** questions, **insightful** questions, **provocative** questions, **physical** questions (a raised eyebrow, a tilt of the head), questions formed by re-pitching the tonality and dozens more besides.

parents can develop specific language techniques and an emotionally intelligent nature in order simply to ask searching, useful questions of the child

Don't think we have to remember all those categories, or even all the examples given below and throughout this book - trust that we will assimilate them naturally over time, and come to recognise them for what they bring to the child. Practice, practice, practice!

So let's examine a few of these categories.

Information Questions

Asking questions generally has the purpose of eliciting information about general things:

"What time does the train leave?"
"How much are those shelves?"

Coaching questions have only one purpose: to enable coachees to find out information about themselves. Here's a good one:

"And what have you learnt about yourself, now you have achieved this?"

coaching questions have only one purpose: to enable coachees to find out information about themselves

Of course, asking coaching questions isn't enough in itself if we don't have backup tools and techniques of how to process the response. Nor if we don't have a healthy philosophy of Emotional Intelligence behind our questions. So make sure we read and practice the previous four chapters (The First to Fourth Ladders) leading up to this one and keep them front of mind - we never know when a 'coachable moment' might jump up and challenge our emerging skills to a duel.

Closed Questions

Some questions elicit a short, yes or no answer. These are known as closed questions. Typically, in the English language, closed questions begin with verbs (do, is, are, have), or modifiers, (might, will, could, should), followed by a pronoun as the second word, (you, they, he, it), and so on. They are used less in coaching than open questions although they have a strong role when they are used well, for example:

When checking understanding: ***"Have I understood that correctly?"***
Checking commitment: ***"Are you happy to help lay the table?"***
Asking permission: ***"Would it be OK to ask you for a few more details about your brother's allegedly 'spontaneous' nosebleed?"***

asking coaching questions isn't enough in itself if we don't have backup tools and techniques of how to process the response

Closed questions are often used when a new insight has been found, to tie it down to an action or a goal:

"Do you want to make a to-do list around that?"

Questions that only give limited options are also in the closed category;

"So do you want to talk to Phillip first, or would you prefer to start writing the letter straightaway?"

In this example the child is given a choice of two by the coach and its mind has very little exploring to do. However, it may well be useful as a call to action. The main problem with 'either/or' questions is that they don't always get an 'either/or' answer - here's an endearing example where my sister, Ellie, was having a 'coaching discussion' with my four year old nephew, Rory, about his behaviour at school, after he'd admitted he'd been told off in his first week at primary school:

Ellie: "So would you like to choose whether you are going to be a helpful boy, or a boy who gets told off."

Rory: (thoughtful pause) "Hmmmm. I can't decide - maybe a bit of both."

Open Questions

The best coaching questions tend to be those that leave an open field for people to find their own answers. These are known as open questions. A majority of the questions used in coaching are open questions, and they stretch the brain to look hard for new insights and understanding. Open questions beginning What, Where, Who, When, and How open up a child's mind and enable it to gain new insights and awareness about itself, (although not 'Why,' as we saw earlier, and will say a bit more about that in a moment):

"How important is that to you?"
"What else is happening?"
"When precisely can you make time to do that?"
"Where else might you find useful information?"
"Who do you know that could help you with that?"

Leading Questions

Sometimes a parent simply needs to tell a child what to do. That is fine; what is not fine is to manipulate young minds into arriving at (our) decisions by asking leading questions. We can and most likely will soon lose their trust and their buy-in to further dialogue opportunities. One example of a leading question is asking our children to find a solution, but not accepting their answer until it tallies with the one we want to hear:

"And what do you suppose happens to young ladies when their parents find out they smuggled vodka into their sleepovers?"

Leading questions are often closed too:

"Surely you should spend a little time at your grandma's after all she's done for you, don't you think?"

"Wouldn't you like to apologise to your sister for burying her doll in the sand pit?"

"Do you think it's a good idea to spend all that money on one belt?"

With a little pause for reflection, leading questions can ***always*** be substituted with more respectful, open questions.

'Why' Questions and **Judgmental Questions**

Questions beginning 'Why...?' tend to put people on the defensive and make them feel they are being judged. Sometimes a judgmental question masquerades as a coaching question, for example ***"What did you do that for?"*** is essentially the same as ***"Why did you do that?"***

It is acceptable to ask 'Why' questions when asking for information which is not personal, e.g. ***"Why do the iPhones sell faster than the Samsungs?"*** This question is fine as long as it is not directed at the person responsible for selling the Samsungs. "***Why did you choose that shirt to wear today?"*** can cause a very defensive response too, while the child wearing that shirt processes whether we like the shirt or not and how he should reply.

However, there is also a well-known and well-used questioning technique known as the 'Many Whys.' This can be useful when 'drilling down' into a child's motivation for something. It is best introduced with permission (and of course we must remember to wait for permission to be granted);

Dad: "Can I ask you a few 'why' questions just to see if we can identify what's happening here?"

Freddie: "OK"

and then ask:

Dad: "Why haven't you made a start on this Medical College application yet?"

Freddie: "Because I'm helping out with the technical stuff for the school play every spare moment"

Dad: "Why are you helping out with the technical stuff for the school play every spare moment?"

Freddie: "Because most people have dropped out, so I'm left to do everything"

Dad: "Why have most people dropped out?"

Freddie: "Because there wasn't really enough for them to do"

Dad: "Why wasn't there enough for them to do"

Freddie: "Because it was quicker and easier when I do stuff, rather than wait for them to learn it"

Dad: "Why was it quicker?"

Freddie: "Because I've been doing it since Year 8 so it's become second nature"

Dad: "Why have you been doing it so long?"

Freddie: "I suppose because I just love being in the theatre"
Dad: "Why do you love being in the theatre?"
Freddie: "Because that's where I feel really alive."

From any point where there seems to be a new energy or insight, Dad can pause the 'Whys' and ask permission to explore more at that point, using open questions again; e.g. ***"When you say "alive," what is that like for you?"*** or ***"What do you notice about your answer 'Because it was quicker and easier when I do stuff, rather than wait for them to learn it'?"*** And so on.

So even though Dad has asked many 'Why' questions, they have been accepted without Freddie becoming overly defensive, and Freddie has answered honestly and with reflection. What is now known is that Freddie seems to have a huge motivation for the theatre, to the point that he is alienating others from helping with any aspect of the production. His Dad could now start exploring Freddie's real motivation towards going to Medical College, or choosing another path, maybe indeed, the theatre.

avoid 'Why' questions as far as is possible - there are always open questions that will achieve the same, if not better, thinking and insights

NOTE - If permission wasn't established before this exchange began, the dialogue could easily have looked like this:

Dad: "So why haven't you made a start on this Medical College application yet?"

Freddie: "Because I'm helping out with the technical stuff for the school play every spare moment"

Dad: "Well you know you better start soon, it has to be done by next week!"

Freddie: "I said I'll do it! Just leave me alone!"

All of this said, my inclination is still to avoid 'Why' questions as far as is possible - there are always strong, robust open questions that will achieve the same, if not better, thinking and insights. Let's plump for them whenever we can.

let's not ignore the inquisitive strength of a raised eyebrow, a tilt of the head, an upturned palm, a smile

Structured silences (in themselves **tacit questions**)

Silence is a rare transaction in everyday conversations, while in coaching conversations it is a frequently traded commodity. When adults do not immediately reply to a question it is usually a sign that the question has given them something to think about. When children do not immediately reply to a question, it may well be that they are pre-occupied with something else or that they don't wish to confront the question. In which case they frequently employ the tried and trusted get-out clause: "I don't know."

As parent-coaches, since it tends not to be commonplace to introduce or accommodate silences in our conversations with our children, it is good coaching practice to ***inform*** the children that:

a) we believe they ***do*** know and ***are*** able to access some solutions and deeper thinking, and

b) that they may have noticed that we are deliberately introducing silences and pauses ***IN ORDER THAT*** they may have uninterrupted time to process their thinking.

Setting their expectations in this way is hugely valuable. When children know they will not be interrupted by an over-zealous parent, and that they are trusted to think for themselves, they regularly produce the sort of wisdom and powerful lateral thinking of which every child is capable.

I call these 'structured silences.' Structured silences therefore give all of us time to process our thoughts and come to a new awareness and understanding. When we are not sure whether our children are processing or simply stuck, or need the prompt of another question, the best way to find out is to ask them a quick, check-in question. Closed questions work well here.

"Would you like time to think about this?"

"Did that make sense?"

"Shall I put it another way?"

Remember: if in doubt about what to do, ask the child.

Silent physical questions

a child will sense little overt judgment in our silence and silent gestures

In the same category of silent questions, small gestures can carry as much weight as an incisive verbal question. Let's not ignore the inquisitive strength of a raised eyebrow, a tilt of the head, an upturned palm, a smile. The power is as much in the minimalism of the movement as in the respectful silence that accompanies it. A child will sense little overt judgment in these gestures, which can be very positively provocative and catalytic. It's true they might provoke little comments like, ***"You don't believe me, do you?"*** or ***"You think that's a bad idea, I can tell,"*** although comments like these give parents opportunities to reaffirm the core principle of coaching which is self-directed learning. We can say,

"I am not making a judgment one way or another. This is your dilemma. I know you'll find the best way through for you. So would you like to tell me more about this...?"

Multiple (stacked) questions

From time to time we find ourselves unsure of the 'right' question to ask and, particularly when we experience hesitation in the child, it is tempting to ask three or four questions in quick succession. In coaching this is known as ***'stacking'*** questions. This temptation is to be resisted as far as we are conscious of it happening. Our goal is to take time to frame each of our questions, and then let each one lie until it has been answered. Work towards keeping our questions simple, succinct and specific and avoid falling into the trap of giving ***"is it this or that?"*** (leading or options) questions.

None of this is particularly easy to accomplish to begin with and we need to be very aware of how we are presenting our questions - once again, the fluency comes with practice.

Television and radio presenters are often poor proponents of this practice. Since their job is to create soundbites we regularly hear long-winded questions, 'stacked' carelessly and without real focus. This is generally to buy a few precious seconds while they attempt to make sense either of an immediate rapidly unfolding situation, or of the response of an expert that they feel they have to decipher for their audience (as if we are not capable of making sense of the interviews for ourselves).

This 'stacking' rubs off on all of us who are exposed to TV and radio bulletins, and our questions can become clunky or fulsome or both:

Mum: "George, would you say you'd be happy to go to the parents' evening with me? Or not? I mean if you did, you could ask your teachers questions too - if you'd like to? Wouldn't that be useful? Or would you like me to ask them for you, I can, if you like or... so what do you think?"

Stay true to a philosophy of creating opportunities for self-directed learning - therein lie a million insightful coaching questions

Apart from being full of closed questions, with many leading questions thrown in for (not so) good measure, these stacked questions could be far more beneficially expressed with a strong, simple coaching question:

"What are your thoughts on going to the parents' evening with me?"

Then allow George to state his thoughts. We can always prompt with ***"...And what else?"*** or ***"What are the advantages and disadvantages...?"*** and other open questions - (but always ***one at a time and after the child has finished speaking***). Then we are perfectly at liberty to state our own preferences or questions, i.e.

"I'd really prefer that you did come with me, so that you can ask and answer any direct questions yourself. How does that sound to you now?"

Stacking questions is often an indication that, Mum, (in our first example), is wrestling with herself to try to keep her own wishes or advice out of her questions, while trying to honour the coaching principle of trust - ceding control of the conversation to the child. She feels that if she doesn't manage to convey her own sense of the best outcome, that the child may very well decide not to come, which goes against her desired outcome. So she searches for the best way to phrase her question, resulting in a very indecisive and woolly set of questions.

The chances are, even if we do ask a question that that we feel is clunky, the children most likely won't notice and will be preparing to continue their thinking with a response. Then, when we interrupt that thinking with a second, third or fourth consecutive question, (often coming back to the first one we chose anyway), the children will be trying to hold on to any question that fits their original thinking and will have 'switched off' their attention to the remainder anyway.

Note to self - try to remember to be ***succinct*** and ***specific.***

Insightful questions

Pretty much any question asked with the right intention behind it can create insight. It's rare that we parent-coaches can plan to deliver a guaranteed insightful question. It will all depend on where the children are with their thinking and their openness to explore their minds. Sometimes a fairly innocuous question like ***"So, what are some of the actions you could consider taking immediately?"*** can open up all kinds of thinking-avenues to one child, while to another child that same question might seem commonplace and expected, and therefore, not so exciting. Alternatively, a more complex, imaginative question like, ***"If you knew you couldn't fail, what amazing goal would you set for yourself?"*** which we might expect to set young minds on fire, may just as easily fall on indifferent ears.

the coach regularly walks a fine line between challenge and provocation; ***the parent-coach even more so***

Let's pick our moments and ask anyway - when the insights do come, they're worth it.

The single most important thing to remember is to stay true to a philosophy of creating opportunities for self-directed learning. Therein lie a million insightful coaching questions, one of which is surely waiting in the wings to spring out onto the stage and ignite our children's imaginations.

Provocative questions

In the same way, provocative questions come from that same space of self-directed learning. The only difference being that they must make sure not to stray into judgment. One key role of the coach is to challenge, as we have noted. The coach regularly walks a fine line between challenge and provocation; ***the parent-coach even more so***. Armed with questions packed with EQ, the aim of coaching provocation is simple and well-intentioned: to encourage, cajole and goad a child into undertaking a difficult or unfamiliar action.

Children find motivation from all aspects of a situation and the parent-coach's job is to identify this and exploit it for the benefit of the child. This may well mean taking risks with language, vocabulary and tonality. A parent will be strongly attuned to the child's sensitivities and will probably err on the side of caution when challenging the child into action. Parent-coaches may be less circumspect, since they are (supposed to be) detached from the child's agenda. When parent and coach are one and the same person the challenge is how to motivate, exhort, provoke ***and listen***, according to the child's current chosen mood-moment.

We are looking to provoke positively through our questions. In resistant mood, nearly any honest-to-goodness question can be received by a child as negatively provocative. Seemingly innocuous questions such as, ***"What do you need to pack for your camping weekend?"*** can result in the child-in-less-than-coachable-mood hearing ***"Why haven't you packed yet?"*** And of course, nearly every 'Why' question can put a child on the defensive as we have seen.

Positive provocation is a concept best achieved when we know the child is in a receptive space and it doesn't hurt to use signpost statements and permission to preface them either. Tell the child,

"I'm going to ask you a few questions now that are designed to be provocative, so don't think I'm judging you in any way, because I'm not. They are just looking to find what levels of motivation and energy you have for this difficult stage of your project. Are you OK for me to ask them?"

When permission is granted, we can 'provoke' to our heart's content...

"What's really stopping you from asking her to go out with you?"

"Name me five good reasons as to what could happen if you don't do that."

"What would your big brother say to you if he was to hear you haven't followed through?"

...and so on.

Clarifying and Reflecting (asking questions without asking questions)

These two techniques are essential tools in the coaching tool bag. Most parents clarify their children's thoughts and statements quite instinctively. Clarifying means repeating the child's words back in a different form. This is to understand what they have said, help them to focus by reducing a long sentence to its key points, and to move them forward.

Clarifying

Clarifying is often interpreted by the child as a question even though it may be a simple statement, e.g.

"So you're saying that you don't really care whether Betty is your friend or not any more..."

"I'm hearing you say that you want to swap Spanish for Drama, give up RE altogether and then do Tai Kwon Do after school on Tuesdays."

Used simply like this, clarifying is an effective way to respond to some of the answers we'll get to our questions without clouding them with our own opinions and thoughts, or sounding like we disagree.

Effective clarifying like this can be delivered as entirely neutral statements. The children may well hear our clarification as if hearing their words for the first time, and it has the same effect as an insightful question might. Here's a possible scenario:

Matt: "When I go into new groups at basketball camp they want us to shout for the ball and I find it difficult to shout to people I don't know. So I just find myself running up and down and waving but they don't always see me so I don't get the ball much and so the coaches took me off the court. Then I come out of the training very frustrated because I haven't showed what I can do."

Dad: "Sounds like you have trouble asserting yourself."

Matt: "Yeah, that's exactly it. With new people anyway. I think I'm quite comfortable with people I know but I want to be more assertive with new groups too. But in a good way or they might think I'm too cocky."

Dad: "So you're saying that assertiveness can be misread as cockiness."

Matt: "Yeah, you're right. They're completely different things, aren't they? Thanks. So I need to just be the same with new groups as I am with people I already know. I'll try that next weekend."

Here Dad has simply used strong clarifying statements to Matt, introducing the idea of 'assertiveness' which resonates well with Matt. Then he simplifies the key points of Matt's next thought into two connected ideas. Although he hasn't now introduced anything that Matt hadn't already mentioned, a lightbulb goes on for Matt as he hears his previous words played back to him with a different slant, and he immediately knows what to do. This is a prime example of a parent not needing to make sense of a situation on behalf of the child - all he needs to do is to listen well and feedback the words or the sense of the words. It would be so easy to listen at Level Three and give advice: e.g.

Matt: "When I go into new groups at basketball camp they want us to shout for the ball and I find it difficult to shout to people I don't know. So I just find myself running up and down and waving but they don't always see me so I don't get the ball much and so the coaches took me off the court. Then I come out of the training very frustrated because I haven't showed what I can do."

Dad: "Hey, just shout more then, you'll soon get the hang of it."

Matt has now had no opportunity to examine his motivations or fears and does not 'own' his actions.

Used adeptly, clarifying statements create the same breakthroughs as well-crafted insightful questions.

used adeptly, clarifying statements create the same breakthroughs as well-crafted insightful questions

Reflecting

Reflecting, sometimes called 'mirroring' or 'parroting' means repeating someone's words back to them exactly. This has a number of advantages to a coaching conversation:

- it obviously shows we are listening;
- it affirms that what we have heard is acceptable and validates it;
- it ensures that both parties have heard and understood – people gain clarity from hearing their own voices and hearing their words repeated back;
- it moves the conversation forward.

Jeannie: "Mum, I'm quitting my Saturday job."

Mum: "You're quitting your Saturday job."

Jeannie: "My Saturday job's chaos!"

Mum: "Chaos?"

Jeannie: "It's mad."

Mum: "Ah, not chaos - mad, then."

Jeannie: "I don't think I'm going to go back this Saturday. The warehouse supervisor's really mean and can't control us. It's embarrassing!"

Mum: "She's really mean and can't control you..."

Jeannie: "Well, she can control us, but she shouts a lot and just loses her temper."

Mum: "OK, so she can control you, but she shouts and loses her temper."

Jeannie: "Yeah. I mean, there are a lot of us in the warehouse, so it's not that easy, probably, but she doesn't have to shout."

Mum: "So there are a lot of you, and it's probably not that easy, you say."

Jeannie: "Yeah. I suppose..."

Mum: "You suppose...?"

Jeannie: "Well I suppose we do all play her up a bit, too."

Mum: "I see. So you all play her up a bit."

Jeannie: "Well she can bring it on herself. It's funny watching her...well, I suppose it's not that funny for her looking for us when they phone from the shop floor for some more stock and we've all slipped into hiding places so she can't find us."

Mum: "So you're all hiding."

Jeannie: "Yeah, thinking about it, I suppose we don't make it that easy for her really. Which is probably why she loses it and shouts. I mean it's not a bad job apart from that. Maybe I should talk to the other girls. She probably feels a bit isolated from us really... I think she's just a bit young for that role, she's not much older than us, so it can't be that easy. I wouldn't like to be in her job, not having to manage all of us anyway."

by standing back from the detail and replaying children's words back to them, children can hear the meaning and effect of their words, and can rationalise them themselves

This seasoned, wise Mum has long ago realised that by just standing back from the detail and replaying her daughters words to her, her daughter can hear the meaning and effect of her words, and can rationalise them herself. Reflecting back the exact words, particularly the highly-charged and emotional words, allows Jeannie to hear herself as if she was going to give her opinion on someone else. Since she is now that 'someone else' she can tone down her own emotions and impetuosity and instead, change her outlook on her situation.

Her Mum never once asks her a new question, although she does reflect back some words or phrases with a quizzical emphasis, e.g. ***"Chaos?"*** and "***You suppose...***" It's the equivalent of raising one eyebrow in a melodramatic fashion. (I've never managed to do this so I have to push an eyebrow up with my finger when I want to do some quizzical, melodramatic reflecting). Or just raise the ***tonality and pitch*** at the end of the phrase. (Like Australians seem to do naturally at the end of just about any sentence, though we won't hold that against them).

A key point to remember is to 'keep it light,' particularly when reflecting energy words and emotions. Parent-coaches are reluctant to accept their children's 'hard luck stories' at face value very often. We prefer to challenge those stories to see whether the storyteller can locate new details and observations around the central characters, and then create a new, happier ending.

For that reason, just as clarifying can create insight, reflecting can be employed in place of a provocative question. It works well when we hear our child make some sort of negative assumption or generalisation too, e.g.

"I suck at maths,"

"Everyone always picks on me,"

"I'll never get picked for the hockey team."

In these situations, reflection can come into its own. Far from trying to negate the child's assumption, we reflect it back, again, often with a slightly playful or amused intonation:

*"I see. So you **suck** at maths."*

*"Ah. **Everyone. Always** picks on you, do they?"*

*"Does one perhaps hear that one assumes **one** will **never** get picked for **one's** hockey team?"*

We can be playful with the theme, as Jeannie's Mum did above, and of course we can always revert to the tried and tested Listening Levels Four and Five at any time;

"Tell me more about sucking at maths,"

"When you say, 'everyone,' who are you talking about specifically?"

"So, what sort of person does get picked for the hockey team?"

And then we are off and running. Reflection often creates the most effective platform from which to start a coaching conversation, because there is no overt contradiction in the parent-coach's reply.

It is all too easy to tell the child:

"Of course you don't. That's nonsense. You're great at maths. Why would you say you suck at it?"

"Not true. Not everyone picks on you. Maybe some people, but that's their problem. Just keep out of their way."

"You can play for whatever team you want, you're a great athlete. It's their loss if they don't pick you."

But in all cases, what the child hears first of all is, ***"You're wrong,"*** or ***"I don't believe you."***

Intuitive and wise use of reflection, particularly when blended with other strong, open questions, can completely transform a child's viewpoint, ***and*** give it ownership of its new set of assumptions. Sprinkle liberally into all conversations and watch the child explore.

THE GROW COACHING MODEL

What is it and how can it be used to best effect by parents?

Experienced coaches know where they are in their coaching conversations at any given moment. They know how much time is left till the end of the allotted session, they know what type of question they are asking, what the purpose of each question is and how to concoct a new question from any response. To an unpractised observer, a skilful coach can hold seemingly seamless and simple conversations, and yet, under scrutiny, we would discover they are highly structured and purposeful.

Models abound in communication skills particularly, as they do in all areas of personal development. When applied to coaching they provide a framework for designated, timed sessions, conversations, or meetings. They enable us to keep moving forwards, towards positive solutions and achievements. They are mostly acronyms, (frequently audacious, naturally - so those of mine that are dotted around this book should fit right in) and, in far too many cases, easily forgettable.

However, there is one that has robustly stood the test of time. The most famous model of coaching communication is known as The GROW Model. It is unique in that it is:

a) very memorable
b) decidedly ***not*** audacious
c) apposite to coaching
d) simple
e) the grand-daddy of all coaching models and acronyms that have followed

There are many models which have been created to attempt to update and modernise GROW, which after all has probably celebrated at least thirty years of keeping coaching conversations in line by now. However, in my opinion, GROW doesn't need updating, nor modernising. It is still as robust as ever, and everybody I have ever worked with using GROW, remembers it and can use it.

So GROW, then. What is it all about? The GROW model was first published and popularised by Sir John Whitmore in his book 'Coaching for Performance.' He generously attributes its creation to a discussion between several coaches of whom he was one, in the offices of a global management consulting firm, McKinsey's, in London and it has been in the public domain ever since.

Whitmore talks about the four main strands to a coaching conversation:

1) Goal or **'G'** questions: finding out what a person's goals might look like
2) Reality or **'R'** questions: finding out what's happening currently around that subject

3) Options or **'O'** questions: finding out what actions might move a person towards their goal
4) Will or **'W'** questions: finding out how committed that person is to complete those actions

In a normal conversation with, say, one's daughter, there are often only Reality and Options strands in evidence. The 'O' strands appear almost immediately, i.e.

Mum: "Hi, Jen. How are you, and how's school going?" 'R'

Jen: "I'm OK. School's OK too although Mrs Styles keeps picking on me for no real reason." 'R'

Mum: "Oh, that sounds a bit unfair. Why don't you have a word with her?" 'O'

Jen: "I did, that's when she told me I was being rude and gave me the detention. I hate this school - I want to leave!" 'R'

Mum: "Well, you can answer back a little too smartly from time to time, sweetie. Are you sure you weren't being just a little cheeky to her? Maybe you should apologise?" 'R' 'O'

Jen: "I knew you'd take her side. There's no point talking to you, you never believe me either!" 'R' 'O'

This is so typical of a conversation where a parent fully intended to be empathetic and helpful. As a parent this is a totally natural and understandable inclination. We love our children, we care what happens to them, we are attached to their development and we are interested to hear about their life. Of course we are. These are primary roles of parents. Love, nurture, protect, educate. All of a parent's actions, questions and support can naturally originate from this backdrop.

Now a coach doesn't have (or doesn't show) emotional concern for the coachee in the way that a parent does. However, whether a parent or not, any person assuming the mantle of coach must understand the ***concept of detachment*** from the child's story, or crisis, or drama, or ambition. To do so is to fulfil a primary role of a coach.

First and foremost, the parent-coaches view their child through the ubiquitous TOPCAT filter. (Remember our Totally Outstanding Person Capable of Amazing Things?) And TOPCATs have all the required answers they need within themselves already. By believing that all the required wisdom, resources, knowledge and motivation already resides within the totally outstanding child, the parent-coach will find the appropriate questions.

So, we are going to revisit the conversation above between Mum and her daughter Jen. Let's identify other structural aspects of the exchange too, which, incidentally, contribute mostly negatively to the outcome:

many people, surprisingly, have never considered that there might be a flexible and productive structure within a conversation, nor that this structure can be learned and re-created for any situation

Mum: "Hi, Jen. How are you, and how's school going?" **'R'**

Jen: "I'm OK. School's OK too although Mrs Styles keeps picking on me for no real reason." **'R' [and Hard Luck Story.]**

Mum: "Oh, that sounds a bit unfair. **[Judgment - taking daughter's side and validating the Hard Luck Story.]** Why don't you have a word with her?" **'O' [and Level Three Listening - offering advice in the form of a Leading Question without being asked and without asking permission.]**

Jen: "I did, that's when she told me I was being rude and gave me the detention. I hate this school - I want to leave!" **'R' [and Hard Luck Story.]**

Mum: "Well, you can answer back a little too smartly, from time to time, sweetie. **'R' [and Blame - and taking the other side this time.]** Are you sure you weren't being just a little cheeky to her? **'R' [and Judgment.]** Maybe you should apologise?" **'O' [and Level Three Listening - offering advice in the form of a Leading Question without being asked and without asking permission.]**

Jen: "I knew you'd take her side. There's no point talking to you, you never believe me either!" **'R' [and New Hard Luck Story.]**

once children know us as parent-coaches they start seeking us out in order to be asked strong, structures questions and to be challenged. They prefer this to being given advice

Before highlighting a GROW coaching conversation, let's familiarise ourselves with each strand and its purpose. Many people, surprisingly, have never considered that there might be a flexible and productive structure within a conversation that can be useful in moving someone towards a goal, and more: that ***this structure can be learned and re-created for any situation.***

I am constantly amazed, during every workshop, that already wonderful communicators - teachers, parents, priests, enlightened managers, good friends - had never considered how their words could be re-structured to be of more use to others. They had never considered putting their questions into categories before. When they do, their conversations are often transformed quite literally ***overnight.***

Whereas 'chatting' and other 'normal' conversations tend to centre around 'R' and 'O' questions, coaching conversations tend to employ 'G' (Goal) questions early on. The purpose of a coaching conversation, as we now know, is simply to be ***useful*** to the other person, so little time is spent on chit-chat. (NOTE - my definition of 'chit-chat,' using coaching terminology, is ***'R' and 'O' questions coupled with Level One, Two Three Listening***).

Once children know us as a parent-coach, however, they start seeking us out in order to be asked strong, structured, effective questions. They come to know we will not indulge them in their problems; rather we will challenge them.

While we are wearing our 'coaching hat,' that challenge aspect is another of our primary roles. When we decide to take off this 'hat' and wear a 'friend hat' or 'parent hat,' we can go back to chit-chat, attachment, empathising, helping, 'shooting the breeze,' and, in all other ways, getting involved with their drama, dilemma or goal from the inside. Otherwise, with our 'coaching hat' on, we must stay on the outside. It's never easy for parents to make this transition one hundred per cent, and many argue it is just not practical or indeed possible to disengage our own agenda from our children's. They are just too intertwined.

When children declare themselves 'stuck,' parent-coaches must wean themselves away from giving advice as a first resort

Maybe, maybe not. You can decide that one and wear as many hats as you feel you need to, simultaneously or interchangeably.

Now, let's break down the GROW model into manageable chunks.

Goal ('G') Questions

So, starting with 'G' questions allows our children to identify what they want to achieve and put them on the path to achieving it. 'G' questions allow the children to focus on the solution rather than the problem. Once we feel more familiar with 'G' questions, we can refer to them at the beginning of each coaching session and continue to defer to them again anytime to keep the focus moving forward, especially if the child becomes stuck.

Here's a strong 'recommendation' (although of course, I'm not attached to it): When children declare themselves 'stuck,' parent-coaches must wean themselves away from giving advice as a first resort. Instead, ask some 'G' and 'R' questions and with patience our children will 'unstick' themselves, and learn that they can do this any time they choose.

There are many Goal questions to help you later in this Chapter.

Reality ('R') Questions

These allow an exploration of the children's current reality, or what is happening at the moment in their lives, that concerns their goal. It is essential to spend a good portion of time asking 'R' questions (often up to ***seventy-five per cent*** of our agreed coaching time), so that the children can find out what needs to be placed on the coaching table for scrutiny. Once the children have everything in view, they will perceive greater clarity and different perspectives, so that ideas will occur naturally on how to move forward.

There are many Reality questions to help you later in this Chapter.

The theory behind asking 'R' questions to enable someone to get clarity on their situation, came from Tim Gallwey, a tennis coach over many years and now considered to be a pioneer of modern day coaching. He is the author of the pioneering book 'The Inner Game.'

One of his key discoveries was that if he asked tennis students to 'watch the ball' or 'hold your racquet in a grip like this,' they would often tense up and under-perform. However, if he asked them more peripheral questions, like counting how many times the ball spun as it went over the net, or by how many centimetres the ball cleared the net, their shots improved significantly.

exploring 'peripherals' thoroughly is central to good coaching practice

Neither of these measurements mattered in terms of his students' tennis techniques, but ***the process of dissecting the reality of what was happening with each shot*** resulted in the tennis player forgetting to 'watch the ball' or 'check their grip' and they tapped instead into their non-rational mind, ***harnessing their intuition***. Their minds then were now ***naturally making decisions*** about speed, positioning, angles, spaces and so on.

In the same way, our peripheral ***'what is happening'*** ('R' coaching questions) are the equivalent of Gallwey's peripheral questions to his students, but applied to our own children's work, activities or lives.

Exploring 'peripherals' thoroughly is central to good coaching practice. It is this present-tense part that is usually missing from every day conversation. We tend to go straight from the past to the future options. For instance, Jen's earlier diatribe went from:

"My teacher told me I was being rude and gave me a detention." (Past tense)

to:

"I hate this school - I want to leave!" (Future tense)

All this achieves is to take the emotional baggage of the past into decisions about the future. Current Reality questions and Goal questions, (which can also be thought of as 'Future Reality' questions) enable children to step away from their emotional track and move forward from a place of greater perspective - the ***Present Tense*** - what is *really* happening *right now*.

The awareness delivered by the initial 'Reality' questions helps children to focus their energy where it will be most beneficial during the Options and Will stages. Parent-coaches can help their children enormously by staying out of the drama and placing the child back firmly in the present to get a more useful overview.

It feels awkward at first to deeply explore current reality, and new parent-coaches tend to fall back on questions about the past or start offering solutions instead, going straight to the Options ('O') stage of GROW. Until the Reality questions become automatic, which they will in a short time with practice, it pays to keep a list close by while coaching to ensure we have asked enough before moving on to 'Options'. I have provided a 'cheat sheet' of all four sections of GROW questions later in this chapter.

If at first we are finding it difficult to follow the conversation ***and*** find spontaneous, pertinent Reality questions, we can allow ourselves to 'cheat' from those questions from time to time. While children are engrossed in this 'R' phase of the coaching, it sometimes may not matter which questions we ask, just as it does not matter how many times the tennis ball spins, or by what margin it goes over the net. What we are doing is getting the children to focus on their issues from different angles. Each new angle will release awareness and insight, emerging self-knowledge and creative energy that will lead naturally into Options and Actions. In time and with practice, our Reality questions will become pertinent and natural.

All these questions help children learn how to dig deeper into their own awareness. Eventually they will hit a bed-rock of understanding and gain an insight they did not have before. They will show signs of energy, for instance, lightness in the voice, brighter eyes, a smile and more upright posture. That is the time to ask them about Options and they will often have started coming up with some already.

If the children genuinely have come to the end of their thoughts for potential actions, this is the time when parent-coaches may offer any appropriate suggestions of our own to their list

Note that we are exploring the present, and although we may ask what someone has done so far, we are not dwelling on the past or listening to hard-luck stories about it. We are focusing on what the situation means to the child more than on the facts. We are not asking questions to find out what has happened, but more, to find out what impact it may be having on the child's work and/or life. When the child reaches a new insight or level of understanding, it is wise to explore that new Reality to embed all new awareness and then to revisit the Goal. Possibly a new Goal or direction will emerge. Then the 'Reality' questions can start all over again.

Options ('O') Questions

Children will move naturally towards the Options stage as their Reality becomes clearer. If they seem to be stuck and are going over old ground, ask them to re-explore their Reality and Goals, always moving the focus forward to break new ground. By continually referring to the Goal or asking some Goal questions, e.g.

"So knowing this now, how does this help you move towards your goal?"

and similar questions, to tap into their 'Future Reality.' This helps to formulate new Options for actions.

There is a distinction to be made here: Options are ***not,*** in themselves, Actions. They are merely ***potential choices*** for actions to eventually be taken by the child. Options only metamorphose into Actions when the child ***commits to do them***, (at the 'W' stage of the conversation), so keep pushing for a wider and wider choice of Options.

Notice that 'O' questions are almost always ***open*** questions. Keep asking open 'O' questions until the children have exhausted all their thoughts. Once it seems that the list may be complete, ask the closed question, ***'Is there anything else?'*** to find out whether it is time to finalise the process and move on to 'W.' This question often results in new Options and can be asked as many times as it continues to deliver results. If the children genuinely have come to the end of their thoughts for potential actions, this is the time when parent-coaches may offer any appropriate suggestions of our own to their list.

Will ('W') Questions

The 'Will' strands of a coaching conversation cover what actions children ***will*** take and ***when*** they ***will*** take them. It is termed 'Will' rather than 'Action' to stress that we must ensure that the chosen actions now are ones the child can really commit to. And of course to ensure that the acronym spells GROW, since GROA would be a little disappointing for such a robust and classic communication model, (especially if we added Now on the end...)

The reason for insisting that children come up with a long list of potential actions in the 'O' phase is simple. We do this so that in the 'W' phase children can prioritise their options in such a way as to create the best possible chance of achieving them and creating strong foundations for their goals. If parent-coaches do **NOT** push for this long list, and simply accept the first option the child mentioned, there is a strong possibility that the child may only attempt the 'safe, comfortable' actions, and a huge opportunity for 'stretching' the child's comfort zones is lost.

The aim of the parent-coach is always to make the actions as accessible as possibe for the child, so once a list of actions has been chosen, the coach will ask a number of questions like, ***"What will you need to make happen before you can do that?"*** and get the child to write that answer down as an action too. There are many Will questions to help you later in this Chapter.

Here is an example we can follow through. A teenager is organising a sponsored swim event, and one of this week's ***options*** (NOTE - it is not yet an ***action***) has been agreed identified as ***"Call to make sure the Sports Centre has enough facilities for one hundred swimmers."***

By asking **'W'** questions to obtain commitment and planning, such as:

"What will you need to do, in order to find this out?"
"What needs to happen first?"
"Is there anything which will get in the way of doing this?"
"What is the timeline for these actions?"
"When will you do that?"
"Are you happy to do all this in one week?"

...and so on, the teenager can now understand that the initial option which seemed like nothing more complex than a phone call may, in fact, break down into a longer list of smaller options. He can arrange these in priority order and name the date and time he will approach each one - now they have become an Action List, rather than options to choose from, e.g.

Make a list of questions to ask the facilities manager. ***(Tuesday lunchtime)***
Find the Sports Hall Reception phone number ***(Tuesday evening)***
Call and ask for the name of the facilities manager. ***(Tuesday evening)***
Make an appointment to talk with the facilities manager ***(Tuesday evening)***
Call the facilities manager and ask questions from list ***(When manager is available)***
Ask to arrange visit to meet facilities manager at the sports centre to view facilities ***(during phone call with manager)***
Make a list of requirements to check at sports centre ***(Friday after school)***
Finish all weekend homework ***(Friday night and maybe Sunday evening if needed)***
Visit sports centre to meet facilities manager Saturday or Sunday ***(depending on manager's availability)***
Ask any questions and check facilities against requirements list ***(during visit)***

So now although there is a much longer list, he can more easily tick them off sequentially, which is satisfying in itself and since there are time slots attached to each action, there is a better chance that he will think to organise his time during the coming week. We will notice that there is a greater acceptance of ***closed*** questions from the parent-coach in the 'W' phase, which is intentional and designed to really test the commitment and planning.

Asking 'W' questions to cement the commitment to these actions is essential - otherwise, when the young man calls or visits the sports centre without considering the accompanying sequence of actions, he may well meet with disappointment, if the sports centre is closed that day, the manager is unavailable, requirements are forgotten about and further calls or visits are needed and so on.

When the time comes to review the initial (complex) option with a parent-coach, he may well have become demoralised because he has not been encouraged to cover all possible bases. Maybe, for example, he had not remembered a big homework project due in that week or a geography field trip taking up most of the weekend. Asking appropriate 'R' questions can also help here, i.e. ***"What might get in the way of completing this action this week?"***

The opposite is true where all the bases have been identified and times have been checked. The young man can now be far more confident that he will be able to fully complete this necessary stage in one week, leaving him well placed to begin a new set of actions the following week. There will be no 'hangover' from unfinished business from the previous week and he will be understanding the necessity of sequential organisation and contingency planning.

Who wouldn't be proud to have a child like that? And he came to all his own conclusions as a result of our well thought-out, patient questions. Which child wouldn't be grateful to have a parent-coach like that too? (Even if they were too cool to actually show it?)

Goal ('G') Questions

What do you want?
In what time frame?
Imagine you are waking up on the day after this has been achieved:
- What does it look like?
- How do you feel?
- What are people saying to you?
- What are the benefits?
- What does a typical day look like?
- What are people saying about you now you have achieved this?
- Who is now in your life?
- What would be different?
- Look back on the journey; how did you get here?
- What will it be like when you become really committed to changing this?
- How do you talk about this achievement now you're living it?
- Who are you now?

How will you know when you have achieved it?
What does success look like for you?
Where are you now and where would you like to be on a scale of 1-10 with this?
How much different would your life be compared to now, with this in it?
In an ideal world what do you really want?
If you knew you absolutely couldn't fail, what would you wish to have in your life?
Can you allow yourself to want more than that?
Is that enough of a stretch for you?
What would be a real stretch for you?
How could you say your goal in a few words?

Reality ('R') Questions

What do you notice about this?
What is happening at the moment?
How important is this to you?
If an ideal situation is 10, what number are you at now?
So if you're at a 4 now, what does 5 look like?
And a 6? (etc)
What impact is this having on you?
What are three key emotions around that?
How do you feel?
Who else is affected?
What have you done so far?
What are you doing that's working towards your goal?
What are you doing that is getting in the way of your goal?
How do you know that is true?
How many...?
How much...?
How often...?
What other perspective could there be?
Where else is this happening?
How can we see if this is a pattern for you?
What themes are you discovering as you describe this?
What habits are forming around this?
What do you notice yourself doing?
What alternative approaches have you tried?
What were the results?
What would it be like if you did that differently?
What does failing mean to you?
What does success mean to you?
What are your beliefs in this area?
What evidence is there to support your beliefs?
How is that habit benefiting/hurting you?
How can you be sure this is working for you?
Would it be OK to ask you a 'drill-down' question?
What resources do you already have?
What could be cultivated further?

When the child reaches a new insight, these and similar 'R' questions are useful:

What do you now know about [it/yourself] that that you didn't before?

What is your insight about that?

What are the most important things you have you learned about [it/yourself] from this?

Where else could you use this in other areas of your life?

What surprised you about yourself when you undertook your actions?

How can this learning be taken to another level?

How do you feel about the fact that you did this?

How do you feel about [....] now you know this?

What is your freshest thinking on this now?

Where can you apply this in other areas of your life?

How can you sustain it?

You can also introduce your own thoughts using permission (sparingly, and only ever at the end of the child's exploration)

Can I give you some feedback on something I've noticed happening?

May I tell you what my intuition is telling me?

(Remember - don't be attached to our feedback, suggestions or intuition. Allow the child to forge its own path from our input).

Options ('O') Questions

What are your options?
What could you do?
What else?
If there were anything else, what would it be?
What has worked in the past?
What has failed in the past that you could revisit?
What steps could you take?
Who could help you with this?
Where could you find out the information?
What might someone else do in your shoes?
Imagine you've achieved your goal; look back on the journey and tell me what you did to get here.
What do you need to do first?
What do you need to do before you can do that?
How do you plan on doing that?
What might be another way?
What more could you do?
How long might it take to do?
What alternative perspectives could be of value?
What would you do next if you couldn't fail?
What would you do next if you weren't afraid of failing?

Will ('W') Questions

What will you do about that?
How committed are you?
What will it take for you to commit?
What could you do to become more committed?
What else you could you do?
How many...?
How much...?
How often...?
How will you..?
When could you...?
Where will you...?
Who will you talk to?
Who could help you with this?
Where will you find that information?
What will you need to do in order to find this out?
What needs to happen first?
Is there anything which will get in the way of doing this?
What is the timeline for these actions?
When will you do that?
Are you happy to do all this in [one week]?
If not, what are you willing to commit to?
How can you apply this new learning/insight as of now?
It sounded like half yes, half maybe, are you really committed to making a change?
Where else in your life can you be taking action rather than waiting for things to happen?
Do you want to write it down as an action?
Can you make a list of people who can help?
What are your instincts telling you to do next?
How could you expand on what you have discovered?
Where can you take a risk instead of playing safe in this goal?

When they haven't completed an action:

When are you going to make these goals your priority?
What are you prepared to do to make this goal happen?
How can you tackle it this week?
What else can you do to make sure you move forward on this?
How can you make sure that the next week is going to be really inspiring for you?
How can you ensure you'll be able to to give it 100%
What is possible if you change this habit?
Is this something you really want to do something about?
What do you need to put aside right now to make this happen?
Are you clear on what you will do this week?
What part of the action will be completed by next week?

* * *

So now we have had a good look at how the GROW model works as a structure in theory, let's compare the conversation our Jen had with her Mum earlier, with a more patient, structured GROW conversation. Initially the conversation sounded like this:

Mum: "Hi, Jen. How are you, and how's school going?" **'R'**

Jen: "I'm OK. School's OK too although Mrs Styles keeps picking on me for no real reason." **'R' [and Hard Luck Story.]**

Mum: "Oh, that sounds a bit unfair. **[Judgment - taking daughter's side and validating the Hard Luck Story.]** Why don't you have a word with her?" **'O' [and Level Three Listening - offering advice in the form of a Leading Question without being asked and without asking permission.]**

Jen: "I did, that's when she told me I was being rude and gave me the detention. I hate this school - I want to leave!" **'R' [and Hard Luck Story.]**

Mum: "Well, you can answer back a little too smartly, from time to time, sweetie. **'R' [and Blame - and taking the other side this time.]** Are you sure you weren't being just a little cheeky to her? **'R' [and Judgment.]** Maybe you should apologise?" **'O' [and Level Three Listening - offering advice in the form of a Leading Question without being asked and without asking permission.]**

Jen: "I knew you'd take her side. There's no point talking to you, you never believe me either!" **'R' [and New Hard Luck Story.]**

Now let's expand it and coach Jen through it using GROW:

Mum: "Hi, Jen. How are you, and how's school going?" **'R'**

Jen: "I'm OK. School's OK too although Mrs Styles keeps picking on me for no real reason." **'R' [and Hard Luck Story.]**

Mum: "So she keeps picking on you for no real reason?" **'R' [and Reflecting.]**

Jen: "Yes, I wasn't doing anything and she picked on me and said I was being rude." **'R' [and Hard Luck Story continues.]**

Mum: "Tell me a bit more about what happened" [**Level Four Listening] - 'R'**

Jen: "Well that was it really, she just said I was being rude and gave me a detention." **'R'**

Mum: "What do you suppose made her think you were being rude?" **'R' [No judgment this time.]**

Jen: "Well, because Cheryl had been pulling faces when Mrs Styles wasn't looking I just laughed out loud once, and she turned round and asked me what I was laughing at, and I said "Nothing really, it was just Cheryl making me laugh," and she said I'd better watch out because people could get the wrong idea when they hear laughter behind their back." **'R'**

Mum: "So what happened then?" **'R'**

Jen: "Well, I said sorry and she said I had better be careful with my attitude." **'R'**

Mum: "So you apologised and she told you, you had an attitude?" **'R' [and Clarifying.]**

Jen: "Yeah, she was really mean." **'R' [and Hard Luck Story.]**

Mum: "Tell me, what would you like to happen here?" **'G' [and ignoring Hard Luck Story.]**

Jen: "Well I just want it back how it was before Cheryl came into our class. And I don't want to do a detention after school. It was Cheryl's fault for making me laugh." **'G' [with half-hearted Hard Luck Story and blame.]**

Mum: So you want it back how it was and it's Cheryl's fault?" **'R' [and Reflecting.]**

Jen: "Well, she's always getting people into trouble but the teachers never see her." **'R' [and blame.]**

Mum: "So you're saying that when Cheryl's around you get into trouble?" **'R' [and Clarifying.]**

Jen: "Well, yeah, actually they do. She always makes me laugh at something and then I get caught and she doesn't." **'R' [and Hard Luck Story.]**

Mum: "It sounds like this isn't the first time that this has happened then?" **'R' [and Clarifying.]**

Jen: "No, there's been a few times this week." **'R'**

Mum: "I see. May I ask you a bit more about Mrs Styles?" **'R' [Level 4 Listening with Permission.]**

Jen: "OK..."

Mum: "Well, you say you want it back how it was. How was it before, exactly?" **'G' and 'R'**

Jen: "Well, we've always got along quite well before." **'R'**

Mum: "May I tell you what I remember?" **[asking Permission]**

Jen: "OK..."

Mum: "I remember you saying you quite liked her at the beginning of term. My experience of her is that she is normally quite supportive of you, and you don't often complain about her like this. Has she treated you like this before?" **'R'**

Jen: "No, it's the first time, although, there was.... oh nothing." **'R'**

Mum: "There was another time?" **'R'**

Jen: "Well, she gave me a warning yesterday when Cheryl was messing about in class." **'R'**

Mum: "So you've already had a warning?" **'R' [and Clarifying with no blame.]**

Jen: "Yeah..."

Mum: "What do you suppose Mrs Styles wants to happen with all this?" **'G'**

Jen: "Nothing. She just wants to teach." **'G'**

Mum: "I imagine you're probably right. So how do you think she feels, having to be interrupted by you and Cheryl a few times this week?" **'R'**

Jen: "OK, fine! So I get the point, but it still doesn't mean I should do a detention." **'R' [and wriggling.]**

Mum: "How do you think you could avoid the detention?" **'G' 'O'**

Jen: "Well you could speak to her and explain. **'O'**

Mum: "OK, that's one possibility. Anything else?" **'O'**

Jen: "Well, Cheryl should really apologise because she's behind it all." **'O'**

Mum: "Right, so I could talk to her and explain, Cheryl could apologise; anything else?" **'O'**

Jen: "Do you want me to say I should talk to her?" **'O'**

Mum: "What's more important is whether you think you should talk to her..." **'O'**

Jen: "Dunno..maybe." **'O'**

Mum: "What do you think would stand you the best chance of avoiding the detention and getting things back to normal?" **'O'**

Jen: "Well, I could talk to her." **'O'**

Mum: "When could you do that?" **'W'**

Jen: "Tomorrow morning at break I suppose." **'O'**

Mum: "You suppose?" **'W' [and Reflecting.]**

Jen: "OK, OK, I will!" **'W'**

Mum: "And what will you say?" **'O' 'W'**

Jen: "I'll just say sorry for interrupting the class and I don't think I deserved a detention for that, but if she wants to give me one then fine!" **'W'**

Mum: "OK, sweetie. That sounds like a plan. Anything else you want to do, or is that it?" **'O'**

Jen: "Well, thinking about it, I'm going to tell Cheryl that I'm not going to sit near her for a while because she's always messing about and distracting me." **'O'**

Mum: "Are you OK to have that conversation with her?" **'W'**

Jen: "Yeah, I don't like falling out with Mrs Styles so I'm not going to mess around in her class anymore." **'W' [and insight.]**

Mum: "Good for you, sweetie. And you talked that through beautifully, I'm really impressed - thank you for staying so calm about it. And I'm sure Mrs Styles will appreciate your apology too." **Appreciation**

when we parent-coaches can notice the structure of our ***own*** conversations, we can start to create strong awareness and responsibility in younger minds too

So now, Jen and her Mum have been able to have a much longer, more detailed conversation about the incident. Mum has managed every time to avoid getting sucked into the Hard Luck Story and blaming, unlike in the first example when she commented, judged the situation, gave advice and took (both) sides.

By staying with 'R' to ascertain some facts and moving to 'G' early on, she is able to switch Jen's focus to explore a little more deeply what the circumstances are and choose a desired outcome. They dance between 'G' and 'R' for most of the conversation before turning to 'O' and then 'W' to commit. When we parent-coaches can notice the structure of our ***own*** conversations in this way, we can start to create strong awareness and responsibility in younger minds too. Witness how the insight seems to pop out easily for Jen right at the end.

NOTE - the components of GROW do not necessarily have to flow in that order - we don't ask all our 'G' questions till they are exhausted, then complete an 'R' section, then 'O' and then 'W'. An effective coaching conversation moves naturally between the elements. A good rule of thumb though is to emphasise 'R' probably more than all the others. Stay in 'G' and 'R' as much as we can – I have earlier suggested up to seventy-five per cent of the time - and generally the 'O' section will emerge by itself when a lot of information and insight has been explored. 'W' evidently comes last.

And it never hurts to wrap up by appreciating the youngsters for their ability to stick to a tricky conversation and see it through, particularly when the outcomes are challenging, like apologising to a teacher or telling home truths to a friend.

Let's familiarise ourselves with the questions in this Chapter and gradually become aware of choosing our responses to family conversations so that the children learn that ***they will be asked questions more than they will be given directions.*** Particularly when they state they don't know what they want, or how to do something; this is the best time to implement GROW.

GROW them and KNOW them.

32.

The Sixth Ladder – The Gift of Coaching Feedback

Feeding back or feeding forward?

This chapter divides roughly in two parts. Well, three actually, if we count my little rant halfway through.

The first section describes traditional thoughts and recognised guidelines for giving feedback. Cannily entitled ***'Section One - Traditional Thoughts and Recognised Guidelines for Giving Feedback,'*** these have been reviewed and finely honed by business educators over many decades and have filtered through into all areas of life, including, quite logically, parenting.

There is much that is well thought out, well considered and useful in this section as we might expect, given the calibre of the contributors. Most people that are exposed to these guidelines and trained in them at work come home to family life at the end of the working day. So please read through at leisure and absorb their principles thoroughly. If we did nothing else but adhere to these guidelines when giving feedback they would serve us well enough.

But, (and there often appears to be a 'but' where feedback is concerned), I'm sure we know where this is leading? Yes of course; to the indisputably superior ***'Section Two - Emotionally Intelligent Feedback. The Way Forward'*** which, when we actually work with it, right through, for the first few times we will probably bounce off the ceilings at its simplicity, grace and power. Indeed, who has ever associated these adjectives with feedback before? So, be patient. Do the legwork and create strong platforms by reading through Section One, first - we will be glad we did, but Section Two - that's where the real growth and development happens.

* * *

SECTION ONE - Traditional Thoughts and Recognised Guidelines for Giving Feedback

Giving and receiving feedback has come to be an integral part of life. In the workplace particularly, managers are highly trained in the theory and practice of giving constructive comments to their team members.

There is a whole etiquette of how and when to give this feedback, depending on the content and gravity of the comments. Let's have a quick overview, and relate this to families.

For example, positive feedback is easy to recognise. Positive Feedback "does what it says on the tin," Feeds back. Positively. For example we might say to our child, ***"You have been working really hard on your French essay, particularly those grammar points. Good for you!"***

Negative feedback however is often more tricky to deliver and many parents think they have to be very diplomatic when doing so. We often find a number of proverbial eggshells appearing under our feet at these moments. For a start we tend to use euphemisms; ***'negative feedback'*** transliterates into ***"learning feedback"*** or ***"developmental feedback"*** or sometimes ***"building feedback"*** or ***"improvement feedback"***.

Many parents have learned to deliver negative feedback by stealth 'between' two pieces of positive feedback in order to lessen any potential demoralising effects; i.e. a child might hear, ***"You have been working really hard on your French essay, particularly those grammar points. Good for you! But..."*** (there's that 'but' again), ***"...I'm not sure you are paying enough attention to putting the accents in all the right places so you're going to lose a few marks there if you're not careful. However, you seem to be making good efforts to remember the vocabulary, so keep it up."***

when listening to positive comments about themselves or their work, children, (adults too), instinctively brace themselves for **'but...'**

This format of giving feedback has become known as, (how to put it more appropriately for our readership), a ***"poo sandwich."*** Good, bad, good. In other words, we spread the negative aspects that we feel we need to comment on, in between two slices of positivity. This has permeated into the way we relay our own opinions on one another's work or behaviour in our families too; we say something general and pleasant, then say ***what we really think they should hear***, then reinforce with a pleasantry or compliment again.

The effect of this is generally that when listening to positive comments about themselves or their work, children, (adults too), instinctively brace themselves for ***'but...'*** We seem to have become conditioned to expect that a negative opinion will follow any positive comments. Which is sad really, since often people give genuine praise without conditions. Listen well, kids. Truly. Many of us parents regularly and sincerely do this, (and it's ***not*** sarcasm, believe it or not).

Parent: "You have been working really hard on your French essay, particularly those grammar points. Good for you!"
Child: "OK...but...?"
Parent: "No, no 'buts.' You've done really well."

Child: "Aren't you going to tell me what I could improve like you normally do?"
Parent: "I don't do that! Do I?"
Child: "Usually."
Parent: "I'm sure I don't. Anyway, no, it's a really good essay...you've done well, I'm just trying to give you positive feedback."
Child: "There must be something to improve."
Parent: "Well, possibly. But I'm..."
Child: "I knew there'd be a 'but.'
Parent: "No, I was going to say, 'but' I'm not looking for mistakes, I'm trying to look for positives. Like you've made a real effort to use more unusual vocabulary, and the spelling's pretty good too."
Child: "Well, that's not going to help me get good marks, is it, if I've made spelling mistakes?"
Parent: "Well one or two, but the real stand-out is your grammar is so much better."
Child: "So what have I spelt wrong?"

So when the child receiving the praise then leaves a pause, and asks for the 'but...?' it can be a deflating experience for the parents too, to have to justify their authentic praise, and work hard to maintain self-belief in the child, who only hears the negatives.

PERMIT ME TO INTERRUPT THIS CHAPTER TO GET SOMETHING OFF MY CHEST...

May I illustrate a parallel with business feedback for a moment? Because I feel that a lot of what is poor about family feedback originates in the harsher world of business.

I ran some training with a company whose sales people were being trained to pitch at Board level. In a role play situation, which I don't relish very much anyway, I and some other coaches were asked to give 'tough' feedback, (by which was meant, 'find fault'). One Hapless Salesman, who I had thought was very impressive in his presentations, was singled out by his real-life sales director, "He's gotten too comfortable – thinks he knows it all," and our instruction was to 'take him down a peg or two'. In fact, the actual words were "Even if you thought he was brilliant, I want him hammered on something."

The implication from this tragically old-school sales director was that sales is a ruthless job and that to be a great salesman, ruthlessness is a quality to be admired. In that environment Ruth was notable by her absence, most definitely persona non grata. Ruth had well and truly left that company's building, long ago.

My question here, as a coach, is how long will Hapless Salesman continue to look for his own innovative, creative solutions in that environment? Everyone needs to work, and most people work hard in their roles and want to do a good job. This Hapless Salesman gave a lot of himself to his company. But to what extent will he continue to offer his energies, intelligence and initiative before his fear of rejection and of 'not being enough' compels him to simply fit in and do what he is told? How long indeed before he decides he is worth more than this treatment suggests and he decides to consider his future at this company and start looking elsewhere?

What parallels are there to an earnest child and an overbearing parent?

An interesting footnote to this sad story of unthinking appraisal techniques, is that this company was already declining in popularity with the powerful City bankers in London and soon afterwards its share price collapsed and the management was sacked.

I am convinced that a large part of the problem with its leadership was this 'tough love' feedback syndrome where giving praise was considered anathema to success. Those neanderthal directors promoted a brutal culture of survival, misguidedly thinking that only the best would rise to the top. Of course the truth was that all the best people left, and only brutal people remained at the top. A 'top' indeed which was significantly compromised by total lack of EQ. No company will survive that for long and this one was no exception.

How often do we focus on the mistake, the negative, the need to improve? Has anyone really taken to heart Ken Blanchard's irresistibly simple maxim from his famous book 'The One Minute Manager?' He urges people to just "Catch people doing something right." How much richer would all our relationships be if we heeded that advice?

Instead, it is an unfortunate indictment of our times that,"May I offer some feedback" has come to be synonymous with, "Can I suggest improvements?" Feedback sessions have become formalised in business and are known variously as Performance Reviews, Appraisals, Personal Development Plans, and so on.

I frequently encounter conversations around these containing an expectation of correction, improvement, judgment, blame or advice.

A number of, no, a majority of people I talk to, at every level of the workplace seem to prepare themselves for this judgment and accept it as a pre-requisite for upward mobility and promotion. It's almost as though they look forward to ascending in the ranks so that they may 'aspire' to become judges and juries over those in the 'lower' orders.

So it's the team leaders and managers upon whom this responsibility falls. How horrendous to have it written into one's job specification that one has to consistently find something one adjudges to be insufficient in the people one works alongside. Not only that, but one is required to identify individualised remedies, insist on their implementation, and follow up to make sure they are having the desired effect.

What enormous pressures. What monumental stresses. What a massively debilitating indoctrination.

Let's follow this through. You've probably guessed where this is leading. All those business leaders are being required to feedback to their teams in that way. Everyone in their teams is expecting to receive feedback in that way. These same leaders and team members then go home in vast numbers as...parents. Who then continue the same judgmental, subjective purveyance of feedback at home because they have been so well trained to do so at work. So who then, might be the final recipients of this avalanche of unsolicited opinion? Ah, that would be our children.

The very same children who then grow up understanding that society rewards those who direct, those who opine, those who judge, those who advise. The very same children who find it almost impossible to establish themselves in this world if they choose, for whatever reasons, not to give advice. The very same children who understandably choose to adopt an advisory, directive nature. The result? Billions of wannabe judges in search of self-eminence. What odds the Age of Aquarius now? What odds the true fellowship of humankind?

Right. That's that exorcism over with. Thanks for listening. Let's get constructive now and take a look at the recognised guidelines for giving and receiving feedback, and see how they can be used to strengthen our family communications.

Feedback Guidelines

1 POSITIVE FEEDBACK	2 ALL FEEDBACK
• As often as deserved • Be authentic • In public, with caution • Tell other people	• Immediately • Direct to the child • Be specific • From I
3 LEARNING FEEDBACK	**4 RECEIVING FEEDBACK**
• For learning not blame • In private • Focus on the positive • About behaviour, not general	• Thank you • No feedback on feedback • Ask for more detail

Reproduced with kind permission of Carol Wilson

GUIDELINES FOR *'GIFTING'* ALL TYPES OF FEEDBACK

don't praise a dog for what it did yesterday

It is considered good practice to deliver feedback of all kinds, whether positive or negative, as ***immediately*** as we can. The closer we can relate the feedback to the actual action the easier it is to make associations, particularly where further action is required. We don't praise a dog for what it did yesterday, it would be meaningless to the poor mutt.

Deliver it ***directly to the person*** concerned, and tell them ***specifically*** what it was that we liked. And ***'own'*** the feedback, i.e. state ***"I think..."*** rather than ***"Everyone here thinks..."*** This makes it more powerful and energised. Of course, if it's a positive feedback and we ***know*** we are speaking on behalf of everyone, by all means say so, ***and*** encourage the others to demonstrate their admiration too, but personally and individually, rather than just group applause.

A former boss of mine had obviously not kept abreast with the latest management guidelines on favourable feedback techniques. Back in the day, when I was fresh out of university, I worked in a translation agency, and he used to make a habit of doing the rounds of the offices, doling out unspecific, random (and often wholly undeserved) compliments. At ten minutes to five, more or less every afternoon he would appear and make cheerful comments to everyone and no-one in particular, to fulfil what he deemed to be motivational behaviour. It amounted to nothing less than a ***feedback frenzy***. We could almost set our watches by "Bernard's Build-ups" as they came to be known.

GUIDELINES FOR '*GIFTING*' POSITIVE FEEDBACK

Where it's positive, give it ***as often as deserved***, not all the time and make sure it's ***genuine and authentic***. So much well-intended feedback is wasted because it is overplayed and general. How many of us overuse words like "Excellent!" "Fabulous!" "Brilliant!" and think we are being motivational?

Most children glow when they receive positive feedback in front of others, so ***deliver it publicly*** if we know the child will appreciate it. Some children though, do have an aversion to being singled out, and can get teased by jealous pals if they are praised too highly or too often, but we will know our children best. And again, most children are thrilled that we will ***let someone else know*** about their triumphs. In my younger days it was always enough if someone validated my efforts to one of my grandparents or my teacher. Currently the nirvana of recognition is to be applauded on social media networks, though this too will likely change again as new media become fashionable.

So the following positive feedback ticks pretty much all the above guideline boxes:

" Super team effort everyone and I think that free-kick goal Andrew pulled off in the match just now was phenomenal, wasn't it? Andrew, how did you make the ball bend so much? You have obviously put in a lot of time developing that - you'll have to give us a masterclass to show us how you did that! I've got the whole match on film too, so I'm going to upload it to Facebook and you can all watch it again!"

This one doesn't:

"Good match everyone - some good shots there from some of you, too. Still work to do though, right - hit the changing rooms!"

GUIDELINES FOR '*GIFTING*' NEGATIVE FEEDBACK

Where feedback is more centred around doing things differently - in other words, *'developmental'* or *'learning'* feedback - the received wisdom is still to apply the etiquette from the "ALL FEEDBACK" box above, and then a few more besides. For example, we are encouraged to give the feedback in such a way as to promote ***learning and not blame*** and make it ***about people's behaviour or work*** rather than a criticism or observation about them personally. So,

"Charlie, I personally think your diagrams need to be in colour rather than black and white,"

is more constructive than

"Charlie, you obviously have no idea how to present your geography coursework, do you?"

Give this form of feedback ***in private***. There is nothing more demoralising than being criticised in public, so see whether we can include ***some aspect of positivity*** with our observations:

"Celia, just while no one else is listening, can I say that normally you take such pride in decorating your cakes? This one seems to me to be a bit more rushed than usual - what do you think?"

is likely to be better received than

"Hey everyone, have you seen this weird blob that Celia has just cooked?"

GUIDELINES FOR RECEIVING FEEDBACK

And finally, there is the challenge of how best to ***receive*** feedback. As we have seen, feedback may be positively or negatively slanted, and children can have difficulties accepting both types. The most important thing to try to remember is to say ***"Thank you"*** when feedback is offered. Regardless of whether the feedback is welcome or unwelcome, encourage children to learn to see it as a well-intentioned gift. What they then do with that gift is entirely up to them.

Imagine a great-aunt has knitted a brightly coloured, stripey woollen cardigan and she presents it to her nephew Charlie, beautifully and lovingly wrapped on our birthday. What would he *always* say? (Apologies for asking such a leading question - of course the answer I am anticipating is) ***"Thank you Auntie!"*** It's a gift; considered, created and delivered ceremoniously. So if it's a gift, it's his to do with as he wishes. He hs a number of choices. He can:

- ***wear it because he likes it***
- ***wear it when his great-aunt is around***
- ***put it in a drawer***
- ***wear it for a seventies costume party***
- ***sell it on e-Bay***
- ***give it to a charity shop***

But whatever his eventual intention, he would certainly have thanked her for it, courteously, I'm sure. As any of us would.

Feedback is that very same cardigan - a gift. Considered, created and delivered ceremoniously. So thank the '*gifter*' of the feedback and assume ownership immediately. My usual phrase is, ***"Thanks for that, I'll bear it in mind."*** And I'm as good as my words; I do bear it mind, although I may well have already decided how I will treat the feedback I've been '*gifted*.'

May I offer a brand new verb to accompany feedback? You may have noticed it creeping in above. From now on I'd like to hear that feedback is being ***'gifted'*** rather than 'given.' Let's promote this idea that feedback is a present, a gift. This is one way of circumventing the notion of judgement that is currently implicit in so much of it.

Let's pick up our earlier scenario where someone kindly commented on the fact that they believed Charlie's diagrams would better serve his geography document if he had used some colour. His initial response, as mentioned earlier, might feasibly be to immediately 'own' the feedback. He may say something along the lines of, ***"Thanks, I'll bear it in mind,"*** and then (in parallel with those cardigan choices) he can:

- ***add colour if he think it will enhance it,***
- ***add colour only when that person is likely to read his documents,***
- ***store the idea away for later,***
- ***create the loudest and most overly colourful diagrammed document ever next time to make a point,***
- ***seek other people's opinions***
- ***reject the idea and continue in black and white.***

The point is the feedback (like the cardigan from his great-aunt) has been given to Charlie. Sorry, ***gifted*** to Charlie. It's now his. He *owns* it. Therefore, legitimately he can do with it as he wishes. The difficulty comes when the feedback is not gifted as an unconditional suggestion, but rather with strings attached. Now it's actually an ***instruction***, an ***order*** or at least a ***recommendation***. How many of us receive these comments *"disguised"* as suggestions from parents, bosses, friends? How many of us *deliver* these comments disguised as suggestions come to that?

The next time we gift some feedback, be clear as to what it really represents. Ask ourselves, how attached are we to the child actually carrying out our "suggestion?" Because where there is confusion over our motive for delivering the feedback, there is normally a push-back from the child.

This can lead to the child having an opinion on our feedback, i.e. ***"I don't agree, I think my diagrams look perfectly good in black and white,"*** and we may find ourselves defending our feedback more vehemently that we had anticipated. So giving ***feedback on feedback*** can result in a ***feedback fight*** which is very unedifying for all and preferably to be avoided.

We can always though, ***ask for more detail*** on the feedback. Nothing wrong there. Simply asking, perhaps with permission...

"May I ask you to expand on that. What specifically do you think would be the benefit of adding colour? And what colours would you suggest?"

...can trigger an open discussion from which Charlie can take whatever he chooses once again from the ensuing ideas.

SECTION TWO - Emotionally Intelligent Feedback. The Way Forward.

OK, hands up. Who has turned directly to this page from the Permission Chapter, ignoring my suggestion to stay on schedule? Of course we are perfectly at liberty to ignore it, it was after all only a suggestion and I have to remain detached from it (or it becomes a 'command in disguise'). Which I can't enforce anyway even if I was of a mind to do so. However, regardless - we are here now, and this is a really exciting moment in the unfolding applications of our coaching skills! Enjoy it.

in a true coaching culture, the term 'negative feedback' is not strictly appropriate as all feedback tends to be received as a useful and positive part of the learning experience

So in short, Coaching Feedback involves asking people to gift ***themselves*** feedback instead of, or before, gifting one's own. What a radical concept, eh? It applies both to positive feedback and what has come to be termed 'learning' or 'building' feedback. (In a true coaching culture, the term 'negative feedback' is not strictly appropriate as all feedback tends to be received as a useful and positive part of the learning experience).

This technique applies to every conversation that seeks to explore a child's behaviour, homework effort, sporting or theatrical performance, fundraising attempt or indeed action of any kind. Applied to adults in similar business situations, I have used it and seen it used in appraisals, performance reviews, exit strategies (a.k.a. firing someone) or any situation where people are being asked to reflect on their personal performance and behaviour.

Here it is. Blink and we'll miss it. Can this simple sequence really live up to this huge expectation? Let's explore and evaluate for ourselves shall we?

The significance of each question lies in its purpose, rather than in the actual words used. Most of the questions are not chronological and could be mixed into a different order, although in coaching it is always useful to start with a future focused question and end with a plan of action. Just using them in this exact sequence though is usually hugely empowering and always appreciated.

All these questions are generic and can be expanded according to the response received and the time available. Asked exactly as they appear here, and receiving even the most sparse replies may only take around five minutes, but will still yield strong insights, trust and reflections. They are guidelines to any number of performance areas needing exploration, and can be modified to suit a particular context, vernacular or style of communication. Let's examine these questions in more detail one by one.

Q1) What did you notice about doing this [performance/ behaviour/ activity]?
Q2) What did you like about [what you did]?
Q3) May I tell you what I liked?
Q4) When you do this or something similar next time, what might you do differently?
Q5) And when you can do it like that, how would it be for you then?
Q6) Would it be useful if I made a (couple of) suggestion(s)?
Q7) Knowing all these things now, how might you use them in [other areas]?

A quick permission pitstop and we'll be away.

It's always a good idea to ask permission before venturing out into open opinion country. So; ***"Would it be OK to talk about your [performance/activity] for a few minutes?"*** is a good opener to a child. Remember to wait for permission to be granted. If it is, continue with Q1. If it is not, ask ***"OK, when would be a good time for you?"*** And assuming we can both pin down an appropriate time, we can then continue too with Q1.

Here's that Q1.

Q1. What did you notice about doing this [performance/behaviour/activity?]

This, like all the questions in this sequence has been carefully worded. Asking *"What did you **think** about your performance?"* is a slightly different emphasis and invites judgement and self-critique, which in turn tends to put people on the defensive. *"What did you **notice...**?"* is a more neutral question requesting information rather than assessment. This can be re-phrased to suit the context of any situation, and if, appropriate, expanded with several further questions, such as:

"What was your experience of [that]?"
"What is happening at the moment?"
"What have you done so far?"
"How do you view what you've achieved?"
"How do you suppose others view what you've achieved?"

Even if neutral questions like these are asked, people still have a tendency to answer by describing ***what went wrong***. We have seen how children associate 'feedback' with 'things to improve.' This feedback exercise is designed to get our children to understand that it is important that they recognise their strengths as much as their weaknesses. They may not feel comfortable 'blowing their own trumpets' at first but we will continue to encourage them to notice their strengths. And if they struggle with this, we can ask them more directly using Q2.

Q2. What did you like about [what you did]?

As the children come to understand that we are happy for them to confidently express their strengths, they soon start their replies to Q1 with what is going well too. In these cases we can ask more expansive questions such as:

"What specifically do you see as your strengths?"
"What are you enjoying about this?"
"What difficulties are you experiencing?"
"How are you overcoming these challenges?"
"What have you achieved so far?"
"What does knowing that you can do this tell you about yourself?"

Another scenario that occurs often in response to Q1 and Q2 is where children reply by talking about failures, and in particular, that the failures were all someone else's fault. In this case we can make the questions more personal, and include some based on Q4 in the sequence:

"What was your own contribution to the success/failure of the project?"

"What might you personally have done differently that would have produced a different result?"

We are now approaching the time for Q3. Regardless of the scenarios we may have encountered so far, make sure we arrive at this Q3 ***after having asked*** Q1 and Q2. It is essential we **do not *start* with this question** - we must allow the child to access and express its strengths and awarenesses ***first. So here comes Q3.***

Q3. May I tell you what I liked?

Perfection! I love this question. It is a model of 'coachingness.' More, I find that this question is nearly always unexpected by the child. And although I ask it with permission I have never met with a refusal and would be amazed if I did. Children are curious; not least at this very point in the coaching feedback sequence. At this point, after baring their souls at Q2, they are expecting to hear an inevitable ***'Yes, but...'*** - that criticism that they have become so accustomed to hearing from parents and friends.

Children are not the only human beings who can tend to dwell on what went wrong, forgetting their accomplishments. How often have we ourselves reported an event where our performance was impeccable except for one small flaw, and that flaw is the focal point for our review of the whole event, blotting out the many things we did well? In many instances, having described what they have done badly, the child now awaits to hear the parent's opinions (i.e. judgments) too.

So to hear at this point ***"What I liked was..."*** often comes as an intriguing surprise. Let's ask ourselves a (pitifully) leading question: "As managers, teachers or parents, would we prefer our employee, colleague or child to express and embody competence or incompetence?"

I also choose to use Permission to preface this question, i.e. ***"May I tell you what I liked...?"*** since permission, as we saw in chapter 30, gives a strong sense of importance, respect and equality to the child.

This element of the process represents a first opportunity for us to gift positive authentic feedback, and to ensure that the child is encouraged to appreciate its own strengths, as perceived by us parents. Here in Q3 we make sure we ***add to the list*** that the child may already have declared, rather than just reinforce and repeat their observations. Q3 is not an exercise to demonstrate to the child that it has been able to spot the same things a parent might also consider important. It is an exercise to show the child that its own observations are valid and will be ***accepted*** without question or undue ceremony.

it shouldn't be a big deal to ask children to confidently identify their strengths

In other words, Q3 underlines that it shouldn't be a big deal to ask children to confidently identify their strengths; that this is what is expected. All we parent-coaches have to do is add to their observations with some more strengths and appreciations to complete the picture. (And there is ***always*** something more to appreciate).

Within Q3 we can also expand their experience of our admiration, by subtly scattering positive comments and observations as frequently as appropriate, i.e.

"How are your teachers responding differently, now you can do it like that?"

"I bet lots of people have noticed how far you've come with this over the last few months. I know I have."

"I've been noticing a real confidence in your team recently."

"Can I tell your Dad what great headway you've made there?"

Now onwards to Q4

Q4. When you do this or something similar next time, what might you do differently?

So far, the child has had three categories of question in their feedback sequence, and not a hint of negativity, blame, criticism or judgment.

Q1 - Notice.

Q2 - You like.

Q3 - I like.

And now a fourth: Q4 - Differently.

Notice the language in all parts of this question, very carefully chosen: *"What might you do* ***differently****?"* rather than *"What would you do* ***better****?"* or *"How would you* ***improve*** *what you have done?"* Using the word ***'differently'*** there is therefore no implication of judgment. We are eloquently implying a trust that the children are in control of their own options and will make some appropriate adjustments. Our opportunity to assist their progress with suggestions comes a bit later in Q6.

In that same clause is the word ***"might."*** Asking *"What* ***might*** *you do differently,"* conveys our confidence in that child's own choice: it can either choose to do it differently, or choose to persevere with the same way, since ***there is nothing in our communication to suggest there is a need to change***. Imagine too, changing the emphasis we put on any of the words; for example:

"***What*** might you do differently?"

"What ***might*** you do differently?"

"What might ***you*** do differently?"

"What might you ***do*** differently?"

"What might you do ***differently***?"

We can experiment all we like, although I'll confess to being fairly pleased, after years of polishing, with my current selection of words.

I like to think coaches are wordsmiths of a sort. We appreciate the inherent mettle of particular words, the changes in tonality and emphasis, and although we generally only contribute less than twenty per cent of the words in most coaching conversations, the words we do contribute are purposeful and astutely selected. And as parents, all of us are fairly well attuned to the language, idioms and fashionable phrases that our children respond best to. So we can build those into our conversations too.

Another message of confidence in this Q4 is the implication that we fully expect the children ***will*** be repeating the experience, or indeed, ***"something similar"***. They can apply any relevant learnings to both scenarios. We ask ***"when"*** rather than ***'if'*** and include a strong inference of ***"next time,"*** leaving the children in little doubt that we have no qualms about their ability to acquit themselves perfectly well, ***once again***.

If our children are in agreement, and we are at a stage where longer coaching feedback sessions don't faze them too much, this section can be explored at length and at leisure. Variations on Q4 can be asked several times and each answer might benefit from being explored through using GROW questions, particularly G and R questions, now we are more familiar with these from chapter 31:

"And where are you with that now?"

"Where would you like to be?"

"What is getting in the way?"

"How might you change this?"

"How will you do that?"

"What can you influence?"

"How would you like it to be?"

The over-riding intention of Q4 is to entice the child to look to a future ideal. In other words it is, in terms of the GROW model, a Goal-oriented, ('G') section of the feedback process.

Now we can open it up further with Q5.

Q5. And when you can do it like that, how would it be for you then?

Here's yet another really strong coaching question. The beneficial effect of the future focus in Q4 can be intensified by this Q5. This is an extremely important part of the coaching feedback process. It directs the children's thoughts to the future, bypassing obstacles that may be obscuring their vision. It creates a sort of verbal visualisation of what the children can reasonably expect, and is really exciting when it starts to sink in.

It is again, a 'G' section question and can usefully be explored at length, using questions like:

"What will the benefits be?"

"How will it impact your friends at school?"

"Imagine you have achieved it – what do you see/hear/feel?"

"What else can you think of that you couldn't do a year ago, that now you can do effortlessly?"

"What do you think about that?"

These questions help the children to place themselves in their future and gain a real experience of how it likely feels. How might we, at this Q5 stage for example, help create a new future reality-vision around children playing a violin solo without mistakes and hearing the applause as they finish the last note? Or receiving the school prize for art from the Head-teacher in front of the entire school?

This type of visioning creates new neural pathways in the brain, in the same way as new habits do. In this respect, the brain is unable to distinguish between fact and fiction – which is why we cry at sad films and squirm at movie violence. The brain will believe that the mistake-free sonata is already achieved, the confidence to produce impressive artwork is already in place. This makes it much easier to go through the process in real life since the brain believes it is simply repeating a well-practised memory. (Recall Michael Phelps' experience in Chapter 7)

This positive visioning process, created by Q5 and supplemented by additional questions is likely to raise a child's energy, motivation and confidence and improve its personal performance far more than focussing on what went wrong.

Try it. You'll like it. So will the children.

Q6. Would it be useful if I made a (couple of) suggestion(s)?

At last, thinks the child. Here comes the advice. ***"Would it be useful if I..."*** and they are waiting to hear ***"...gave you some advice?"*** But, no. Not 'advice.' Instead, "Would it be useful if I...made a couple of '***suggestions***?'

Suggestions, eh? Is that 'advice in disguise,' rearing its head again, as we noted earlier? But, no again. When a coach offers suggestions, it is without conditions or attachment. We may accept or reject a coach's suggestion. Coaches don't insist we comply; that's a director's role. (Or should that read 'Dictator's'..?) Gifting genuine suggestions and having them received as just that - a ***suggestion*** that can be accepted or rejected at face value is a mark of real deep down trust between the two parties.

If someone offers me a suggestion, and allows me to receive it, consider it and reject it, without any attachment or insistence or come-back, I know I have found a confident coach. Regardless of whether they lay claim to that title. And strangely, a huge number of these confident coaches are actually under ten years old. I have received dozens of suggestions from young children on a variety of activities, considered them and either adopted or rejected them, and the children have accepted my decision happily and without demur.

Teenagers have offered me advice, and generally been far more vociferous if I have declined their counsel. Conversely, where I have embraced it, they tend to be sure to let people know that it was them that suggested it. The need for recognition seems to be more apparent as the ego develops at this age.

However, parents I meet seem to have learned to build advice into most sentences. They may say to me, ***"You know what you should***

try...?" or ***"Why don't you...?"*** or ***"You could always..."*** If I acquiesce, they follow through, to check I have succeeded and done justice to 'their' idea, and if I spurn the advice, they pout and tell me they were ***"only trying to help."***

Come on parents, let's re-discover that carefree detachment we used to exhibit so nonchalantly. Let's stop trying to ***'help'*** and start with being ***'useful'*** again. Let's allow others to take responsibility for their decisions, their choices and their mistakes if need be. There is so much valuable learning in all of them - who are we to deny others that education?

Coaching doesn't promote suggestions but it doesn't prohibit them either. It doesn't necessarily follow that our suggestions and advice will not be useful. They may well be, and if we genuinely have good ideas it would, indeed, be unchivalrous in many cases not to offer them. But for them to be true coaching suggestions, we must stay ***detached from the outcome.*** Trust that the children will make good learning choices from all their available options, many of which will have been gleaned from its own mind. And the more the merrier.

We probably all know children who would rather not do something of obvious benefit to them if it meant conceding that the idea came from us, right? A little ego moment clouding their judgment perhaps? Let's rise above it, smile inwardly and say sweetly,

"It was just a thought. You can use it if it fits, or leave it. I'm not attached to it. I'm sure you'll find the right solution for you."

So, depending upon the context of the coaching feedback conversation, this Q6 is an opportunity for the coach to offer any suggestions and advice or to gift any 'learning' feedback. With any luck, the children will already have come up with their own learning feedback in Q1 or Q4, negating the need to deliver it at all.

A *'couple of things'* we may have noticed:

We do say, ***"Would it be useful if I made a (couple of) suggestion(s)?"***

We don't say, ***"Would it be useful if I made seventeen suggestions?"***

Let the child focus on one or two things at a time. We can always review those adjustments at a later time and then make another one or two suggestions when it's appropriate.

We may also have noticed that the theme of Q6 is intentionally placed near the end of the feedback sequence. We perform best when we are in control of the pace of our own ideas, so once we have been given the space to say all we want to say, we will be more receptive to input from others.

Expanders at Q6 might be:

"Would it help to hear something from my own experience?"

"Could we discuss the reports we have received from your teachers?"

"Could I share with you what is coming up for me here?"

"I have an idea that might help. Would you like to hear it?"

All these expanders are accompanied by asking permission. This helps children to relax and think more clearly in sensitive situations, because here too, they feel more in control.

In workshops, the question is often raised about what to do when the children are, according to the parent, definitely deluded about their actual perceived ability and are reporting their progress through spectacles with more than just a tint of rosiness. It's true, in such cases this feedback process can appear to raise a dilemma; namely, the child appears to believe that its performance was of a very high standard with little to adjust going forward, while the parent actually believes it is mightily misguided. The dilemma therefore is how to offer learning without appearing to judge.

Knowing is all we know. Therefore it's neither acceptable nor possible to not know

It's a worthwhile scenario to consider, as in this case the integrity of the coaching feedback process is at stake. My view is that we would work through Q1-5 as normal, accepting everything the child says without contradiction or sarcasm and offering our own 'likes.'

Then at Q6 it is perfectly acceptable for the parent-coach to deviate slightly and step back into a parenting role, saying something like,

"I'd like to just take my 'coach's hat' off for a minute and put my 'parent's hat' back on, because I want to ask you to [...do the following actions]. My view is that it's important you spend some time [...doing these actions] before continuing with this task."

In this way, the parents are still being transparent in their needs to steer, protect and give instructions, and are not 'disguising' them as suggestions, a tactic which seriously dilutes the trust that is being cultivated. We note too, from this minor deviation from the 'script,' that the parent can still avoid passing judgment while wearing the parent 'hat.'

Q7. Knowing all these things now, how might you use them in [other areas]?

Finally we embark upon the 'Options' and 'Will' (actions and commitment part of GROW) to tie down reflections and ideas into a solid pathway forward. If this is attempted too soon, without a thorough exploration of the present situation and the future, the children will not have enough insight or reflection on their current situation with all the associated implications. In that space, children will tend to just announce they are "stuck" and report that they "don't know" how to resolve their challenges or change their behaviour.

However, do we parent-coaches buy that? Oh no. Knowing is all we know. Therefore it's neither acceptable nor possible to not know.

There is a psychological state known as 'learned helplessness' which children enter when asked to form an action plan without a rich base of current awareness. If we want to tackle a child who is in this 'I don't know' place, try this simple tactic: using strong and respectful permission, ask,

"Would it be OK to continue to ask a few more questions [on that subject?]"

If permission is granted, continue with some G and R questions. By teasing out new areas of exploration, new insights appear. It is really valuable to complete a feedback session not simply with a sense of what went well and what could be done differently, but also with a notion of ***how that information can be used in other areas of the children's life*** so as to expand their horizons of what's possible.

Of course, permission may equally likely be denied. This is quite probable as children tend to enjoy the control they have discovered in this 'learned helplessness' state. After all, the parent can't easily break through the armour of 'I don't know.' If this happens, just go along with it, saying,

"OK, although my feeling is you probably* do *know, and I'm sure you'll definitely be able to piece it together when we have had a little more time to explore what else is happening. I'll ask you later on, or if anything comes to you in the meantime just give me a shout, OK?"

And then be sure to remember to ask again later on, otherwise the opportunity may be lost.

Further 'O' expander questions here might be:

"Where else could you apply this?"

"What else could you do with these skills?"

"Who do you know that you could share these skills with?"

"How could you apply this in other subjects at school?"

There it is - coaching feedback for the future. It's simple. It's respectful. It works. And, as the immortal Forrest Gump would likely say: "That's all I have to say about that."

Epilogue

"Every child should be coached to within an inch of their lives!"
Richard Tyrie, Founder and CEO, GoodPeople

Coaching is finding its way into all walks of life now; industry, government, education, personal relationships and family life. Since it is natural for people to emulate role models as they grow and learn, whether consciously or otherwise, I await the day that parents become recognised as the most cherished role model of all.

one day the world's social structures will be modelled on exquisite parent-coach-leaders

Generation by generation, and country by country, my vision is that one day the world's social structures will be modelled on exquisite parent-coach-leaders. Parent-coach-leaders, like us, who aspire to embody a respectful, enlightened philosophy of communication, who make time to listen to our children, who appreciate their sincere, earnest efforts to make a difference in their worlds and who give them space to do so.

I believe everyone gets to a place at some point in their lives when they totally understand who they are, and how they fit in life. It may be just for a fleeting moment and appear unsustainable or it may be nurtured throughout the rest of their life but I believe it arrives and is always recognised, even if it's not acted on. And in that moment is the realisation that every choice open to us is within our power to make, and so we can forgo the wisdom of others, in favour of our own intrinsic knowledge.

it never hurts to keep a healthy dose of theatrical incredulity handy for coaching emergencies

The chances are high that this realisation will come sooner rather than later if we have had parents who have loved and trusted us enough, who have believed in us at every moment, who have given us space to screw up regularly AND have kept a playful perspective on things. It never hurts to keep a healthy dose of theatrical incredulity handy for coaching emergencies.

We are all, unavoidably, former children ourselves. How many of us, as parents now, wonder how things might have turned out differently, had our own parents and teachers known to really invest time to talk and listen to us? Especially since we didn't possess the communication skills to articulate our sense of our deep down talents and aspirations? Nor our sense of our deep down motivations, or our fears? How might things have turned out differently if, back in the day, our parents had known to create an environment where these talents and aspirations stood the best possible chance of being truly acknowledged, understood and nurtured?

So we now hold the coveted title of parent ourselves. Do we now fully realise the implications of denying our own children the opportunities to level the same disappointments at us? The good news is that we now have our chance to show what we have learned and what it has meant to us.

My feeling is that combining coaching skills with parenting brings about respectful relationships. In fact it's not just a *feeling* - my ***experience*** has convinced me that it's an inevitable consequence.

combining coaching skills with parenting brings about respectful relationships

In this book I have made various analogies with designing and constructing a house. In fact I decided to depict it as a Chateau. Every brick of this Chateau is imbued with Emotional Intelligence, and these are laid especially densely in the foundations and the basement floor upon which the rest of the house stands. The ground floor is open-plan and airy so we can see from one end to the other as there are few dividing walls. It's easy to access and exudes warmth and relaxation and the promise of intrigue and exciting discoveries upstairs.

On the first floor reside all the protocols of Permission; above that, the second and third floors, where Listening and Insightful Questions are everywhere. The higher we go, the more we see through the windows. And the fourth floor is where the real treasures lie - every room filled with positive and appreciative wisdom and self-belief - the Gifts of Coaching Feedback. Needless to say the panoramic views over the gardens that we are continually landscaping, as far as, and beyond our staked perimeter are dramatic and unforgettable.

Signing up for parenting, certainly as a first-timer, is a leap in the dark. It's emotional, it's fun, it's painful and it's an education. Most parents survive the experience with good grace and humour. That part at least is a choice. Let me make a parallel to the FISH! Philosophy, with which some may already be familiar.

After nearing bankruptcy in 1986, John Yokoyama, the owner of a Seattle fish market known as Pike Place decided with his employees to change their way of doing business and become "World Famous" in the process. Using a coach to help them explore what was important to them, they began looking for more fun ways to fill their customers' orders and sell fish.

They began to interact and play more with the customers, flinging the wet fish to each other, inciting laughter from the customers as well as compliments (and commiserations) about their throwing and catching abilities. Employees would often invite customers to wear an apron and join the fish-flinging fun. The Pike Place employees gave their complete attention to each of their customers and ensured each had an enjoyable visit.

Four years later, they were featured repeatedly in the national media and television shows. The store became a popular tourist destination in Seattle, attracting up to 10,000 daily visitors, and is often billed as, yes - "World Famous." In an interview, Yokoyama stated, "We took a stand that we were going to become world famous. We just said it and it became so."

On a visit to Seattle, a business writer, John Christensen, observed how animated and happy the employees at Seattle's Pike Place Fish Market were in their work. He created the FISH! Philosophy as a workplace management system and published it as a film, with a spin-off series of books. These have been translated into 17 and 34 languages respectively. Christensen realised that not only were the workers making a mundane job fun for themselves and their customers, they also were selling tons of fish.

play is the spirit that drives the curious mind

Christensen's FISH! Philosophy, as it has become known, has four elements.

1) Choose your attitude

Choosing one's attitude means taking responsibility for how we respond to what life throws at us. As one of the fishmongers says,

"If I choose to stay out until 4 a.m. one night, partying, I still have a responsibility to my customers at the fish market the next morning at 5 a.m. They don't want or expect poor service just because I decided to have fun and hardly sleep the night before."

playfulness is a mindset we can bring to everything we do

Once we are aware that our choice of attitude impacts everyone around us, we can ask ourselves, ***"Is my attitude helping my family or my friends? Is it helping me to be the person I want to be?"*** The FISH! Philosophy recommends for us to choose to be cheerful and friendly every day, so our feel-good factor will spread to others.

As parent-coaches, this is always going to be a tough call. In testing moments, if we can hang on to our values just that fraction longer than children can to theirs, we can model strength and calm and purpose, and questions will surface from a productive, supportive place, rather than commands from a place of irritation.

2) Play

there is little more important that we can achieve as parents than truly ***'being there'*** through good times and bad

Play taps into our natural way of being creative, enthusiastic and having fun. Play is the spirit that drives the curious mind, as in ***"Let's play with that idea or situation!"*** and makes our children around us feel as though they can have fun with us too. Levity and fun are huge motivation drivers and playfulness is a mind-set we can bring to everything we do.

3) Be there

This is about giving our full attention to a task as well as to our children. Often while at school or home, we will be there physically although our mind isn't ***'present.'*** There is little more important that we can achieve as parents, than truly ***'being there'*** through good times and bad. Being there means being emotionally present for our families. It's a powerful message of respect that improves communication and strengthens relationships and helps the children maintain a positive attitude as well.

4) Make their day

Making their day is achieved by finding simple ways to assist or delight our children in a meaningful, memorable way. It's about contributing to their lives, not because we want something out of it, but because that's the parent-coach we have chosen to be. Creating a "filter of incredibleness" and making warm eye contact towards our children through that filter, is a big part of this and makes our children ***our single focus.*** Their friends love to be included in this way when they visit our house, and of course their teachers at school too. Making our children's days, and indeed, other people's days cannot do otherwise than to reflect back well on us too.

young people are offering us the responsibility and the privilege of guiding their education – the least we can do is pay attention

So I think those fishmongers in Seattle have it about right. We can of course always choose our attitude and the way in which we communicate. Maintaining a sense of humour, detachment and playfulness is essential. When our kids' days are "made", doesn't it feel as if we have had a good day ourselves? By being fully present and looking at our children through a permanent filter of awe and empowerment we can allow ourselves to see the entire, glorious, wise young person who shares our lives. These young people are offering us the responsibility and the privilege of guiding their education – the least we can do is pay attention.

Being right is overrated
Being open is brave
Being attentive and fully present is everything

Of ***course*** our children can work things out. Let's step aside and allow them to have a go. They are wonderful young people capable of fabulous achievements. Even amongst all these searching questions we are starting to ***ask*** now as parent-coaches, the one thing we can always give ourselves permission to ***tell*** them, whether wearing our parent, coach, teacher, mentor or friend 'hat,' is that they are amazing, beautiful, intelligent, fun, able, trusted and loved.

Let's never, ever stop telling our children that.

Further Appreciations

Having come into the parenting role relatively late on in life I find myself to be more than a little in awe of parents. Especially those of you who have been parenting for a dozen years already, twenty perhaps, or even several decades.

In awe of the fact that your parenting has been based purely on an intuitive, minutely tested love for your children; a love that they probably won't come to really understand or fully appreciate until they begin parenting their own children (Hmmm where have I heard that statement before...?)

In awe of the fact that you have first bought, and second *read through,* a book like this, to be able to better relate to your children.

In awe of the fact that you have been working through the day-by-day challenges of educating, motivating, stimulating, placating, commiserating, playing, financing, sacrificing, loving...all for other people...once again, your children.

Fabulous.

In a scruffy, modest part of South West London, known as Streatham Hill, live an elderly couple, Lisa and Martin. When I say elderly, I mean that chronologically, rather than energetically, speaking. Now together for nearly sixty years they have no intention of moving to a different or more comfortable area. When you put down roots, you put down roots.

Lisa was a high school drama teacher for some thirty-five years, and has staged innumerable plays and large scale musicals with dozens of characters in every one, and continues still to do so. She is now almost eighty years old. Her ethos was and is, one of inclusivity; if anyone asked her whether they could be in one of her school or church plays, she would write them a part, or include them in a chorus or dance team or backstage crew. Shakespeare's Tempest has probably never before had so many entertainers at Miranda's wedding, nor ever will again.

She retired from teaching and dedicated her life to her church, just as her father, a priest, had done. She trained and studied to become a Deacon, the highest office then available to women in the Church of England. She wanted to go higher, to become a full priest, but the laws didn't allow it and she had no expectation of the men-only rule changing in her lifetime.

Like a number of other women in the late 20th Century, she refused to accept the spurious and sexist reasons put forward by poorly informed religious thinkers of her time. "I want to become a priest," she said. "You can't, women can never be priests in the Church of England," said the closed-minded religious thinkers who, at the time, had established church law on their side.

In the 1990s there was increasing pressure for a vote to challenge that law and one was duly organised. Given the enormity of the change to the church and the likely repercussions to its congregations world-wide, it was ruled that a massive sixty-six per cent majority would be required from the Laity and a staggering 75% majority needed from the incumbent Bishops to secure a historical yes-vote for women priests.

The vote, as we now know was successful, and Lisa achieved a lifetime's ambition of becoming a full-time priest in the Church of England, aged sixty-one. She was ordained in Southwark Cathedral, London, in 1994, with dozens of other like-minded, dedicated women; the first group of women ever to be allowed to assume that title since Jesus was still alive and preaching, two thousand years before. It will only be a short generation to wait before women are 'allowed' to become Bishops too; the out-dated fuddy-duddies who currently oppose it won't live forever.

Lisa worked, daily, tirelessly as a priest for the next ten years, finally 'retiring' to preach occasionally and stage the occasional street passion play, inevitably with a cast of hundreds, through the streets of South West London to keep her occupied. Oh yes, and launching her third career in her seventies, performing one-woman shows to sell-out audiences at the Edinburgh Festival, based on her book, Spilling the Beans, a wonderful, amusing and heart-warming perspective of life in their East London vicarage immediately after World War Two.

Never let anyone tell us our dream is unrealistic or unachievable.

Martin has been an unswerving pioneer in prison reform, victim support, mediation and restorative justice for much of his life and he too, continues to be so. Now well into his eighties, he still flies around the world, giving talks to conferences and symposia and talking about it to everyone who shows even a slight or polite interest. His passion to educate and inform people of the positive merits of finding alternatives to prison sentences is as vibrant as ever.

If you ever have occasion to be browsing one of the huge volumes of Who's Who, a vast directory of people of occasional note, his name is included as a former Director of the Howard League for Penal Reform in the United Kingdom. You will probably also spot in his brief bio, listed as a hobby, an entry of "Making Helpful Suggestions." *

Until the mid-1950s the law was pretty black and white - we transgressed, we were locked up, and society conveniently overlooked many of its responsibilities towards our human rights. Successive governments and law-makers were reluctant to change the *status quo* for fear of losing votes. Penal reform was not up for discussion. "People want security," they said, "and with criminals behind bars we will all feel safer."

"I want to create more humane prison conditions," Martin said. "That's crazy, prisoners should be made to suffer," they said. "I want victims of crime to have their pain recognised and supported even by bringing criminals and victims together to talk through their feelings and understand one another. I want to find alternatives to prison where criminals can contribute back to the communities they have wronged, and give them a better chance of becoming useful to society," he said. "You can't," they said, "the law doesn't provide for that."

Finding ever more humane and respectful ways for people who have crossed legal boundaries to be given opportunities of righting their wrongs within their communities, rehabilitating and reinventing themselves and working to stay on the right side of the law has been his lifetime's work.

In 2012 he was presented with an Award at a European conference in Finland, in recognition of his contribution to Restorative Justice. Today, successive British and world governments are listening to the ideas and examining the benefits of prison reform, victim support schemes, mediation and restorative justice. They have become electoral issues, open to debate.

Never let anyone tell us our goal is unrealistic or unachievable.

Put these two independent, stubborn, hardworking luminaries together; add their principles, dogmatic outlooks, values and yes, even those irritating 'helpful' suggestions and we have a fair portrait of the cultural backdrop surrounding me and my brothers and sisters as we grew up.

Lisa and Martin - Mum and Dad - I'm in awe of all you stand for and all you've done for me too. I'm so grateful to you both for being so true to yourselves all through my life. Your wisdom has been to continue to do what made most sense to you, and allow us children to simply notice that, and then let us pick our own paths, which we have all done, and they have inevitably taken us in many different directions. It occurs to me that, in fifty years, I've never asked you what aspirations you might have had for me. I suspect if I did you would simply say, as good parent-coaches would, you'd be happy for me to make good sense of the world in my own way. And then leave it at that.

So. Consider that box ticked then. Still being there, still doing that. Be happy for me. I am.

* Case in point: while reading through an early draft of this book, he commented on its title; ***"Kid Pro Quo? Sorry, I don't think it really works. How about "Parenting with a SMILE?"***

Helpful, suggestive habits die hard. Thanks though, Dad. I'll bear it in mind.

Bibliography

Apter, Terri (2002) *The Myth of Maturity: What Teenagers Need From Parents to Become Adults,* Norton

Berne, Eric (1964) *Games People Play,* Random House

Blanchard, Ken (1982) *The One Minute Manager,* William Morrow

Doidge, Norman (2008) *The Brain That Changes Itself* Penguin Books

Duhigg, Charles (2012) *The Power of Habit: Why We Do What We Do, and How to Change,* Random House

Eriksson, Anders (2003) *Non Campus Mentis,World History According to College Students,* Workman

Faber, Adele & Mazlish, Elaine (1999) *How to talk so kids will listen and listen so kids will talk,* Avon Books

Gallwey, Timothy (1986) *The Inner Game of Tennis,* Pan

Gladwell, Malcolm (2002) *Outliers – the story of success,* Little, Brown & Company

Goleman, Daniel (1999) *Working with Emotional Intelligence,* Bloomsbury

Gray, John (1992) *Men are from Mars, Women are from Venus,* Harper Collins

Harris, Thomas (1967) *I'm OK - You're OK,* Harper & Row

Kline, Nancy (2009) *More Time to Think,* Fisher King

Lovegrove, Megan & Bedwell, Louise (2012) *Teenagers explained: A Manual for Parents by Teenagers*, White Ladder Press

Rosenberg, Marshall, (2003) *Non-Violent Communication: A Language of Life,* Puddle Dancer Press

Whitmore, John (4th Ed; 2009) Coaching for Performance, Nicholas Brealey Publishing

Wilson, Carol (2007) *Best Practice in Performance Coaching,* Kogan Page